MAY EVERYONE IS WRONG

REVELATIONS, CONSPIRACY, AND THE KINGDOM OF HEAVEN

TERRY WOLFE

Maybe Everyone Is Wrong
Copyright © 2020 by Terry Wolfe

tellwell 🖋

Tellwell Talent
www.tellwell.ca

ISBN
978-0-2288-3777-0 (Paperback)
978-0-2288-3778-7 (eBook)

TABLE OF CONTENTS

1

ABOUT THIS BOOK

Hypothesis (n): a proposal made with limited evidence, intended as a starting point for investigation. A tentative supposition.

This document is not a publication of factual claims about past, present, or future events, organizations, people, or systems. The views contained within are the product of an ongoing study exercise of Revelation, organized and presented as a proposal for your consideration. It is a radical "what if" examination, seeking to interpret the prophetic vision of John the disciple in a new way that makes better use of the fascinating details and literary structures of the book. Rather than seeing it as a description of some magical end time of chaos and punishment, or a jumbled metaphor that connects the church age to ancient Jewish archetypes, I believe it is the most intricately and perfectly designed puzzle in the history of the world. This book is an attempt to solve as much of the puzzle as possible, following the hints created by God in a very specific order, using very specific symbolism, to help believers understand that Jesus Christ and God the Father have been in total control of world history ever since Jesus ascended to heaven. Therefore this book examines on our own world's history (as well as our present age and possible future) not as modern historians who obsess over complicated tangles of circumstances and luck, but as a unified, perfect, necessary plan of God, cryptic and hidden from understanding, yet beautiful and poetic in so many ways.

As I explore this view I will be challenging popular conceptions of Revelation and show, if nothing else, that there is still room for fresh interpretation in the otherwise stale conversations surrounding the most exciting and challenging book of the Bible. Whether this hypothesis is closer to the truth than any other interpretation God alone will know.

I will happily advertise here that important sections of this book are hugely speculative, academically dubious, impossible to prove, ungenerous to certain historic characters, and deeply subjective. Nobody should mistake this for a formal or rigorous treatment of the subject, or accept its proposals as if they have undergone professional scrutiny. All of the research underpinning these views has been done on a layman level with an unsystematic methodology, using intuitive guesswork at times, in my limited spare time. I have no special education, resources, journalistic access, or scholarship. I do not claim to be an expert on anything. Far from it. I would describe it as a sort of "meditation" on the text:

> *Meditation (n): continuous, profound contemplation on a subject of a deep or abstruse nature.*

All Christians believe things we can't possibly verify, and call it a religion. But this does nothing to diminish it. On the contrary, it is our strength and our joy. We listen to a higher voice, which is called discernment. Our spirit is not factual. It resonates with God's Word not by intellect or information, but by a personal awakening of our spirit. This allows us to test ourselves and each other's ideas through the spirit, in prayerful questioning. Scholarship has never persuaded me to live better, love people more, or suffer persecution with grace, and if they were completely honest even scholars would admit that they pick and choose which facts and narratives suit their personal tastes. No academic proof has ever shown me the gates of heaven, nor pulled me from the fires of hell. The heart hears what is heartful. Change is not chosen, but chooses us, overcoming our nature through conviction, beyond reason. My findings are driven by the feeling of being struck by possibilities, and following them into a powerful appreciation of poetry, irony, and beauty. My study of interlinear Greek, Hebrew, and Aramaic manuscript passages has been fascinating and helpful, and so has expert testimony on various topics, but all of it has been subjected to my own heart's discernment. If my own lack of training has disqualified me to speak on the Bible, so be it. But what shall we say about the experts and their conclusions? I've seen the end result of their work. They all contradict each other, talk in circles about dull questions, and have altogether offered the church a worse tangle of half-baked guesses than I have in this lowly hypothesis. Indeed, this study did not begin wanting to make anything new, or to be a contrarian, but only to take stock of what was already understood by my superiors. Upon closer inspection, I was profoundly disappointed that even the biggest, oldest, and most highly respected views were shabby and ready to fall apart at the slightest jostle. It has forced me to reconsider everything and start over from the beginning.

This book, therefore, is not "a study of religious views", or an attempt to analyze any of them in particular, but a religious document itself, written in a religious mode of thought by a religious man. It is by no means scripture, prophecy, or divinely inspired, though it is written in the strength of my own spirit. In other words, it does not try to prove anything. It is the realm of discussion and personal exploration. Where it deals with factual questions of history, it is certainly missing detail and could be improved, but I have gotten it as accurate as I can with my limited time and resources so far. Think of it as one possible path through Revelation, and one that I continue to question. The most important word in this book might be the very first one you see: "MAYBE".

QUESTIONS OF OFFENSIVENESS

As a citizen of Canada, I'm very grateful for our Charter of Rights, which gives us religious freedom to proclaim our beliefs as long as we're not depriving others of their rights. In the Canadian Charter of Rights and Freedoms, Section 2(A), titled "Freedom of Religion", we see religious freedom defined as: *the right to entertain such religious beliefs as a person chooses, the right to declare religious beliefs openly and without fear of hindrance or reprisal"*. This book entertains religious beliefs, declaring them, not even to be true necessarily, but possible.

As Christians we must be willing to separate ideas from people, and people from their backgrounds or institutional connections. Only God judges mankind; but we can discuss ideas and institutions while we ask what the Bible is warning us about. When we condemn an idea or an institution, we do not condemn people, nor imply that everyone attached to them are evil, unworthy, or inferior. The Bible establishes God's standards, and thus it inherently comments on every institution's beliefs, priorities, and ideas. Even without mentioning names, the Bible stands in judgment of mankind. When interpreting or applying the Bible's mysterious symbolism and prophetic passages, therefore, we must be even more willing to let the logic of the Bible shine forward without indicting any person or group, either categorically or individually. As for myself, I have always appreciated Christ's teaching when it comes to tolerance, discrimination, bigotry, and hate:

> *When Jesus heard it, he saith unto them, They that are whole have no need of the physician, but they that are sick: I came not to call the righteous, but sinners to repentance. (Mark 2:17 KJV)*

The principle behind this is simple: Christians are supposed to offer and invite, not bully or force others, even if we think it is best for them. I do not advocate anyone to discriminate against anyone. Even if the Bible condemns Catholicism by showing it to be an abomination, I treat Catholics with love. I do not treat them badly or wish for anyone else to pile against them either. Even people who disagree fundamentally on religious matters need to respect each other's legal rights, and this is what the Bible teaches us as well. Anabaptists live peacefully with many people who are atheist, agnostic, Hindu, Catholic, Jewish, or some other faith, if said Anabaptists adhere to the Bible. Many Catholics claim that the Catholic Church is the only way to be saved, but does this count as "hatred" and "intolerance"? As long as we are allowed to have our own faith, and preach our own message, I don't believe so. Not even Jesus Christ himself sought to forcefully convert anyone, or wage some kind of war against those whose practices and beliefs he condemned, but said that he seeks those who will gladly hear him. That is love in truth. With this book, I also wish to speak to those who will gladly hear, and have no interest in disparaging those whose ideas or institutions I oppose.

Furthermore, spreading the Gospel and defending the Bible is an act of love for those we sympathize with, not an attack on a person. As a Canadian, I value that we are allowed to contest ideas and beliefs, as millions of people participate in arguments about ideas in a free society, including groups fundamentally opposed to each other on religion, politics, or any number of matters. Those who reject the Bible or the Gospel are free to do so, and we do not want to harass those who disagree, even if they harass us. Those who have another interpretation can be disagreed with, but this is not intolerance. I welcome disagreements, and in the future I may disagree with this hypothesis myself. Intolerance and discrimination goes beyond sharing beliefs, or trying to persuade people with arguments and evidence. If sharing our beliefs counts as hatred or intolerance, then the gospel and Christianity itself have been outlawed—which would be true intolerance and discrimination! Preaching and talking to others, or writing as scribes who belong to God's Kingdom, is fundamental to Christianity. For anyone who reads this book and disregards this message of love, tolerance, and non-confrontation, I disavow their actions.

QUESTIONS OF WRITING STYLE

With respect to the writing style, I'm afraid it is the only way I know how to write. I have tried to avoid unnecessary hedging language, and instead preferred a straightforward approach of pouring out the ideas from my heart, and advocating for them strongly. I do this without constant disclaimers, although it would be warranted. Let this first chapter be the disclaimer for it all. Many ideas are asserted flatly without citations or a methodological breadcrumb trail to follow. I encourage you to dismiss any and every point that is unconvincing, or to look up the claims and reason among yourselves.

2

INTRODUCTION

THE RULER OF THIS WORLD

Now is the judgment of this world; now the ruler of this world [Satan] <u>shall be cast out.</u> (John 12:31 EMTV) I will no longer speak many things with you, for the ruler of the world <u>is coming</u>, and he has nothing in me. (John 14:30 EMTV) And when he [the Holy Spirit] comes, he will convict the world of sin, and of righteousness, and of judgment: of sin, because they do not believe in me; of righteousness, because I am going to my Father and you see me no more; of judgment, because the ruler of this world <u>has been judged</u>. (John 16:8–11 EMTV)

Three times in the same discourse Jesus talks about the ruler of this present world as a fundamentally evil being who has no part with him. He has been judged, along with this present world, and he has been "cast out" and "is coming", but what does that mean? It's obvious when we read Revelation:

And there was war in heaven: Michael and his angels fought against the dragon; and the dragon fought and his angels, and prevailed not; neither was <u>their place</u> found any more <u>in heaven</u>. And the great dragon was <u>cast out</u>, that old serpent, *called the Devil, and Satan, which deceiveth the whole world: he was <u>cast out into the earth</u>, and his angels were <u>cast out with him</u>. And I heard a loud voice saying in heaven, Now is come salvation, and strength, and the kingdom of our God, and the power of his Christ: for the accuser of our brethren is <u>cast down</u>, which accused them before our God day and night. And they overcame him by the blood of the Lamb, and by the word of their testimony; and they loved not their lives unto the death. Therefore rejoice, ye heavens, and ye that dwell in them. Woe to the inhabiters of the earth and of the sea! for the devil is <u>come down unto you</u>, having great wrath, because he knoweth that he hath but a short time. And when the dragon saw that he was <u>cast unto the earth</u>, he persecuted the woman which brought forth the man child. (Revelation 12:7-13 KJV)*

So we see that the "ruler of this world" is Satan, cast out of heaven after the war with Michael and God's faithful angels. Apparently Satan and his angels had their own place in heaven before Jesus came up. Once he loses the battle and gets cast down to earth, he rages and looks to make war with the church.

Fear none of those things which thou shalt suffer: behold, <u>the devil shall</u> cast some of you into prison, that ye may be tried; and ye shall have tribulation ten days: be thou faithful unto death, and I will give thee a crown of life. (Revelation 2:10 KJV) "I know your works, and where you live, <u>where Satan's throne is</u>. And you hold fast to my name, and did not deny my faith in the days in which Antipas was my faithful witness, who was killed among you, <u>where Satan is dwelling</u>. (Revelation 2:13 EMTV)

Look closely. Here Jesus tells the churches that the **devil** is the one who will cast believers into prison and have them killed. Not only that, but he has a throne placed in a geographical region on earth, and Jesus knows where it is. It's important to notice that Jesus does not say that Jews will imprison them, or the Romans, or the Greeks, or any humans at all; although obviously human authority figures will be the ones to carry out the conspiracy on behalf of Satan. Jesus does not even comment on them, because he knows that Satan is behind it all.

> *Wherein in time past ye walked according to the course of this world, according to the prince of the power of the air, the spirit that now worketh in the children of disobedience: (Ephesians 2:2 KJV)*

Who is the "prince of the power of the air"? Once again it is Satan, of course. He has earthly power to influence the world, to the point where the "course of this world" is dictated by him. It's a conspiracy against the church by the children of disobedience. Satan has his own deceiving spirits that can accomplish this.

> *and every spirit which does not confess that Jesus Christ has come in the flesh is not of God. And this is the spirit of the antichrist, which you have heard that it is coming, and now is already in the world. (1 John 4:3 EMTV) For many deceivers are entered into the world, who confess not that Jesus Christ is come in the flesh. This is a deceiver and an antichrist. (2 John 1:7 KJV)*

John confirms that Satan's deceiving spirit is in the world during the early church period already. He uses the term "antichrist" for it because they have already "heard" some folklore tale about it; we'll discuss the antichrist in detail in later chapters. What matters here is that the spirit of Satan is already in the world and active during the lifetime of the disciples, not some distant scary future.

Not only are we taught when Satan is coming to earth to make war and by what methods he will use, but we're actually told the time where Satan's conspiratorial world system stops controlling world affairs and starts to be governed by Christ and God:

> *And the seventh angel sounded; and there were great voices in heaven, saying, The kingdoms of this world are become*

> *the kingdoms of our Lord, and of his Christ; and he shall*
> *reign for ever and ever.*
> *(Revelation 11:15 KJV)*

Jesus "shall" reign, but currently his Kingdom is spiritual and heavenly, not earthly. Until that day, the world and its kingdoms are the domain of Satan. We're even told at which prophetic point Satan decided to give his power, throne, and authority to a certain empire described as a "Beast" that has body parts of a leopard, bear, and lion:

> *And the Beast which I saw was like a leopard, his feet were like the*
> *feet of a bear, and his mouth like the mouth of a lion. The dragon*
> *[Satan] gave him his power, his throne, and great authority.*
> *(Revelation 13:2 EMTV)*

There are a lot of questions around the timing of these things, and so we will deal with those as we explain the amazing, deliberate structure of Revelation. What's important to understand right away is that the Bible never teaches that Satan is the ruler of Hell, or some spiritual place where he punishes sinners. That is a myth created by false teachers hundreds of years ago, and a tradition that needs to be destroyed. Satan was cast out of heaven (the divine realm) to the earth itself, and has been building an empire against the church ever since.

REVELATION AS OUR GUIDE TO GLOBAL EVIL THROUGH THE AGES

In this book I will take seriously what Jesus and the disciples taught about the global Satanic conspiracy, and more importantly I'll analyze how Revelation beautifully expands on this world view to give us clues. Revelation tells us what manifestations Satan's empire will take throughout history until Jesus reclaims the world from him, and what the destiny of believers really is, contrary to the outward appearances of being destroyed and unloved by God.

Once we put Revelation into context, it becomes simple and clear. The context is Jesus' teachings and ministry, which was about proclaiming the Kingdom of Heaven to be imminent in the spiritual realm, and Satan's empire to be imminent in the carnal world, which has been judged already. The events of Revelation therefore teach us what God will be doing in heaven after the time of John's vision, and what Satan will ultimately do on earth until he is destroyed. Then it goes beyond and describes the fulfillment of the many promises and prophecies God has made to reward the faithful.

The truth is, all Christians are conspiracy theorists if they truly believe the Bible. To say that Satan himself is the ruler of this planet we're currently living in, conspiring all the time to destroy the church, means we should look at history and our current day very differently than we've been taught. If we really believe what Jesus says, we need to examine the world in light of his teachings, not go along with secular propaganda and government education.

Notice what Revelation says: *"**Now** is come salvation, and strength, and the kingdom of our God, and the power of his Christ: for the accuser of our brethren is cast down, which accused them before our God day and night."* What this means is that, until Satan was kicked out of heaven and no longer able to accuse the brethren before God, neither salvation, nor strength, nor the Kingdom of Heaven, nor the power of Christ could be fully established. This is why Jesus taught not only about the coming of the Kingdom, but also warned about the arrival of the "ruler of **this** world" being cast out and coming to earth. And Satan didn't come alone. His angels are kicked out too, but instead of sending any of them to hell, God exiles them to earth with Satan, where they wage war in ignorance, not knowing what God's plan is anymore because they have lost access to the divine realm!

Revelation is not some spooky book about the end of the world, but rather a major comfort to the faithful, who might be confused why Satan seems to be winning against Christianity in every era. It is a guide to future generations to recognize how everything is happening according to God's ultimate strategy, not Satan's. The church is supposed to have tribulation, and Satan is supposed to carry it out. This is not an accident, an oversight, or a failure on God's part. God allows Satan to become more powerful in this world, and therefore test each generation of believers to see whether they are willing to resist and die for the gospel and the Kingdom.

DEALING WITH MYSTERIES AND MISCONCEPTIONS

There are many amazing mysteries in Revelation and the Bible, and this book will try to tackle as many as it can without being too long. For one, how is it that Satan seems to actually think he can win against God somehow? I think it might be due to a single unusual promise made by God thousands of years ago in connection to Israel's fate, and I'll explain how it connects to the bizarre, complicated conspiracy Satan's servants are involved in today. Beyond that, we must deal with the many flawed interpretations regarding the Antichrist, the Rapture, the Mark of the Beast, the Four Horsemen of the Apocalypse, the Beast itself, the Whore of Babylon, the Day of the Lord, the Tribulation, and God's promises about Jerusalem and the Third Temple, the Millennial Kingdom, Heaven, and Hell.

If this book's hypothesis is true it means that many scholars have been wrong despite their best intentions. I would never accuse them of being lazy, stupid, or malicious, because:

> So then each of us shall give account concerning himself to God. Therefore let us no longer judge one another, but judge this rather, not to put a stumbling block or an offense before our brother. (Romans 14:12-13 KJV)

And again, Paul himself admits that he only knows things partially, and that partial prophecies will pass away and be replaced by better ones. And that he understands things only as if looking at an enigma:

> Love never fails. But _whether there are prophecies, they shall pass away_; whether there are tongues, they shall cease; whether there is knowledge, it shall pass away. _Now we know in part, and we prophesy in part._ But when that which is perfect has come, then _that which is partial shall_

*pass away. ….. For now <u>we see through a mirror by reflection</u>
["enigma" in Greek], but then face to face. Now <u>I know
in part</u>, but then I shall know just as I also am known.
(1 Corinthians 13:8-12 EMTV)*

Not only that, but look at what Jesus teaches:

*Then he [Jesus] said to them, "Therefore <u>every scribe</u>
having become a <u>disciple in the kingdom of heaven</u> is like a
householder who brings <u>out of his</u> treasure <u>new and old</u> things."
(Matthew 13:52 EMTV)*

He tells us that all future scribes who are disciples in the kingdom
of heaven will bring out old and new treasure from their own household:
meaning some of the old teachings, and some new ones, with their own
perspective. Jesus is telling us that there will be a continual, gradual, and
partial improvement of our understanding. Furthermore, Paul teaches
that we have permission to build on the foundation of Jesus Christ, but
warns us to take heed. "By fire" it will be revealed for what it is.

*According to the grace of God which was given to me, as
a wise architect I have laid the foundation, <u>but another
builds</u> on it. But let each one take heed how he builds on it.
For no other foundation can anyone lay, other than that
which is laid, which is Jesus Christ. Now if anyone builds
on this foundation with gold, silver, precious stones, wood,
hay, straw, <u>each one's work shall be made manifest; for the
day shall reveal it</u>, because it shall be <u>revealed by fire</u>; and
the fire shall <u>test each one's work</u>, as to what sort it is. If
anyone's work which he has built remains, he shall receive
a reward. If anyone's work is burned up, he shall suffer
loss; but he himself shall be saved, but so as through fire.
(1 Corinthians 3:10-15 EMTV)*

What we build might be "gold, silver, precious stones, wood, hay,
straw", indicating a wide range of quality and resilience. This again
shows that the Holy Spirit does not reveal all mysteries to anyone fully.

It shows that there is no black-and-white, binary dichotomy between those who teach perfectly with the Holy Spirit and those who are wicked, deluded, or unsaved. There are gradations in all things, and they all get tested.

I here bring forward new treasures and old ones, carefully building on the foundation of Jesus Christ and the Bible, knowing that I myself will be saved even if I am wrong, and the day will have to reveal the quality. The fire is not the opinion of men, but the day itself.

Checking the text

This document is comparable to most Bible studies or commentaries, in that it provides Biblical quotations and cross-references passages and ideas without quoting the entire text. Some parts will be summarized and skipped, but our study will generally progress from the beginning of Revelation to the end. The reader might wish to follow along in their own Bible if they're concerned about something being overlooked. Different translations are used for the sake of clarity at different points. The King James Bible, English Majority Text, and American Standard Version are primarily used, with a Strong's Concordance version of KJV being used to check the Hebrew and Greek original text wording. I would recommend the reader to download and use the free Bible program, "e-Sword", then use its Bible download function to download these versions to easily check between them. For an even more pinpoint breakdown of the original manuscript language of a verse or passage, consider using BibleHub.com and their "interlinear" tool, available at this URL: *biblehub.com/interlinear/*

3

JUDGING INTERPRETATIONS

B efore I give my interpretation, we should ask ourselves: what makes one interpretation better than another? The following criteria is what I have judged other interpretations by, which caused me to realize the need for a better one. Although I know my own is not perfect, this was my metric:

1. **It makes use of every choice in the material**
   - ✓ Exact wording matters more than paraphrasing or summaries
   - ✓ Every mention or instance of something is shown to be important (there is no redundancy or pointless mentions)
   - ✓ Conspicuous omissions are shown to be deliberate and revealing
   - ✓ Timing, pacing, and progression of the material is shown to be important, not accidental or random
   - ✓ The overall structure is shown to be deliberate and meaningful
   - ✓ Patterns and smaller sections are shown to be important
2. **It is compatible and poetically tied in with the rest of Scripture**
   - ✓ Harmony with other literal and direct teachings
   - ✓ Principles and themes resonate strongly together
   - ✓ Continuity of metaphors, principles, and symbols

3. **It presents a strong utility and purpose for the material**
   - ✓ It shows the material to be very useful to past Christians
   - ✓ It shows the material to be very useful for today's Christians
   - ✓ It shows the material will be very useful to future Christians
   - ✓ Its usefulness generates more appreciation of older mysteries
   - ✓ Where obscure, the obscurity serves/served a good purpose
4. **It greatly prefers the actual words and meanings in the text**
   - ✓ English words and phrases are taken seriously
   - ✓ Greek words and phrases are taken seriously
   - ✓ Buzzwords and "tradition terms" are not respected

4

LOGIC OF THE SEVEN-SEALED BOOK

And I saw in the right hand of He that sat on the throne a
scroll, having been written inside and outside, and having
been sealed with seven seals.
(Revelation 5:1 EMTV)

Not only is this divine document in the right hand of God, it is sealed shut tightly, and has seven signets or royal seals on it, and therefore is supremely important, holy, and secretive. It is written on the inside and the reverse, meaning it is packed with writing. What this document represents is crucial to differentiating it from the seven trumpets and seven vials that will come later. It is not a generic metaphor. It is not interchangeable. Nobody in heaven or earth is worthy to even look upon the book, causing John to greatly wail and sob.

We can see that the seven-sealed book is the centerpiece of Revelation, serving as its entire structure of prophecy. In fact, the seven trumpets are specifically said to be events that happen *after* the seventh seal is broken, and the seven vials are only released *after* the seventh trumpet sounds, which means the whole book of Revelation is one timeline, moving in a linear direction, from beginning to end, and the book is the framework for the entire thing.

If it's a book that God has written and keeps in His right hand, secret from everybody, we should ask ourselves what the subject could possibly be. Why is nobody worthy to look at it except Jesus, who is now shown to have seven horns and seven eyes, which are said to be the seven spirits of God sent through the whole earth, showing his complete observation and power? Many assume that the book is the judgment of the world, or the "Apocalypse", because the events that happen seem frightening and dire. This is a mistake. Let us note that the tradition term of "Apocalypse" has caused a lot of confusion because it has become so deeply associated with cataclysmic judgment, final retribution, battle, etc. that it blinds people to the reality that there is no Biblical support for Revelation being only a distinct period of extreme judgment or wrath. John is simply witnessing what must "shortly come to pass" and what "shall be hereafter":

> *The Revelation of Jesus Christ, which God gave unto him, to shew unto his servants things which must <u>shortly come to pass</u>; and he sent and signified it by his angel unto his servant John: (Revelation 1:1 KJV)*

> *Write the things which thou hast seen, and the things which are, and the things which <u>shall be hereafter</u>; (Revelation 1:19 KJV)*

It's important to note that Jesus takes the book personally out of God's right hand. The call was sent out by the mighty angel, but this is still Christ's choice to take or not take. God allows this to happen, and apparently it is a magnificent celebratory event in the kingdom of heaven. The living creatures and elders fall and worship again, like they already did before, only this time they have harps and golden containers full of fragrance, which represent the prayers of the saints. This clearly distinguishes the elders from the saints as well. As of yet, no saints are here, only their prayers.

GOD'S ETERNAL PLAN, AND THE ENIGMA OF ITS TIMELINE

The seven-sealed book is nothing less than the grand, global, eternal strategy playbook that God has devised ahead of time. Nobody is worthy to look upon it because it specifically permits the rise of Satan's influence and power over the precious saints, even though they are sanctified and washed in the blood of the Lamb. Think about how shocking that must have been to first century believers, and even the angels themselves! Who could possibly be worthy of such a serious, powerful, and unhappy task except Christ, who was himself sacrificed, and who loves the churches more than anything? Only Jesus knows the full weight of this grim strategy. He doesn't want his followers to be killed, imprisoned, and falsely persecuted by Satan. But nevertheless, because it is God the Father who has ordained what must come, he alone must bear the burden. (Of course, once we truly understand the Kingdom of Heaven and Christ's ministry, we know that suffering and dying for the Lord is not a bad thing at all, but a joyous blessing.)

> *But of that day and that hour knoweth no man, no, not the angels which are in heaven, <u>neither the Son</u>, but the Father. Take ye heed, watch and pray: for <u>ye know not when the time is</u>. (Mark 13:32-33 KJV)*

Not even Jesus knew the timing when he was on earth. It's true that the descriptions of the end times throughout the New Testament contain important details and sometimes even the order in which they must happen, but there is a consistent pattern of *these same authors* admitting that they don't know *when they will happen*. Two thousand years later, we can see that God's plan was far beyond what anyone could have imagined.

> *Knowing this first, that there shall come in the last days scoffers, walking after their own lusts, And saying, <u>Where is the promise of his coming?</u> for since the fathers fell asleep, <u>all things continue as they were</u> from the beginning of the creation. (2 Peter 3:3-4 KJV) But the heavens and the earth, which are now, by the same word are kept in store, reserved unto fire against <u>the day of judgment</u> and perdition of ungodly men. But, beloved, be not ignorant of this one thing, that <u>one day is with the Lord as a thousand</u>*

years, and a thousand years as one day. The Lord is not slack concerning his promise, as some men count slackness; but is longsuffering to us-ward, not willing that any should perish, but that all should come to repentance. (2 Peter 3:7-9 KJV)

Clearly, Christians have always been mystified about the timeline of God's plan, even the authors of the Bible. But even before this, look at the great prophet Daniel's strange conversation with the angel regarding the timing of things:

But thou, O Daniel, shut up the words, and seal the book, even to the time of the end: many shall run to and fro, and knowledge shall be increased. (Daniel 12:4 KJV) And I heard, but I understood not: then said I, O my Lord, what shall be the end of these things? And he said, Go thy way, Daniel: for the words are closed up and sealed till the time of the end. Many shall be purified, and made white, and tried; but the wicked shall do wickedly: and none of the wicked shall understand; but the wise shall understand. (Daniel 12:8-10 KJV)

And Jesus tells us only to look for a fulfillment, not to calculate the days:

Now learn a parable of the fig tree; When his branch is yet tender, and putteth forth leaves, ye know that summer is nigh: so likewise ye, when ye shall see all these things, know that it is near, even at the doors. Verily I say unto you, this generation [by implication, "age"] shall not pass, till all these things be fulfilled. (Matthew 24:32-34 KJV)

He tells his own disciples that it's not for them to know the times:

When they therefore were come together, they asked of him, saying, Lord, wilt thou at this time restore again the kingdom to

Israel? And he said unto them, It is not for you to know the times or the seasons, which the Father hath put in his own power. (Acts 1:6-7 KJV)

The seven-sealed book is the ultimate mystery, and the timing of it may be the most mysterious aspect of it. That may be why, when God allows Jesus to take it from Him, the living creatures and elders fall and worship again, because the time seems to be at hand.

KEEPING THINGS SEALED, AND BREAKING SEALS

God needed to keep His strategy book sealed for many reasons, but among the most important must have been keeping his plans secret from Satan and his angels. They were in heaven until the war, when he was cast with them down to earth, around the time of Jesus' ministry. If Satan had been allowed to know the plan it would ruin the whole thing, because Satan actually needs to be furious and ignorant. He doesn't realize that he'll fulfill God's plans by waging war on the church. We are also told that Jesus could not send the Holy Spirit until Satan came down and Jesus went up to heaven. There is a very real relationship between these things, implying that Satan was an obstacle to the plan. Again, in Revelation 12:10 we are shown how the heavens rejoice as soon as Satan and his angels are gone, and how *"salvation, and strength, and the kingdom of our God, and the power of his Christ"* finally manifest at that point. It is not just symbolism, but a real metaphysical conflict that has huge implications for how to read the Bible.

After Satan is gone from heaven and Jesus arrives to take the book and begin breaking the seals, he becomes in charge of the fate of the church. Breaking a seal means Jesus unlocks a portion of God's plan each time, allowing it to play out in the world. This isn't merely symbolism either. The book has the power to alter the course of the world and change the future! But before we can explore the contents of the book, we need to recognize that this is a common pattern we see both in Revelation, and the Old Testament: first there is a heavenly discussion or decree, or symbolic fulfillment of an event, and then the literal events are arranged to happen in the world according to God's plans. This obviously happens in Genesis when God speaks to His divine council and the universe obeys His Word. But we can see it later on too, dealing with worldly events:

> *And he said, Hear thou therefore the word of the LORD: I saw the LORD sitting on his throne, and all the host of heaven standing by him on his right hand and on his left. And the LORD said, Who shall persuade Ahab, that he may go up and fall at Ramothgilead? And one said on this manner, and another said on that manner. And there came forth a spirit, and stood before the LORD, and said, I will persuade him. And the LORD said unto him, Wherewith? And he said, I will go forth, and I will be a lying spirit in the mouth of all his prophets. And he said, Thou shalt persuade him, and prevail also: go forth, and do so. Now therefore, behold, the LORD hath put a lying spirit in the mouth of all these thy prophets, and the LORD hath spoken evil concerning thee. (1 Kings 22:19-23 KJV)*

God poses the question to his divine council, and then when He's satisfied with their solution He authorizes them to carry out the plan on earth. Likewise, prophecies such as the seven-sealed book are commandments made in heaven that must be fulfilled on earth. But how, when, and how many times they must be fulfilled are mysteries. Some of the most important descriptions of events in Revelation happen in heaven first, symbolically, divinely foreshadowing what will happen on earth soon after.

What, then? It ultimately means that everything that happens is God's plan, and the timing and authorization is in the hands of Jesus, and throughout the history of the church this has been a comfort. This is a beautiful message for believers, to know that Our Lord Jesus, who was persecuted and killed for our sins, is the one controlling the allowance of tribulation, pacing it so that everything can be fulfilled as the Father desires. He can limit or expand Satan's worldly power, one step at a time.

This is the same reason we are shown the throne room as well: it has a giant crystal floor, where God and Christ can look down on us and see the events of the world clearly. It means they are not at all ignorant about our suffering, our prayers, and our hopes. In fact the elders and beasts have our prayers as fragrances and instruments, and seems to cherish them! The whole scene so far speaks to how God observes us, loves us, hears us, and cares about our future, even though He requires there to be a gradual building of evil in this world. This is also why Jesus acknowledges the seven churches, and admits that Satan is already busy imprisoning and killing them on earth. He cares deeply and he promises them great rewards for being patient. Instead of thinking of themselves as failures and victims, they are victors in Christ, guaranteed rewards.

So then, the logic of Revelation and John's visions revolves around the duality of the wonderful, caring, and righteous Kingdom of Heaven where we eventually go when we die, contrasted by the Satanic conspiracy and tribulation on earth. The longer God's plan goes on, the more evil the world becomes and the more anticipation builds in the Kingdom of Christ's return and overthrow of Satan's empire on earth.

5

LOGIC OF THE KINGDOM
OF HEAVEN

Jesus answered, My kingdom is not of this world: if my kingdom were of this world, then would my servants fight, that I should not be delivered to the Jews: but now is my kingdom not from hence. (John 18:36 KJV)

And from the days of John the Baptist until now the kingdom of heaven suffereth violence, and the violent take it by force. (Matthew 11:12 KJV)

Therefore say I unto you, The kingdom of God shall be taken from you, and given to a nation bringing forth the fruits thereof. (Matthew 21:43 KJV)

And he said unto them, When ye pray, say, Our Father which art in heaven, Hallowed be thy name. Thy kingdom come. Thy will be done, as in heaven, so in earth. (Luke 11:2 KJV)

And I appoint unto you a kingdom, as my Father hath appointed unto me; That ye may eat and drink at my table in my kingdom, and sit on thrones judging the twelve tribes of Israel. (Luke 22:29-30 KJV)

The main subject of Jesus' teachings was the Kingdom of Heaven, and yet it is still greatly misunderstood today. The Bible teaches that the Kingdom of Heaven is a place that is not on this planet, but is eventually supposed to arrive here. Thirty-three times the term "Kingdom of Heaven" is used, but only in Matthew. Seventy times the term "Kingdom of God" is used in the New Testament, but we will use the term Kingdom of Heaven here because it more clearly speaks to the divine nature removed from this world until the "kingdom comes".

Notice above that Jesus said the Kingdom of Heaven was suffering violence between the time of John the Baptist until Jesus was speaking. This is an amazing statement that many don't know how to interpret. But we must piece it together with the other passages about the war in heaven, and recognize that he's talking about Michael and God's angels fighting against Satan and his angels. "The violent take it by force" he says, indicating that it is not some kind of formality or benign concept. How this war was carried out is unknown, but I would be surprised if it was physical violence; a spiritual war in heaven between angels is impossible to comprehend. But we do see interesting remarks that may provide some clues:

> *And there was war in heaven: Michael and his angels fought against the dragon; and the dragon fought and his angels, and prevailed not; neither was their place found any more in heaven. (Revelation 12:7-8 KJV)*

What if the violence and war in heaven was more of a **legal dispute** than literal violence with weapons and hitting each other? We're told that their "place" was not "found any more in heaven", which could imply that **his role was no longer needed there**. Because the Messiah had arrived on earth and was about to redeem mankind, Satan the accuser was out of a job. His "place" (or throne) was sent down to earth so that he could continue that role on earth—becoming the accuser of Christianity in this world instead, conspiring and conquering in order to invalidate God's plans if he could.

SEVEN ANGELS, GUARDIANS OF THE KINGDOM ON EARTH

We know that God speaks to His divine council in the divine realm, which we simply call heaven. The divine council predates creation itself. In the divine realm, God makes decrees and allows them to carry out His plans in creation. But the "Kingdom of Heaven" is a different concept. The Kingdom only gains power once Satan is cast out and Jesus takes his seat next to the Father. That's when Jesus becomes judge of the world and guides the churches with full authority. He uses seven angels, which are in his right hand:

> *The mystery of the seven stars which thou sawest <u>in my right hand</u>, and the seven golden candlesticks. <u>The seven stars are the angels of the seven churches</u>: and the seven candlesticks which thou sawest are the seven churches. (Revelation 1:20 KJV)*

Jesus keeps the seven angels of the churches in his right hand, symbolically and spiritually. When he gives his instructions to the seven churches (in chapters 2 and 3) he seems to speak first to the "angel of the church" each time, **not** the church itself. What this means is unclear, but apparently there is a divine representative watching over churches on behalf of Jesus at all times, and they can be held accountable for what the church is doing wrong.

> *<u>Unto the angel</u> of the church of Ephesus write; These things saith he that <u>holdeth the seven stars in his right hand</u>, who walketh <u>in the midst of the seven golden candlesticks</u>; (Revelation 2:1 KJV) Nevertheless I have somewhat against thee, because thou hast left thy first love. Remember therefore <u>from whence thou art fallen</u>, and repent, and do the first works; or else <u>I will come unto thee</u> quickly, and will <u>remove thy candlestick</u> out of his place, except <u>thou</u> repent. (Revelation 2:4-5 KJV)*

Curiously, we can see clearly **Christ's** message is directly pointed to the **angel** of the church, and that if the angel doesn't "repent" and recover its "first love" Jesus will personally come quickly and "remove" the "candlestick" in that angel's command, delivering a punishment. Notice that Jesus again makes a clear difference between the stars he holds in his hand and the candlesticks he walks in the midst of. If the candlestick is the church and the star is in his hand, this makes a clear distinction. And if the angel isn't careful, Jesus will remove that candlestick (or church) from him. This is language intended to contrast. Meanwhile the message to the **churches** is always said by the **Spirit:**

> He that hath an ear, let him hear what the _Spirit saith_ unto
> _the churches_; To him that overcometh will I give to eat of
> the tree of life, which is in the midst of the paradise of God.
> (Revelation 2:7 KJV)

And then the same pattern repeats, with Jesus speaking to the angel, but the Spirit speaking to the churches.[1] Due to the nature of John's writings the churches will see the messages written to the angel, and this is clearly intentional, with some passages directly referring to human events such as being imprisoned by Satan, which wouldn't happen to an angel, but that doesn't mean the angel is interchangeable with the church itself. The message is to humans and to angels, who are working together for the Kingdom, but with different roles.

> No man, when he hath lighted a candle, covereth it
> with a vessel, or putteth it under a bed; but setteth it on

---

[1]   And <u>unto the angel</u> of the church in Smyrna write; These things saith the first and the last, which was dead, and is alive; (Revelation 2:8 KJV) He that hath an ear, let him hear what the Spirit saith unto the churches; He that overcometh shall not be hurt of the second death. (Revelation 2:11 KJV) And to the angel of the church in Pergamos write; These things saith he which hath the sharp sword with two edges; (Revelation 2:12 KJV) He that hath an ear, let him hear what the Spirit saith unto the churches; To him that overcometh will I give to eat of the hidden manna, and will give him a white stone, and in the stone a new name written, which no man knoweth saving he that receiveth it. (Revelation 2:17 KJV)

a candlestick, that they which enter in may see the light.
(Luke 8:16 KJV)

Jesus uses the metaphor of a candlestick in his ministry to illustrate how he views the role of the church. They are a natural source of **light** to the world. And because we know that the world is ruled by Satan and his conspiracy of darkness and blindness, our lights are meant to help people **see** a preview of the Kingdom of Heaven on earth!

You may think it's strange that Jesus would rebuke angels as if they are flawed and can be guilty of negligence. But you shouldn't. Satan and his angels were not only flawed, but violently opposed to Jesus Christ! And if angels were perfect, all-knowing, and wise, they wouldn't have flawed ideas in 1 Kings and need to discuss various strategies as if it were up for debate. The Bible actually teaches that angels are **not** perfect; only God the Father is perfect, all-knowing, omnipotent, and purely righteous. Even in the divine realm, God is infinitely superior to every other being. Angels can be ignorant, or make mistakes.

> *Of which salvation the prophets have enquired and searched diligently, who prophesied of the grace that should come unto you: Searching what, or what manner of time the Spirit of Christ which was in them did signify, when it testified beforehand the sufferings of Christ, and the glory that should follow. Unto whom it was revealed, that not unto themselves, but unto us they did minister the things, which are now reported unto you by them that have preached the gospel unto you with the Holy Ghost sent down from heaven; which things the angels desire to look into.*
> *(1 Peter 1:10-12 KJV)*

Angels witness events on earth and in heaven, giving them a unique vantage point to see creation, but God alone knows His plans; they can only participate as authorized. They are not worthy of being worshiped, and they are not worthy to judge humanity. In fact, **we** are going to judge **them**!

Does any of you, having a matter against another, dare go to court before the unrighteous, and not before the saints? Do you not know that <u>the saints will judge the world</u>? And if the world will be judged by you, are you unworthy to judge the smallest matters? <u>Do you not know that we will judge angels</u>? Let alone ordinary matters! (1 Corinthians 6:1-3 EMTV)

So then, how can the angels be judged by us, if they are already perfect? If they were perfect, they could judge us! But they are not. God is the sole judge of mankind, which was made in His image: not angels, and not Satan who blasphemes God by wishing to be like Him. Satan wants the ability to judge mankind. The fact that Satan is a mere angel and wishes to rule mankind is exactly why he's hated and punished by God! So therefore saints can be superior to angels, and even powerful ones. And if so, it's no wonder Jesus would rebuke angels he has put in charge of his precious, beloved church; their job is to guide and protect God's children!

It makes perfect sense in historical context as well. Suddenly, after thousands of years, the age of the human priests and sacrifices in the temple are gone, and there is no more earthly system of rules and laws to govern anything about God's people, only the Holy Spirit and angels. The Kingdom is taken from the corrupt rulers of the Jews and given to the new priesthood of saints who hardly know what to do. This would have been a surprise even to the angels! They desire to look into the nature of this new Kingdom and know its timings. Remember that none of them knew what God had planned. They are not all-knowing, or able to guess exactly what God will decide. They are usually sent to do special tasks on behalf of God, or have a role in heaven. Now they are suddenly put in charge of earthly churches full of flawed, sinful, confused humans who are reborn with the Holy Spirit but needing guidance and protection. Even an angel can become lax or insufficiently disciplined, needing warnings from Jesus. And this doesn't even factor in the reality of competing spirits that are sent from Satan; spirits such as the spirit of antichrist.

ON EARTH AS IT IS IN HEAVEN

So what is the Kingdom of Heaven? It is the divine realm after being rid of Satan and his angels, purged clean, and revived in strength because Jesus the Messiah reigns as King forever. There he makes judgments with mercy, and gives humanity time to repent and be saved. He instructs the angels how to help the church, and chooses his recruits from among mankind and causes them to be reborn, beginning their lives anew as spiritual infants, growing to be new men and women whose names are written in the Book of Life. They are reserved to be co-heirs, priests, judges, and future kings themselves in the Millennial Kingdom. If we can picture the divine council as a vast body of angels working on behalf of God, deciding the fate of nations and having their own roles and tasks, we can picture what the Kingdom of Heaven is like. Jesus seeks more souls to serve him, but this time it won't be angels. We must remember that Jesus became an actual human himself, and then was given authority over the whole universe! This would have been the first time in the history of creation that a human was elevated above everyone in the divine realm except the Father. Therefore, it should not be surprising when we are reborn in the Spirit and recruited to follow his example. We can fulfill our roles and be part of God's new council in a sense. We will be like Christ, having authority over nations. He gives us limited command here on earth until then, with gifts and previews of what we will be able to do when the kingdom is established on earth.

The Kingdom of Heaven is therefore a place of judgment and of rest, overlapping between heaven and earth. When a saint dies on earth he is transported to heaven, increasing the population of the Kingdom there and reducing it here. Death is our ticket to the heavenly side of the Kingdom, in other words. But it is only a place of rest and judgment, **not** the eternal paradise itself.

And they sung a new song, saying, Thou art worthy to take the book, and to open the seals thereof: for thou wast slain, and hast redeemed us to God by thy blood out of every kindred, and tongue, and people, and nation; And hast made us unto

our God kings and priests: and we shall reign on the earth.
(Revelation 5:9-10 KJV)

Do you see how people in heaven are waiting to come to earth? But here we see Jesus inviting a sinner to go with him to paradise in heaven:

And he said unto Jesus, Lord, remember me when thou comest into thy kingdom. And Jesus said unto him, Verily I say unto thee, To day shalt thou be with me in paradise. (Luke 23:42-43 KJV)

It's easy to see why people think heaven is the **eternal** paradise and resting place of all saved souls, but Revelation clarifies that heaven is not permanent. In fact, those who are in heaven are just waiting for events on earth to be completed (in accordance with the seven-sealed book) so that Jesus can come back down to earth with his saints and reign on earth for a thousand years!

And I saw thrones, and they [who?] sat on them, and judgment was given to them, and the souls of those who had been beheaded on account of the testimony of Jesus, and on account of the word of God, and those who had not worshipped the Beast or his image, and they did not receive the mark on their forehead or on their hand. And they came to life and reigned with Christ for the thousand years. But the rest of the dead did not come to life until the thousand years were finished. This is the first resurrection. Blessed and holy is he that has part in the first resurrection. Over these the second death has no power, but they shall be priests of God and of Christ, and shall reign with Him for a thousand years. (Revelation 20:4-6 EMTV)

We must discuss who sits on the thrones, as well as the resurrection, the second death, the Beast, the image, the mark, and the thousand years, and that which follows. But what's important to notice here is that the saints in heaven end up on earth when they come down with Jesus for the battle of Armageddon, which is also called the "marriage supper". Jesus gets "married" to the bride of Jerusalem (inhabited by the church) on earth, reclaims it, and saints in heaven are given new bodies, living on the earth again! Therefore, we should not imagine that we will stay in heaven forever. Everybody in heaven is excited about what's going to happen on earth! And not only will we be back on earth, but we will reign with Jesus Christ over the remainder of the nations, as priests and kings, receiving the rewards that we earned during our lifetimes, probably in direct proportion to how much we served the Kingdom of Heaven in our lives, receiving the rewards Jesus taught about.

> *And when he was demanded of the Pharisees, <u>when the kingdom of God should come</u>, he answered them and said, The kingdom of God cometh not with observation: Neither shall they say, Lo here! or, lo there! for, behold, <u>the kingdom of God is within you</u>.*
> *(Luke 17:20-21 KJV)*

Until Jesus comes again, the Kingdom of God is found only in the churches, where the Holy Spirit resides in those reborn, serving the Kingdom on earth. It is a personal, internal mystery that Satan cannot figure out, because he is blind to the working of God's Spirit and his seven-sealed book plan. The saints will not only be with God, but will reign with Jesus, making the "kingdom" very real:

> *To him that overcometh will I grant to sit with me in my throne, even as I also overcame, and am set down with my Father in his throne.*
> *(Revelation 3:21 KJV)*

So we see that there is a secret Kingdom of Heaven building on earth, subject to persecution, guided by angels, and governed by Jesus and the Spirit. Then there is the spiritual side in heaven that watches over us and makes divine judgments in conjunction with us on earth, insofar as we have limited authority here. This disparate Kingdom will be united and return to earth. Jesus himself will conquer, and that's when the heavenly paradise will no longer be needed as a resting place.

6

LOGIC OF THE RIDERS

And I saw when the Lamb <u>opened one of the seals</u>, and I heard, as it were the noise of thunder, one of the four beasts saying, Come and see. And I saw, and behold <u>a white horse</u>: and he that sat on him <u>had a bow</u>; and a <u>crown was given</u> unto him: and he went forth <u>conquering</u>, and <u>to conquer</u>. (Revelation 6:1-2 KJV)

Jesus rules of the Kingdom of Heaven and is entrusted with the greatest secret in the history of the world. He is given authority to break the seals of the book that no other entity in the universe was worthy to even look at. This act empowers Satan to become more organized and effective at persecuting the church. Even though Satan has placed his throne in a geographical region and started influencing human authorities to imprison and persecute the church, God wants him to gain more influence and begin conquering the world. Why? Because God needs to separate the righteous from the ungodly before He can judge the world properly.

> *<u>I came to cast fire to the earth</u>, and how <u>I wish it were already kindled</u>! But I have a baptism to be baptized with, and how distressed I am till it is completed! <u>Do you think that I came to give peace on earth</u>? I tell you, <u>not at all</u>, but rather <u>division</u>. (Luke 12:49-51 EMTV)*

Another parable put he forth unto them, saying, The kingdom of heaven is likened unto a man which sowed good seed in his field: But while men slept, <u>his enemy</u> came and sowed tares [today called "darnel"] among the wheat, and went his way. But when the blade was sprung up, and brought forth fruit, then appeared the tares also. …. The servants said unto him, Wilt thou then that we go and gather them up? But he said, Nay; lest while ye gather up the tares, ye root up also the wheat with them. <u>Let both grow together until the harvest</u>: and in the time of harvest I will say to the reapers, Gather ye together first the tares, and bind them in bundles to burn them: but gather the wheat into my barn. (Matthew 13:24–30 KJV)

Jesus says that he wants to set the world on fire and have it divided. He wishes that it already was burning, and we know that God wants to divide the holy from the godless. But Satan is going to sprinkle "tares" among the churches, and this will make it hard to separate them until they're fully mature. God does not want to "harvest" either of them until they are easy to separate, which means that evil must become more evil, and good must become more good. Tares are today called "darnel" and are not simply weeds, but a counterfeit plant that looks a lot like wheat, but doesn't actually have wheat grain when it's matured. In other words it's a false church; a blasphemous imitation. A church that doesn't produce good fruit and proper Christian results. This is very important.

In order to make sure Satan can plant the false church on earth instead of openly waging war, Jesus needs to break one of the seals and authorize him to do so. Satan has very little power that isn't granted to him. Let us also remember that the term "four horsemen of the Apocalypse" is an incorrect tradition term that has no basis in the Bible whatsoever. It is an unbiblical myth to say that these riders must only appear at the end of the world, or all together. People assume wrongly because they misunderstand the seven-sealed book to begin with.

As we study the evolution of Satan's empire on earth, it may be important to note that God's declarations are often simple and vague, but what we see in history is extremely complex. In order to understand the four riders that appear with the breaking of the seals we must examine history in broad strokes, looking for the parallels and clues, and leave the complicated disputes to secular scholars who don't have the beautiful guide of the Bible to help.

WHITE: THE DELUSION AND MISSION OF THE ANTICHURCH

As we look at how and when the first four seals are broken, we see an interesting pattern. Each time a seal is broken it triggers some kind of miraculous, unlikely conversion of a powerful, godless military figure to the side of Satan, who then becomes part of the counterfeit church, which we will call the Antichurch as a reminder of its evil nature. This military power then uses their immense skill and tenacity to establish a new office on Satan's behalf, which conquers more of the world and ultimately persecutes the Kingdom of Heaven while blaspheming and pretending to be holy and good. This new power always ends up having a particular color associated with it. When the power begins to wane and collapse, Jesus breaks a new seal and reinvigorates Satan's empire with a new addition to its conquest machine.

The first seal releases a rider on a white horse. We're told that the rider has a bow, but receives a crown and goes to conquer. The miraculous event in this case is the "conversion" of Constantine the Great around 300 AD. He was a Roman general who received a vision in the sky in the shape of a cross, with a Latin inscription underneath that said, "With this, conquer". This is a very well known historic account, and cannot be disputed as the claim of Constantine himself. Being a rational pagan, he believed this was a sign from one of the many gods, and so he literally painted the symbol of the cross on the shields of his troops, obeying the instruction in the most outward and non-spiritual sense. Immediately, his army began to win their battles against the odds, and this confirmed to him that the sign in the sky was a true message from a new god. He began conquering everything he could with that symbol, turning it into his god's icon. This was easy for him to believe, since Roman pagans had no issue with believing that one god could be stronger than the others. In fact they already had ideas of how the divine pantheon operated, and who was stronger than whom. They also wouldn't be too surprised if a god would directly communicate with Roman emperors and heroes, since Romans believed that emperors were like gods themselves, and had cults to worship them as such. He was given a mission by this god and immediately went to work conquering with the sign of the cross.

But think: what does the cross represent to a Roman general? Certainly not the gospel of Jesus Christ and the sacrifice for the sins of mankind, but a symbol of Roman authority and capital punishment, killing those who defied Roman law. It was a familiar symbol, showing the ruthless public humiliation of criminals who dared to defy Rome's absolute power. The fact that Jesus had been crucified was not special to Romans, just another example of a dangerous person who failed to escape the punishment. Constantine would have had to ask his counselors and scholars about the religious meaning of the cross, but for him it had a special meaning tied to his "divine" vision of conquest. Before Constantine, Christians were considered a strange, dangerous cult in Rome, brutally killed by Nero hundreds of years earlier (60 AD or so) and since then hiding in the catacombs of Rome which they were creating as safe haven, or in the mountains. Systematic attempts to find and kill them had turned the church into a secret society, gathering at night in the tunnels to worship. They refused to cremate their dead or bury them, but instead laid their dead in the hollows of the walls because they believed that the resurrection could happen at any time and the revived brothers and sisters would have to be able to stand up and walk out of the catacombs! For Romans, however, all they saw were people sneaking dead bodies into tunnels at night, and hearing them call each other brothers and sisters even while married. So they believed it was a death cult oriented around incest and witchcraft. Constantine overturned that by publicly declaring himself a Christian, and authorizing the safety of Christians, and the worship of Jesus, in Rome.

It is likely that Constantine himself never once realized that he was worshiping Satan and creating a false church. He dutifully conquered the other pagan temples and erected crosses in them, showing to

Rome that his god was greater than theirs. Eventually all of the most powerful people in Rome were calling themselves Christian too, seeing that the emperor was singleminded and determined to convert the Roman empire. They created councils to discuss the dogma of the new religion, and greatly twisted the meaning of the Bible to suit their pagan ways because they weren't true followers of Christ. None of them were born again, or filled with the Holy Spirit. It was an intellectual bastardization of Christianity, and true Christians at the time knew it. This false church incorporated Mary as a replacement for their own female goddesses, and the disciples as replacements for the various gods they knew and preferred. Statues of demigods and pagan figures were simply renamed to Saint Peter or some other Biblical figure. This is why Roman Catholicism is rightly called "baptized paganism", because it was never a true church, only a blasphemous perversion.

> Now there arose during that time a serious disturbance concerning the Way. For a certain man named Demetrius, a silversmith, who made silver shrines of Artemis [the Roman version of Diana], providing no little trade for the craftsmen, whom he gathered, with the workers of similar occupation, and said: "Men, you know out of this trade is our prosperity. And you observe and hear that not only at Ephesus, but almost in all of Asia, this Paul has persuaded and turned away a great multitude, saying that they are not gods which are made by human hands. And not only is this business of ours in danger to come into disrepute, but also the temple of the great goddess Artemis may be despised and also her magnificence, about to be destroyed, she whom all Asia and the world worship." (Acts 19:23-27 EMTV)

Pagan craftsmen greatly profited from statues, temples, idols, silver works, and elaborate commissions they received. Great patrons of the ruling class in Greek and Roman societies would pay the guilds to create statues, and some of these exist to this day in museums. This created an economy of pagan worship that had no equivalent in Christianity, and was blasphemous. Rome hated Christianity and refused to destroy the idols and pagan temples, but instead "conquered" them by pretending they were suddenly part of Christian worship. This is the function of the white rider, which seeks to always conquer other religions as if it were Christian, while actually being Satanic and deluded.

It's difficult to understand history by going according to Revelation because the Bible never dignifies the lies of Satan, which is what we've been taught as history. God does not dignify Satan's Antichurch as legitimate, which then forces us to put aside our own misconceptions and see history from God's point of view, because He won't meet us in the middle. Paul already established a church in Rome hundreds of years before Constantine, and we even have accounts of him in the Bible preaching to Roman authorities such as king Agrippa. The so-called "church fathers" who claimed to come from Paul and the disciples were not necessarily even believers, and went on to have influence that we don't need to respect or account for. Revelation leaves the description of the rider vague, using the symbolism of white (holiness) and to show that it is a false version of Christianity—the tares that Jesus warned about. The true rider of the ultimate white horse is Jesus himself, when he comes down in the clouds in the Day of The Lord. The first rider is not Christ, but an impostor who will deceive many, and this deception will be how he "conquers" with the aid of Satan and his meddling spirits.

Constantine is the first Pope of Rome, despite what Catholic scholars claim, and white has been the established color of the Papacy for millennia. To this day the Pope wears white, and seeks to conquer the world with the Roman symbol of the cross, absorbing other religions as if they were compatible. But unlike the strict punishment of ancient Roman law, when conquest involved military occupation, Popes love to be "ecumenical", partnering with and assimilating other beliefs into the Catholic Church. Rome was always incorporating new gods from different regions into their pantheon, and this much didn't change. According to the dictionary, the very term "Catholic" means "free from provincial prejudices or attachments", though it is more commonly translated as "Universal". But this is the very opposite of Christianity, which is obsessed with rejecting everything and remaining pure. The word "holy" actually means "separated" in the sense of being sanctified, set apart, and purified from whatever is common and vulgar.

The rider of the white horse therefore represents both Constantine and the office he creates for Satan's growing empire. It will continue to ride onward to conquer, and subsequent riders will only add to this power, and expand with new roles, while always having the same goal of conquest.

Red: The militarization of the Antichurch

We cannot address the infinite blasphemies and false doctrines of the Catholic Church, so instead I will draw your attention to the sermon on the mount where Jesus teaches what God prioritizes and blesses in the real Kingdom of Heaven:

> *Blessed are the poor in spirit, for <u>theirs is the kingdom of heaven</u>. Blessed are those who mourn, for they will be comforted. Blessed are the meek, for they shall inherit [not conquer] the earth. Blessed are those who hunger and thirst after righteousness, for they shall be filled. Blessed are the merciful, for they shall obtain mercy. Blessed are the pure in heart, for they shall see God. Blessed are the peacemakers, for they shall be called sons of God. <u>Blessed are those who have been persecuted for righteousness' sake, for theirs is the kingdom of heaven</u>. "Blessed are you whenever they revile you, and they persecute you, and they say all kinds of evil against you falsely for My sake. Rejoice and be exceedingly glad, for great is your reward in heaven, for so they persecuted the prophets who were before you. (Matthew 5:3-12 EMTV)*

The Kingdom of Heaven is for those who are poor in spirit and persecuted for being righteous, meek and mourning, hungering for righteousness. Not for ornately dressed priests in lavish robes, sitting in thrones and carrying golden scepters, or commanding armies. Satan's

Antichurch always persecutes the righteous, accusing them falsely, just as Satan accused the brothers of Christ day and night in heaven until he was kicked out. That's why as Satan's empire grows, so will his strategy for finding new ways to make Christians seem evil in the world's eyes so they can be killed without too much backlash. Unlike Jesus, Satan wants the world on his side; he needs to appease them or at least justify his brutality to some extent.

As we move forward, we must remember that Constantine the Great radically transformed Rome. This included the establishment of a new capital city in the east, called Constantinople (modern day Istanbul, Turkey) after his own name. This eastern empire of Rome was considered Roman territory as well, but was eventually called the Byzantine Empire by historians to make a distinction. Despite creating a kind of schism in Roman religion and politics, Constantinople thrived during the downfall of western Rome for centuries, carrying on its own version of Constantine's religion, prospering and holding on to many artifacts and examples of Roman greatness. Today that religion is called the Greek Orthodox, or Eastern Orthodox.

The second seal is broken during that downfall of western Rome.

> And when he _opened the second seal_, I heard the second living being saying, "Come!" Another horse went out, _fiery red_, and it was granted to him that sat on it _to take peace from the earth_, so that they might _kill each other_; and there was given to him _a great sword_. (Revelation 6:3-4 EMTV)

The miraculous event that followed the second seal's breaking took place around 800 AD, in the Frankish kingdoms, who were the ancestors of French and German tribes. The Romans had tried to conquer "Germania" as they called it many times, but the warrior tribes there were too resilient and defiant for it to ever be properly incorporated into the empire. As a result, the Europeans knew and respected Romans, but were still sovereign. By 800 AD the king of the Franks was Charlemagne the Great. Western Rome was being destroyed by barbarians and Rome itself was in danger of being totally overrun and conquered. The Pope at the time, named Leo III, feared for his life and fled to the north, seeking the aid of Charlemagne, whose father, Pippin, had previously defended Rome and reclaimed territory on its behalf. Pippin believed in Rome's Christianity, and wanted to save their great historic city. The Pope therefore devised a trick, to get Charlemagne his son to permanently vow service to the Vatican itself, turning his unstoppable warrior armies into a weapon of Rome. In order to pull this off, the Pope's servants apparently forged a document that was said to be sent by God, declaring that Charlemagne should become the new Holy Roman Emperor, the protector of Roman territory. The plan worked, and Charlemagne was flattered to receive his new title and supposedly divine favor. Like Constantine before him, Charlemagne immediately set to work saving Rome with his armies, establishing the "Papal states", and then returning to Europe to conquer it in the name of the Holy Roman Empire as well. As he forced the people to convert—both to ancient Roman idealism and Roman Catholicism—he tried to create in them a new love for the classic Roman glory, hoping to revive Greco-Roman literature and Latin as a language. It was a mixed success, but the conquest nevertheless handed Europe to the Vatican on a silver platter.

As a result of this miraculous militarization of the Vatican's authority, the Pope was now able to "excommunicate" kings and princes at will, having them killed as heretics if they did not obey the commands of the Catholic Church. The brutal reign of the Vatican over Europe and its armies became known as the Dark Ages, due to the extreme oppression, ignorance, plagues, and corruption that resulted. The Inquisition, which was a systematic slaughter of anyone who questioned the Papacy, was just one of the Satanic innovations during the reign of the red horseman. The Crusades, which sought to conquer Jerusalem with the Templars, ultimately set up the modern banking system in the process and created a new way for international wars to be waged. This period of extreme spiritual darkness also saw the rise of exorcisms, stigmata, and shared visions of Mary statues coming to life in some way. Then there was the "falling sun" miracle, in which large groups of people saw the sun fall out of the sky to earth only to rise back up instantly. This was all part of a new period of Satanic conquest. Of course, anyone who challenged the priesthood by being a true Christian was killed as well, and their property seized, even if they were nobles, royals or wealthy merchants. It was called the Holy Roman Empire, but it was neither holy, nor Roman. It should be called the Satanic European Empire, and it oppressed the church for hundreds of years, forcing Christians to once again become a secret society living in the fringe, hunted by Satan's antichrist slaves.

Charlemagne himself was called the Holy Roman Emperor, but the true office of military power in the Vatican belonged to the Cardinals, who are directly beneath the Pope in the hierarchy of the Catholic Church, followed by Archbishops and then Bishops, Priests, and finally Deacons. As a term, "cardinal" priests had existed already, much like how the position of "Pontifex" and the place called "Vatican" existed before Constantine, during the pagan era. Catholicism was less about invention, and more about reinvention. It allowed Satan to consolidate European power into the hands of the Vatican, which meant that the Cardinals would eventually become the church's equivalent to kings in terms of power and authority.[2] This meant Cardinals would reign over a kingdom as if it were theirs, and commanded the kings to use their military on behalf of the Papacy to kill "heretics", wage wars, and conquer lands. They coordinated the bloody Crusades and Inquisition, "taking peace from the earth" while not personally waging war themselves. Notice that the rider of the red horse does not attack or destroy anyone, though he has a giant sword in his hand. This is because the Cardinals—who always wear red!—only needed to speak a word and kings would tremble and obey. The fiery red of Cardinals is so iconic that the color "cardinal red" was named after them, not the other way around! It represents blood, military power, and blatant oppression.

The horrors of the Dark Ages were defined by the Cardinal system. Satan's conspiracy was greatly multiplied, allowing him to destroy, plunder, and murder as he pleased, making pacts with various kings and armies to subjugate the people and monopolize the economy. The European people were sick of it, hated the Pope, and longed for some

---

[2]   The Pope is said to be above all kings, the king of kings, the equivalent of Jesus Christ on earth. Popes are therefore counterfeit Christs, and they worship the counterfeit version of God, Satan, who considers himself the equivalent of God the Father.

kind of relief, but were constantly being monitored and threatened. The "Holy Roman Empire" was thus a Satanic deception never before seen in the history of the world; except perhaps the Tower of Babel itself.

BLACK: THE DARK SCIENCE OF THE ANTICHURCH

> *O Timothy, keep that which is committed to thy trust, avoiding profane and vain babblings, and oppositions of science [Greek: "gnosis"] falsely so called: (1 Timothy 6:20 KJV)*

The Satanic European Empire reached its peak during the reign of the Medici family in Italy in the late 1400's and early 1500's. The Popes at the time had filled Europe with absolute dread. Despite the Age of Sail bringing in riches and treasures, it also created a powerful merchant class, trade, and a desire for freedom and exploration, not dogma and ignorance. Spain rose as a Catholic powerhouse in the midst of this transformation, sailing the world in the name of the Pope, stealing from and conquering the natives with a message of Catholic supremacy. This is where the Conquistadors came from. Other countries were sick of the greed and despotism of the Cardinals, and wanted reform.

Gnostic sects were forming behind the scenes, sharing mystic heresies from the Far East, India, Africa, and antichristian Judaism with its Kabbalah practices. The Spanish Inquisition had to work overtime to slaughter those who challenged the dogma of the church, trying to uncover other members of these groups, tracing their funding, and directing the governors and princes to torture them horribly. Meanwhile, in Germany, Martin Luther brought forward his criticisms of the sale of indulgences—the Satanic blasphemy doctrine of selling forgiveness for the dead. The church reached a critical point of no return. Murdering and martyring people was not going to be a solution forever.

The Protestant Reformation loomed large thanks to Martin Luther and other reformers pointing out the extreme hypocrisy and corruption of the Catholic Church. The invention of the printing press also allowed the Bible to be printed in the common tongue and mass-distributed. As soon as regular priests and normal folks understood God's Word, their pretense of legitimacy would vanish. The Vatican was panicked. It was at this time, around 1500 AD, that Jesus broke the third seal and saved Satan's empire from collapsing.

This time, the miraculous event took place in Spain, when a military general by the name of Ignatius Loyola was struck by a cannonball in the leg and sent to the hospital. Despite being a brave and successful army leader on behalf of the immensely powerful Catholic kingdom, he was secretly a member of a black magic secret society known as Los Alumbrados, or "The Illuminated". His story and conversion would unleash the third rider.

When we keep in mind that the Protestant Reformation would not happen for a few decades and would take place in another European country, it shouldn't be a surprise that the Spanish Inquisition was focused mostly on forcefully converting Jews to Catholicism. They were a visible minority who refused to conform. They wanted to remain independent, because they operated powerful banks and trade operations, and sent tithes back to their Jewish homelands. The Cardinals did not appreciate this rogue sect operating at a high level in their countries. But after being forced to convert, these "conversos" naturally reacted by becoming a sort of secret society; outwardly they professed to be passionate servants of the Pope, but privately they created their own network of spies and secret communications to operate independently in the shadows. Between these conversos and the many other Spanish nobles who despised the stifling Catholic empire, they formed Los Alumbrados as a way to unite and empower each other, ensuring that their banking, politics, and military ambitions aligned in favor of their own gnostic interests. Members belonged to powerful and well-connected families, and these traveled easily, made personal and business connections, arranged marriages and strategic partnerships, recruited, and expanded the secret society under the nose of the Inquisition. In order to deflect attention away from themselves and their evil, they often pointed even more vigorously at the rumblings of other "heretics" who, for example, dared to question the authority of the Pope. Accusing others was a good way to remain free from suspicion yourself.

This group loved forbidden manuscripts and foreign mysticism, which was being imported from far away lands constantly. They were practitioners of sex magic, blood magic, and gnosticism, believing that God did not really exist, but rather that humanity could unlock powers by indulging in enough discipline and depravity. To them, "illumination" was Satanism:

> For such are false apostles, deceitful workers, transforming themselves into the apostles of Christ. And no marvel; for Satan himself is transformed into an <u>angel of light</u>. Therefore it is no great thing if his ministers also be transformed as the ministers of righteousness; whose end shall be according to their works. (2 Corinthians 11:13-15 KJV)

Just how elaborate and international their society was is unknown, but sail, commerce, and travel would have allowed for a vast network. Los Alumbrados and its international spy nobility were one reason Spain was so successful in its military efforts in the first place; they whispered things to each other across state lines, financed armadas of ships, and pooled their knowledge at all times.

When the Spanish Inquisition came for Ignatius Loyola during his hospital stay, agonized and doomed as a military commander, he knew his days as a secret enemy of the Catholic Church were over. They knew something about his secret society, and were prepared to torture him until he exposed their secrets and brought down the whole system. But when Jesus broke the third seal, Loyola experienced a type of epiphany. Instead of confessing his sins and participating in the inquisition, he pleaded to speak with the Pope himself. He was granted an audience, and recovered enough to visit. There he pledged the entire network of Los Alumbrados to the service of the Pope if they would give him a new office and incorporate him as the leader of his own "militia". By explaining the extent of their reach, power, and gnostic wisdom, the Pope agreed to spare him and create a new branch of the church known as the Society of Jesus, the Militia of the Pope.

And when he opened the third seal, I heard the third living being say, "Come." And behold, <u>a black horse</u>, and he who sat on it had <u>a pair of scales</u> in his hand. And I heard a voice in the midst of the four living beings, saying, "A quart of wheat for a denarius, and three quarts of barley for a denarius; but do not harm the oil and the wine." (Revelation 6:5-6 EMTV)

All interpretations seem to agree that this rider commands the trade prices of the world, if not its food supplies. But balances are also a symbol of taxation, money lending, legislation and justice systems, regulatory power, and careful technical measurement. All that this strange rider seems to be doing, according to the verse, is holding some balances and talking about the prices of things. To any outward appearance he doesn't seem to be evil or destructive at all, does it? This is because they are covert, preferring indirect methods for their conquests.

Amazingly, the "Jesuits" (the derogatory nickname given to the Society of Jesus by other Catholic orders, which they happily accepted) were totally free from the Inquisition's scrutiny, meaning they were allowed to do and say anything they wanted, including totally contradicting and criticizing the Papacy and the Vatican itself. This is still true today, where Jesuits often raise the ire of Catholics by being contrarian, progressive, modern, and scientific. They were given a blank check to serve as "reformers" in their own way, establishing elaborate front organizations such as schools and hospitals around the world in order to spy, scheme, and research as much as possible. Imagine how utterly intimidating and powerful the Los Alumbrados must have been in order for the Papacy—able to make kings tremble—to grant them this kind of license to disgrace the clergy as much as they pleased!

As a matter of fact, at one point (in 1773, to be exact) the Vatican did officially abolish the Jesuits from existence because they were considered "too independent" and a huge threat to Vatican control. A close study of this period will show how, immediately upon being banished from the Catholic nations, the Jesuits used their international spy network to enact revenge, orchestrating the rise of Napoleon Bonaparte to conquer Europe, invade Italy, humiliate the Pope in the Vatican, and spread the ideology of nationalism, revolution, deism, and other "Enlightenment" principles so that the Vatican would learn its place. The Pope was now a follower of Satan's plans, not the leader. The Jesuits were "restored" a few decades later. It's no coincidence that "the Illuminati" was founded by an actual Jesuit, Adam Weishaupt (pretending to be an ex-Jesuit and sworn enemy of theirs) in 1776—only three years after the Jesuits were officially abolished. "The Illuminati" is nothing other than the extension of the Jesuits in the secular world, and a blatant allusion to their original form as "Los Alumbrados" hundreds of years earlier in Spain.

So the Jesuits became their own secret society within the church, bitterly hated by the other Catholic orders who were stuck following the unpopular dogma and fighting the Reformation the old fashioned way. The Jesuits would instead lead the "Counter-Reformation" (the plan to undermine, destabilize, and destroy all "heretic" churches who believe the Bible and love the truth) and spread the Satanic gnostic madness far and wide in the name of Jesus. There is no more wicked, inverted, pure enemy of Christ than the Society of Jesus, who claim to do all of their assassinations and evils "for the greater glory of God".

Gnosis means "knowledge", but it has a scientific connotation. It is not simply knowledge from experience or teaching, but a type of study and systematic organization. Gnosticism is therefore an attempt to organize the secrets of the universe into a proper school of thought, leading to a type of "illumination" or salvation through learning and science. Already in the Bible we see Timothy warned to avoid it by Paul, who must have realized the danger thanks to his past as a devout Pharisee. Jewish gnosticism was carried on after Jesus through Jewish scholars, culminating in Kabbalah mysticism, which merges Satanism with the Bible, trying to unlock the exact knowledge of how the world works. This group's merging of Spanish merchant gnostics was central to the Los Alumbrados success, and became fundamental to the Jesuits as well.

The secret mission of the Jesuits has always been science and "illumination". They traveled the world in the guise of Christian missionaries—always dressed in black!—teaching and learning at the very cusp of scientific discovery. They take vows of poverty, refuse to be ornately dressed, and prefer to control from the shadows. This gives them the appearance of humility, although they are more devious and egotistical than any other group in the world. The color black represents evil, Satanism, dark magic, the occult, secrecy, subtlety, and a kind of purity that is opposite to holiness. The Jesuits are a highly educated, lethal, trained military society, and might be best categorized as an occult intelligence agency, operating worldwide long before the CIA and other imitators even existed. They saved the Vatican from becoming powerless worldwide through their bloody revolutions and warped science, although they often clash with them in terms of politics. They created the "Enlightenment" that seemingly weakened the Vatican. (We will explain this mystery yet.) Many have said that the Jesuit General[3] is more powerful than the Pope himself, earning him the nickname of "Black Pope".

So let us return to the scales in the hands of the black rider. In reality, the rider of the black horse holds a pair of scales because this represents measurement, which is the foundation of science (gnosis). Everything that can be measured can be deconstructed, tamed, controlled, and turned into a weapon eventually. The black rider doesn't carry any outward weapons because the Jesuits are not outwardly violent. They are scientists, occultists, and mystics. The voice talks about the price of food and the treatment of natural resources because this is also the end result of the Jesuit conquest: total economic control of the world, and technocratic revolutions that lead to centralized planning, popularly known as the New World Order. We are at the height of their accomplishment today.

GREEN: THE DEATH EMPIRE OF THE ANTICHURCH

As of the writing of this book I believe the fourth seal has been broken, unleashing the beginning of the reign of Death. Based on the pattern of the last three seals, and the description in Revelation, it is

---

[3]   Yes, the proper title of the Jesuit's leader is "General", showing that it is a military order.

very interesting to speculate on what it will mean, and we believe it is possible to guess.

If the pattern we've seen so far is consistent, it means that the power and public credibility of the previous rider should have reached its zenith and become in danger of collapsing. This is happening today thanks mostly to the Internet, which has allowed Christians and other truth-seekers to expose the Satanic conspiracy and make humanity aware of the evil powers behind modern society. There is a crisis in the New World Order plan, as humanity rejects centralized global government and technocracy, and demands sovereignty, reform, and a return to sanity. Satan is still controlling the world powers and his conspiracy, but it's becoming very hard to make the world play along with it anymore. If Jesus has broken the fourth seal, it means that we should expect a powerful, influential (though not necessarily well-known) figure to "convert" to the side of Satan and begin creating a system of control, conquest, and opposition like never before. Obviously nobody in history was aware of the breaking of a seal at the time, and the creation of this power was hidden behind complex world affairs and mysterious private interactions, so we shouldn't expect it to be easy to notice in terms of who has "converted" and what they're doing exactly.

> *And when he opened the fourth seal, I heard the voice of the fourth living being saying, "Come." And behold, a pale [Greek: "chloros"] horse, and he who sat on it was named Death, and Hades was following him. And authority was given to him over a fourth of the earth, to kill with the sword, and with famine, and with death, and by the wild beasts of the earth. (Revelation 6:7-8 EMTV)*

The first thing we must note in this passage is that the word translated "pale" is the Greek word "chloros". This literally means "green" or "verdant". The chemical chlorine is named after the word because concentrated chlorine is bright yellow-green. When applied to horses it can be thought of as a pale grayish-yellow dun color, but I think the color green is much more appropriate. The second thing we must note is that the rider is simply called Death, which seems to indicate that it will be openly known to the world as this. While the black rider was mysterious and seemingly harmless, the Death rider will be blatantly obsessed with killing humanity. How will this work, and how does it fit into the conspiracy of Satan and his minions?

Satan is today conspiring to create a massive "population reduction" in the name of the "Green Movement". Hundreds of examples of this rhetoric can be easily found online and in newspapers, magazines, and mainstream discussions of academia. Saving the planet requires a huge portion of mankind to be killed according to the evil "scientists" who dictate our world from on high, like priests. Environmentalism has gone completely out of control, being turned into a religion with cultists who are funded by billionaires. Every day, a coordinated religion is being created in public, preaching the death of industry, personal freedom, and humanity itself. Children are being taught that the world won't exist by the time they reach adulthood, and it's the fault of the older generation who failed to protect nature. It is earth worship, even though the people orchestrating it are the ones who pollute, destroy, and rape the earth more than anyone in history. The richest men in the world are obsessed with population numbers and being "green" suddenly. Is this a coincidence? You can answer that yourself.

We must recognize that God only authorizes this rider to kill 25% of the world. Whether that refers to geographic territory or population percentage is unclear. It's also unclear whether that 25% is a single landmass or demographic, or distributed across the whole world. But in any case, the rider's powers will be limited, though devastating and horrific. He has the power to kill with weaponry, famine, "death" (a mysterious cause), and "wild beasts", which might be a metaphor for something other than literal animals, such as terrorists.

The Death rider is also followed by Hades (the "grave") in the same seal, indicating that this won't be a long period of history. The rise of the Green Priesthood and its population agenda will be relatively quick, and Hades will then be dominant. This could represent the reign of the death cult that follows in the wake of the rider, or it could simply indicate that the end of the world is coming soon after; I lean toward the latter interpretation myself for reasons that will become clear as we continue.

It's unlikely that the reign of the Death rider will be very organized or official, but the climate alarmism cult already has ties to the Vatican and their Jesuit Pope. The governor of California flew to the Vatican some years ago to beg Pope Francis to preach on climate change. The Pope has become quite obsessed with the "green movement" and advocates for a more socialist, science-driven world order. It would be no surprise to me if the Catholic Church officially ordained a new office or branch dedicated to "environmentalism" and the global government of the world's population numbers yet, dressed in green robes. We may have a "Green Pope" yet.

Because the green movement and its cult is so closely tied with New Age beliefs, Mother Earth worship, and primitive spiritism, it would not be surprising to see other New Age beliefs rise to world prominence, such as so-called "aliens" or spiritual beings who could have green color. Whatever it is would be a deceptive hoax, aimed at demonizing Christians and justifying their murder. It's hard for us to imagine today because we are at the zenith of the dark science age, but all it would take is for more disclosures of UFOs and alien information to trick much of the population into fearing and believing in New Age beliefs and abandon traditional notions of God and religion. Many self-proclaimed Christians would go "green" if there was a convincing world event that seemed to debunk the Bible and unite humanity under one government of some revolutionary spirituality.

In any case, the Death rider will not be able to kill the whole world. The majority will survive, and then the fifth seal will be broken, returning us to a heavenly scene where the dead Christians cry out for vengeance. This is a clear hint that Christianity will be hit hard by the Death empire. We know this is one of Satan's goals, and it is his world to rule. But here we come to the question of the Rapture, the Antichrist, and many other controversies that must be dealt with.

7

EVIL DELUSION

These things have I spoken unto you, that ye should not be offended. They shall put you out of the synagogues: yea, <u>the time cometh, that whosoever killeth you will think that he doeth God service</u>. And these things will they do unto you, because they have not known the Father, nor me. (John 16:1-3 KJV)

I pray for them: <u>I pray not for the world</u>, but for them which thou hast given me; for they are thine. (John 17:9 KJV) I have given them thy word; and <u>the world hath hated them</u>, because <u>they are not of the world</u>, even as <u>I am not of the world</u>. I pray not that thou shouldest take them out of the world, but that thou shouldest keep them from the evil. <u>They are not of the world, even as I am not of the world</u>. (John 17:14-16 KJV)

Then saith Pilate unto him, Speakest thou not unto me? knowest thou not that I have power to crucify thee, and have power to release thee? Jesus answered, <u>Thou couldest have no power at all against me, except it were given thee from above</u>: therefore he that delivered me unto thee hath the greater sin. (John 19:10-11 KJV)

Pontius Pilate represents Rome, not only in the sense of being an official, but symbolically. He has no power over Christ except that

51

it was granted by God above. He also says that the Jews who delivered him to be punished have a "greater sin". He specifically prays to God and says that he does **not** pray for the world, but only for his followers. This world is hopeless, but his followers are beloved. He knows that soon people will be killing him and his followers while genuinely believing that they're doing service to God. A painful thought.

This has greater implications for the whole church, and its future. When Satan takes control of the world he always accuses Christians before he kills them. He loves to accuse the righteous, as we know. His servants, beguiled by the spirit of antichrist, do not know the Father and truly think they're serving God by killing them, whether they are Jews or Romans. Satan hides behind religious sensitivity and sanctimoniousness, to accuse Christians before killing them. The rulers of the Jews and their adherents believed Jesus was blaspheming and deserved to die according to the law. The Roman Catholics believed that Christians are heretics, betraying God by not respecting the clergy and proper "Kingdom of God" (as they see it) on earth. Either way, we must remember that Jesus does not blame the humans themselves as much as Satan, who is directing the conspiracy. They have sins, and some are greater than others, but yet it is part of God's plan.

THE GREAT BLINDFOLD: ENIGMA OF THE STATUE AND THE STONE

And in the days of these kings shall the God of heaven set up a kingdom, which shall never be destroyed: and the kingdom shall not be left to other people, but it shall break in pieces and consume all these kingdoms, and it shall stand for ever. Forasmuch as thou sawest that the stone was cut out of the mountain without hands, and that it brake in pieces the iron, the brass, the clay, the silver, and the gold; the great God hath made known to the king what shall come to pass hereafter: and the dream is certain, and the interpretation thereof sure. (Daniel 2:44-45 KJV)

This amazing dream of king Nebuchadnezzar, which he received in Babylon a few hundred years before Jesus was born, and which was interpreted by the prophet Daniel, has been the source of huge divisions to this day. Everyone wants to know what the eternal kingdom is, but first we need to know when "the days of these kings" are:

> And whereas thou sawest the feet and toes, part of potters' clay, and part of iron, the kingdom shall be divided; but there shall be in it of the strength of the iron, forasmuch as thou sawest the iron mixed with miry clay. And as the toes of the feet were part of iron, and part of clay, so the kingdom shall be partly strong, and partly broken. And whereas thou sawest iron mixed with miry clay, they shall mingle themselves with the seed of men: but they shall not cleave one to another, even as iron is not mixed with clay. (Daniel 2:41-43 KJV)

It's a confusing description. Everyone recognizes that the "stone cut without hands" is related to the Messiah, but Jews believe that this day has not come yet, because Jesus seemingly failed to destroy Rome, which was clearly the iron kingdom. In fact, after Jesus, Rome only grew in strength, to the point of conquering the known world like nobody before! Jews are very aware of the huge power of the Catholic Church, and believe they will smash the empire and bring about the arrival of their Messiah, to whatever extent they take it literally. Catholics believe the church is the stone, which becomes the eternal kingdom. However, they believe this is fulfilled as Constantine "consumed" the other pagan religions and kingdoms. By conquering their pagan temples and incorporating them into the "Universal" church, they believe it fulfills Daniel's prophecy.

To support this view, Catholics obsess over this famous passage:

> And Jesus answered and said unto him, Blessed art thou, Simon Barjona: for flesh and blood hath not revealed it unto thee, but my Father which is in heaven. And I say also unto thee, That thou art Peter [Greek: "stone"], and

upon this rock I will build my church; and the gates of hell shall not prevail against it. And I will give unto thee the keys of the kingdom of heaven: and whatsoever thou shalt bind on earth shall be bound in heaven: and whatsoever thou shalt loose on earth shall be loosed in heaven. (Matthew 16:17-19 KJV)

Not only does he bless Simon, but he renames him "Peter", which is a certain sized stone. Plus he says that upon "this rock" he will build his entire church, making it unclear whether he's talking about Peter or the statement Peter made, which was that Jesus was the Christ. Jesus also says that the gates of hell will not prevail against it, and seemingly authorizes Peter with great power to affect heaven itself. It's not hard to see why a Roman Catholic would be confident that Peter—the "stone" who was blessed and authorized with the keys to influence heaven— would be the same stone that demolishes the statue in Nebuchadnezzar's dream, according to Daniel's interpretation. It aligns perfectly, to the point where it can't be an accident. Jesus must have made this statement deliberately as a trap for Satan to use in the future. Plus the Roman Catholic Church has survived ever since its creation, which seems to prove that they are the Kingdom. And why has it survived? We know that it's because Jesus Christ himself is breaking seals on the book to give it more power and prevent it from collapsing! So the Romans can truly believe that they are righteous and fulfilling the mission of God, expanding and conquering the world forever, "consuming" the kingdoms it meets. It truly believes it is immortal, holy, and was given the keys to affect things in heaven. That's why Popes can make rules about how humanity should live, sell indulgences to change people's fate in the afterlife, and so on.

In other words, both the Jews and the Romans believe they are serving God by conspiring against each other and the saints. Jews want to collapse the power of Rome and establish the Kingdom for the first time, and Romans want to keep conquering until they fill the whole world and there is no more resistance.

As Christians, knowing that Satan is behind all these conspiracies, we should not hate any group or people. They are ignorant, deceived, deluded, and think they are serving God. Only the truth can cause them to see the error of their ways and convert them one at a time. But even so, let us never forget that it is God the Father who preordained all of this with the seven-sealed book, and that Jesus is in control of breaking those seals. We are moving towards God's victory, not Satan's, no matter what happens.

DANIEL'S TRUE MEANING: COMBINING STATUE AND BEASTS

If you're familiar with Daniel, you know that he not only documented the vision of the statue and the stone that smashes it apart, but had his own dreams about giant beasts with strange descriptions. One of the beasts in particular worries him: the "fourth beast", which is hard for him to identify. It's more powerful than all the others, and is said to have the power to destroy the saints and reign until the end of the age. He wants to know what it means, but the angel does not tell him the full meaning, only more enigmatic hints.

If we properly interpret the statue and the stone, we see that Rome is the iron legs of the statue, breaking apart everything before it. But the kings of those final days before the Kingdom arrives are described as the feet and toes of the statue, mixed with iron and clay. This describes the Jewish (clay) King Herod and his shared governance with Rome (iron). It was partially strong and partially weak. Herod was a king, but he was under Roman authority. The Jewish priests had to bring Jesus to a Roman authority to have him executed. Herod expanded the Second Temple, but only in order to make it more like a Roman military fortress. He tried to mingle together God's kingdom and Rome's. The ten toes show how divided and confused it all was. And that's how the region was when Jesus began to preach there.

Furthermore, we must think about the statue of Nebuchadnezzar's dream as a a timeline; the Bible clearly shows that we should. And if it is a timeline, then the feet and toes need to be **proportional** to make any sense at all. The feet and toes can't possibly represent thousands of years, because the statue is proportional and the toes don't stretch on for miles! The timeline runs out once it reaches the toes, which immediately follow the iron legs of old Rome. That is to say, before Jesus smashes it, and before Satan then "heals" it from death by giving it his throne and authority.

Jesus destroys the whole statue eventually, but the description does not suggest it is immediate. It breaks apart all at once, but it doesn't simply vanish on the spot. It turns into chaff and eventually blows away in the wind. Likewise, Christ's kingdom begins small, and eventually fills the whole world:

> *His legs of iron, his feet part of iron and part of clay. Thou sawest till that a stone was cut out without hands, which smote the image upon his feet that were of iron and clay, and brake them to pieces. Then was the iron, the clay, the brass, the silver, and the gold, <u>broken to pieces together</u>, and <u>became like the chaff of the summer threshingfloors; and the wind carried them away</u>, that no place was found for them: and the stone that smote the image <u>became</u> a great mountain, and filled the whole earth. (Daniel 2:33–35 KJV)*

What Nebuchadnezzar's statue really represents is the powerful pagan religious-political systems that ruled over the Mediterranean region where Jerusalem is located. Religion and political systems were always deeply connected before our modern day, and so it makes sense why the destruction of this statue represents not only the fall of empires, but of religions and false gods. But taken in the full context of the Bible, this passage also speaks of Jesus overcoming Satan. His angels are outcast from heaven, and this is what allows the power of Christ and his Kingdom to come into fruition, right? Jesus comes to earth in order to powerfully smash the giant idol and destroy it, and cleanse the heavens in the process, while Satan is cast to earth after losing the war, and is cast to earth from heaven as well. These two opposing forces both arrive on earth in the same small time period, when the old world is destroyed and reduced to rubble, allowing for a new start to the world. Who will win? Who is more clever? Who has more secret power? Whose angels and spirit is greater? Whose followers are more devout?

> *And he said unto them, I beheld Satan as lightning fall from heaven. Behold, I give unto you power to tread on serpents and scorpions, and over all the power of the enemy: and nothing shall by any means hurt you. Notwithstanding in this rejoice not, that the spirits are subject unto you; but rather rejoice, because your names are written in heaven. (Luke 10:18-20 KJV)*

Mankind is blind to the spiritual domain, but Jesus Christ proved that he is truly God in the flesh with his transfiguration on the mountain. This showed the angels and the spiritual world that he was the real thing, and that a new age had arrived. He had the power to overcome everything. Satan's decision to save Rome from collapse and turn it into his own Antichurch miraculously "healed" it from death, despite being fatally wounded. It should have been destroyed along with the rest of the statue, but it miraculously came back to life and has never truly diminished. Countless people have been deceived by this ever since.

But now that we have established this context, we can finally explore the mystery of Daniel's fourth beast, and how it aligns with Rome and the greatly-misunderstood "Beast" of Revelation:

> *After this I saw in the night visions, and behold a fourth beast [Rome], dreadful and terrible, and strong exceedingly; and it had great iron teeth [Rome's metal in the statue]: it devoured [incorporated while destroying] and brake in pieces, and stamped the residue with the feet of it: and it was diverse from all the beasts that were before it; .... I beheld till the thrones were cast down [the war in heaven], and the Ancient of days did sit, whose garment was white as snow, and the hair of his head like the pure wool: [the glorified Jesus] his throne was like the fiery flame, and his wheels as burning fire. A fiery stream issued and came forth*

*from before him: thousand thousands ministered unto him,
and ten thousand times ten thousand stood before him: the
judgment was set, and the books were opened [Judgment
Day]. …. I beheld even till <u>the beast was slain</u>, and his
body destroyed, and <u>given to the burning flame</u> [lake of fire].
(Daniel 7:7-11 KJV)*

So the fourth beast of Daniel's vision has "iron teeth", just as the
fourth kingdom in the statue was made of iron.[4] The fourth beast is
certainly Rome, and its empire will last until the Kingdom of Heaven
comes… But which time? This is clever, because even though Christ's
Kingdom spiritually arrived with Jesus the first time, and old Rome was
in a sense weak and destroyed, the Kingdom of Heaven hasn't yet come
down to earth, and neither has Rome's empire truly been destroyed and
cast into fire!

Once we appreciate the timing mystery of the seven-sealed book
in Revelation, and God's plan to magnify Satan's earthly empire after
the Kingdom of Heaven is first established above, we can understand
why the destiny of the fourth beast is mixed up and seemingly
contradictory. Both the Kingdom and the Beast are destined to battle
again. Immediately after this vision, Daniel has a separate vision more
specifically regarding a heavenly event:

*I saw in the night visions, and, behold, one like <u>the Son of
man</u> came <u>with the clouds of heaven</u> [Jesus' ascension], and
<u>came to the Ancient of days</u> [this time God the Father], and
<u>they brought him near</u> before Him [to receive the seven-sealed
book]. And there was given him dominion, and glory, and <u>a
kingdom</u>, that all people, nations, and languages, should serve
him: his dominion is <u>an everlasting dominion</u>, which shall not
pass away, and his <u>kingdom that which shall not be destroyed</u>.
(Daniel 7:13-14 KJV)*

---

[4]   Babylon (gold/lion), Media-Persia (silver/bear), Greece (brass/leopard), and
Rome (iron/mystery beast).

He sees that the "clouds" bring the "Son of man" up to the "Ancient of days" and he is brought near to receive dominion, glory, and a kingdom. To a Jew in Babylon, hoping for the arrival and glorification of the Messiah, this is indeed a magnificent comfort and vision. It confirms that God will fulfill his promise to Israel and create the kingdom, even if Daniel doesn't understand how this can be possible with that pesky fourth beast roaming around until the end of the world! Only after Jesus do we appreciate the trick God played on Satan and the world.

As for the nature of the fourth beast, it gets further described. It will be given the ability to make war with the saints and overcome them, speak great blasphemies, and prevail until the end of days. Sound familiar? As we read Revelation it certainly will. Let's read what the angel tells Daniel:

> *I Daniel was grieved in my spirit in the midst of my body, and the visions of my head troubled me. I came near unto one of them that stood by, and asked him the truth of all this. So he told me, and made me know the interpretation of the things. These great beasts, which are four, are four kings, which shall arise out of the earth. But the saints of the most High shall take the kingdom, and possess the kingdom for ever, even for ever and ever. Then I would know the truth of the fourth beast, which was diverse from all the others, exceeding dreadful, whose teeth were of iron [Rome], and his nails of brass [Greece]; which devoured [consumed], brake in pieces, and stamped the residue with his feet; And of the ten horns that were in his head, and of the other which came up, and before whom three fell; even of that horn that had eyes, and a mouth that spake very great things, whose look was more stout than his fellows. I beheld, and the same horn made war with the saints, and prevailed against them; Until the Ancient of days came, and judgment was given to the saints of the most High; and the time came that the saints possessed the kingdom. Thus he said, The fourth beast shall be the fourth kingdom upon earth, which shall be diverse from all kingdoms, and shall devour the whole earth, and shall tread*

it down, and break it in pieces. And the ten horns out of this kingdom are ten kings that shall arise: and another shall rise after them; and he shall be diverse from the first, and he shall subdue three kings. And <u>he shall speak great words against the most High, and shall wear out the saints of the most High, and think to change times and laws</u>: and they shall be given into his hand until a time and times and the dividing of time. But the judgment shall sit, and they shall take away his dominion, to consume and to destroy it unto the end. <u>And the kingdom and dominion, and the greatness of the kingdom under the whole heaven, shall be given to the people of the saints</u> of the most High, <u>whose kingdom is an everlasting kingdom</u>, and all dominions shall serve and obey him. (Daniel 7:15-27 KJV)

The Beast in Revelation also has ten horns, is comprised of the various beasts of Daniel, and is the final kingdom that will make war with the saints, speak blasphemy, have Satanic power, and become "healed", even though it should have died from the arrival of the Messiah, who was meant to rule the world. Look at the description:

And I stood upon the sand of the sea, and saw <u>a beast</u> rise up out of the sea, having seven heads and <u>ten horns</u>, and upon his horns ten crowns, and upon his heads <u>the name of blasphemy</u> [the Antichurch counterfeit]. And the beast which I saw was like unto a leopard, and his feet were as the feet of a bear, and his mouth as the mouth of a lion [it is diverse from the other beasts of Daniel, but incorporates them]: and <u>the dragon</u> [Satan] <u>gave him his power, and his seat, and great authority</u>. And I saw one of his heads as it were <u>wounded to death</u> [from the victory of Christ]; and <u>his deadly wound was healed</u>: and all the world wondered after the beast. And they worshipped the dragon which gave power unto the beast: and they worshipped the beast, saying, Who is like unto the beast? <u>who is able to make war with him</u> [Pax Romana]? And there was given unto him <u>a mouth</u>

speaking great things and blasphemies; and power was given unto him to continue forty and two months. And he opened his mouth in blasphemy against God, to blaspheme his name, and his tabernacle, and them that dwell in heaven. And it was given unto him to make war with the saints, and to overcome them: and power was given him over all kindreds, and tongues, and nations. And all that dwell upon the earth shall worship him, whose names are not written in the book of life of the Lamb slain from the foundation of the world. If any man have an ear, let him hear. (Revelation 13:1-9 KJV)

So while the Roman Catholics truly believe they are the stone that will fill the world and "consume" or "devour" the other kingdoms, they are actually the Anitchurch, the empire of Satan, the blasphemers who make war with the saints and think they are doing service to God.[5]

All this is according to God's plan, and all of it is because the wheat and the tares need to both grow and mature before the harvest can happen. The Jews rejected Christ, so God needed to spread the Kingdom of Heaven around the whole world, not just establish an Israelite empire. But once the Kingdom is spreading around the world among gentiles, pagans, and the godless sporadically, unconventionally, through preaching and conversion, it's no longer possible to cleanly divide the holy from the evil. Remember that God needed Lot to flee Sodom before He could destroy it? And that Noah and his family needed to have an escape before he flooded the world and destroyed it? God's wrath is not surgical and individual. It's a collective punishment, vast and destructive to entire cities, nations, or the whole world. He can't pour out his wrath on the world properly until the holy people are fully separated from the evil. That's why history is being allowed to continue, Satan is being allowed to grow more powerful, and why the church is

---

[5] I am not saying anything about individual Roman Catholics, or even groups of them, but the institutional powers and authorities over the centuries who have, in their delusion, worked against God. We ought to love and care for those stuck in the Roman Catholic system as we would for any other precious human soul in need of redemption.

going to ultimately be targeted and reduced until God doesn't have to worry about collateral damage.

SATAN'S LOOPHOLE: THE TRUE ROLE OF DARK SCIENCE

Let's return to the topic of Los Alumbrados. Remember that they were born out of a hybridized gnosticism of Jewish Kabbalah and Spanish mystics in the Age of Sail, in the 1400s. Their obsession with occult and scientific knowledge, or "gnosis" in Greek, was not driven by a rational curiosity or a pure love of knowledge; there was something deeply sinister and dark about their inquiries. It was about control and power. Most Christians can't even comprehend that somebody would believe the Bible was powerful and true, and yet abandon its doctrine and use it as a weapon for selfish gain. But that's what thousands of scholars have done throughout history, and continue to do to this day. They treat it as a mysterious holy book, full of magical riddles for those cunning enough to exploit them. They reject literal interpretations, and invent all sorts of backwards and inverted meanings while still regarding the book as sacred. Satan knows that the Bible is powerful, but evil will always pervert what is good and pure.

Gnostics see the Scriptures as supernaturally powerful, but only so that they can use it for secret schemes. And the Jesuits continued this tradition by reading the Bible carefully, but only to glean and twist the meaning of things. Many books have been written exposing the hypocrisy and deceit of the Jesuits, mostly produced in the 1800s when European intellectuals were becoming sick of them. We must remember that even your typical Roman Catholic priest commits blasphemy and sacrilege on a daily basis as they deign to absolve sins in place of God, claim to convert wine and crackers into the literal blood and flesh of Jesus Christ for communion, and instruct ignorant followers to worship Mary and make their prayers to saints instead of praying to Christ or God directly. But the Jesuits were masters of cunning and subtle propaganda, rising to the occasion of the Protestants and their newly discovered love of Scripture in the 1500s. Ex-Jesuits who have been converted to Christ, such as Alberto Rivera, have attested that their brainwashing was so complete that they could not even read the words of the Bible without distorting it automatically and seeing things in the verses that weren't there. To give the reader some idea of how this wicked blindness works, below is an example of how a gnostic Jesuit might see a Biblical passage:

> and _to the Jews I became as a Jew_ [pretending to be Jewish and marrying into Jewish bloodlines to gain their secrets and riches], in order that _I might win_ [dominate] Jews; …. _to those outside the law_ [secular, heathen], _as one outside the law_ [pretending to be secular and atheist and making secret societies like Freemasons to gain their obedience] …. in order that _I might win_ [dominate] those outside the law; _to the weak I became as weak_ [feigned meekness and humility], in order that _I might win_ [dominate] the weak. _I have become all things to all men_ [secret agents, able to camouflage in any culture or society], that I might _by all means_ [including murder, theft, fraud, lawsuits, deception] save [subjugate] some. (1 Corinthians 9:20-22 EMTV) And _everyone who competes_ [struggles for dominance] _exercises self-control_ [extreme military training and cunning] _in all things_. Now they compete in order that they may receive a perishable crown [temporary local authority], but we compete for _an imperishable crown_ [eternal world domination]. Therefore I run thus: not as without a goal, thus _I box_ [physically attack, kill]: not as one beating the air. But _I treat my body roughly_ [harsh discipline and rituals], and _I bring it into subjection_ [occult self-mastery], lest, having preached to others, I myself should become disqualified. (1 Corinthians 9:25-27 EMTV)

The symbol of the Jesuits has been around since their creation, and is used to this day, though exact details vary. The basics are always the same: the whole symbol is contained within a sun, which is a direct homage to the Jesuit's roots as "Alumbrados" and their Satanic "enlightenment". Three nails, showing the eternal power to crucify and dominate Christ, and a cross above the letters "IHS", are inside the sun. The letters IHS are supposedly a "Christogram" that refers to Jesus. Roman Catholics carry on the tradition of Constantine, who obsessively used the image of the cross as a symbol of Roman spiritual power to conquer. Jesus Christ was nailed to the cross and died on it, showing Rome's power to kill the Messiah and defy God. For true Christians we never need to see the cross, wear it, or glorify it with symbols or adorn our churches with it. The story of the cross is only one of many important phases of Jesus' ministry, and symbolizes the fulfillment of his mission and the forgiveness of our sins, accomplished once and forever; after which Jesus was resurrected and now lives in heaven, victorious and glorified. But that does not make the nails and the cross any less potent for the Beast system, which sees it from the other point of view: it shows Satan's power to make war with Christ's church and prevail. They continually advertise the Roman cross, not as a sign of redemption, but of the dark power of Rome, the continual persecution of Christians, and an attempt to humiliate Jesus by keeping him symbolically in a state of eternal suffering.

To gnostics, nothing is what it seems. They think the plain language of the Bible hides a mystery that often means the **opposite** of what it says. In Canada, the Jesuits have a special document called a "Jesuit Dictionary" that explains that they have their own language, dubbed "Jesuit-speak".[6] They are proud of being double-talkers, able to subtly confuse their listeners. I can attest that, in my own life, I have personally met a student of gnosticism who loved to twist the meaning of words around and tried to recruit me into his occult view of the Bible, saying that Jesus was an Egyptian magician who was trying to teach mankind about the secrets of mysticism. To them, "love" can secretly mean hatred and murder; "faith" can mean atheism. Every good promise of God

---

[6]   http://image.jesuits.org/CANADA/media/Jesuit-Dictionary.pdf Here we see an entry entitled "Alumni of Jesuit Education". It says, "Included would be Rousseau, Moliere, Voltaire, Alfred Hitchcock, James Joyce, Descartes, Arthur Conan Doyle, Fidel Castro, and President Bill Clinton among others." This shows that the Jesuits take personal credit for all those leaders who were educated in Jesuit universities such as Georgetown. They love to be the schoolmasters of the elite to this day, just as they were in the 1500s.

makes can be turned into a trap against humanity, if leveraged properly. By using their knowledge of the Old Testament and other ancient texts, Kabbalah practitioners are experts on looking for ways to undermine God's plans, just as Satan always does. Even in the Garden of Eden, the serpent used God's own words to deceive humans, and again when Christ was tempted by Satan in the wilderness.

This is important to understand because, as you're about to learn, there are some promises in the Bible that have staggering implications to gnostics, which we would overlook as practically impossible to exploit. Shortly before the age of science and materialism, Los Alumbrados discovered something that would potentially allow Satan to have the ultimate victory over God, in their minds. This became their main goal. Although it is completely overlooked by scholars and Bible teachers alike, there is a single verse in the Bible that has the power to cancel God's entire covenant with Israel and, by extension, the Messiah. This was not told to me by anyone, but having some knowledge of how they operate, and seeing their plans unfold in the world, I understood it myself. This promise has become the number one priority of the Jesuits and their cadre of obsessed scientists ever since the 1500s, during the rise of men like Ignatius Loyola and Francis Bacon:

> *Thus saith the LORD; If heaven above can be measured,*
> *and the foundations of the earth searched out beneath, I*
> *will also cast off all the seed of Israel for all that they have*
> *done, saith the LORD.*
> *(Jeremiah 31:37 KJV)*

Read it again carefully if you must. Most Christians would read this and believe that it's a promise of eternal faithfulness to Israel, because the thing being discussed is an impossibility, meant to show how God's loyalty to Israel is permanent and unbreakable. After all, humans could never measure the heavens or search out the foundations below… can they? It may be impossible to believe, but Satan and his evil servants take this deadly serious. After all, it is a promise of God Himself, meaning He cannot ignore it or pretend it doesn't exist if somebody were to fulfill it. To the gnostics who love Satan, this is an actual loophole that, if they could pull it off, would invalidate all the prophecies concerning Israel and therefore Christ's victorious return to earth. Everything changes.

Does it seem ridiculous that an ancient Catholic religious order from the 1500s, during the height of the Spanish Inquisition—when all radical ideas were punished with torture and death—could somehow be arrogant enough to believe they could measure the heavens, or search the foundations of the earth? It shouldn't. Once you know about the Jesuits you will see that it's exactly what they believed they could do, and they used the full power of their secret international finance and spy network to pursue it.

There are two dedicated fields of science related to the measurement of heaven and the foundations of the world. They're called **astronomy**, and **seismology**.

> *Astronomy (n):*
> *1. The branch of physics studying celestial bodies and the whole universe.*

> *Seismology (n):*
> *The branch of geology that studies earthquakes.*

It turns out that these are the two scientific fields that the Jesuits are most recognized worldwide as being pioneers of! Seismology has been called "the Jesuit science" in fact. They were some of the earliest, best, and biggest researchers, dating back centuries. They tried to create a new and corrected calendar in 1582, based on observations of the heavens. They introduced astronomy to the Chinese around the same time, reviving their scientific interests. They built multiple advanced observatories in the 1700s around Rome. They tried to map the whole sky in the 1800s. They built major laboratories in the early 1900s. In 1981 they moved to Tucson, Arizona because the skies were much more clear, and according to VaticanObservatory.va, "the Vatican Observatory Research Group (VORG), in Tucson, Arizona in the United States" is "one of the world's largest and most modern centers for observational astronomy." The website boasts that "The VATT [Vatican Advanced

Technology Telescope] has pioneered the new technology of creating large, lightweight, stable mirrors in a rotating furnace." As recently as June 2020, another Jesuit priest was honored by having an asteroid named after him. According to an article at *thedialog.org*[7] dated June 22: "One more Jesuit has had an asteroid named for him." It goes on to describe how the 74-year-old Jesuit priest built and maintained special cameras to image the cosmos. He joined the observatory staff in 1983, and has a degree in astronomy from the University of Toronto. He studied "galactic structure" and "star formation". He is quoted as saying, "I am very much a star man. But realizing that stars are in our galaxy, I'm also interested in galactic structure and history of star populations in our galaxy. My way of probing all this is through the individual stars." But it adds that "The Jesuit's current research focuses on the characteristics of human sentience in the context of evolution." Deconstructing the human mind in the context of **evolution** is an interesting thing for a Roman Catholic priest to be studying, don't you think? Other Jesuit "contemporaries" who have had asteroids named after them are Brother Guy Consolmagno, director of the Vatican Observatory, Father Richard Boyle, Father Jean Baptise Kikwaya, and Father Robert Macke, a "meteorite curator". Previously, asteroids have also been named after Father Christopher Claviu, who made mathematical measurements "that helped develop the Gregorian calendar", and so on.

This is no joke. You can look it up yourself. The Jesuits have won awards and been recognized by scientific institutions for their amazing insights into the field of measuring the heavens, and searching the foundations of the earth beneath. Seismology observation stations are manned by Jesuit priests. They created and operated some of the most prestigious universities in the world, such as Georgetown. They want to know how to measure the heavens and figure out the foundations of the world. However, because scientists discovered that the universe is not static, but changing and expanding constantly, it's impossible to simply measure it once and have an accurate map. There are so many variables and mysteries (such as "dark matter") that nobody could ever say it has a defined size. Rather, the only way to really "measure" it

---

[7]   http://thedialog.org/international-news/vatican-observatory-astronomer-father-chris-corbally-becomes-latest-to-have-an-asteroid-named-in-his-honor/

would be figuring out the exact formula behind all of creation itself, producing some kind of formula that predicts and explains the trajectory of the cosmos.

In order to break through this mystery scientists have moved on to "quantum" science. This is science that is mostly theoretical and based on particles, waves, and math more than natural observation. By unlocking the secrets of molecules and energy, scientists developed nuclear power, atomic bombs, transistors, wireless communication, genetics, and many more incredible things. In a sense they are accidental byproducts of this endless gnostic pursuit of the Jeremiah 31:37 loophole. It explains why scientific discoveries always get used for warfare, control, and evil first, and the benefits to mankind are secondary: because those who truly pioneer the sciences are often occultists belonging to secret societies, and desperately want to enslave mankind and undermine God, not help humanity.

> *And God said, Let there be lights in the firmament of the heaven to divide the day from the night; and <u>let them be for signs</u>, and for seasons, and for days, and years: (Genesis 1:14 KJV)*

The truth is, astronomy/cosmology have always been an obsession of gnostics, even before ancient Egypt existed. The exact movement and cycles of the heavens were known to be related to the destiny of mankind, which means they telegraphed the plans of God and the fate of the earth. "Astrology" (as opposed to astronomy) says that our personalities and relationships are supposedly derived from the stars and planets. Whether you believe there is any legitimacy to that or not, you can't deny that ancient "scientist priests" were geniuses who created amazing monuments and discoveries related to the heavens. They took it very seriously many thousands of years before the supposedly materialist science of today. They were religiously-motivated science cults, and that's exactly what top experts still are today. It has always been gnosticism rooted in a quest for power on behalf of false gods.

By scientifically observing the universe, sending out probes, and studying the movements of galaxies and asteroid fields, scientists have found out when the next giant asteroid field will threaten the planet, and can engineer earthquakes themselves using technology. These are powerful things to understand. It makes us wonder if God created the Jeremiah 31:37 loophole specifically to entice gnostics and evil people to keep studying, and never give up!

> But thou, O Daniel, shut up the words, and seal the book, even to the time of the end: many shall run to and fro, and _knowledge_ [gnosis, cunning, science] _shall be increased._ (Daniel 12:4 KJV)

God wants humanity to come closer to understanding the mysteries of creation. He wants Satan's empire to believe they have a genuine loophole that will invalidate His prophecies and promises. Much like psychology and the dream of Artificial Intelligence, the more scientists have studied, the more they realize they have no idea how things work. God is glorified by mankind's hubris. He wants the most genius minds in the world to be obsessed with invalidating Him. Why? Because the more they struggle in vain to thwart Him, the more they must admit that they are unworthy and incomparable to His infinite wisdom. He will have the last laugh no matter what. But there's another reason: because the more they discover, the more they unlock horrific power, and show the world their true nature as villains.

As we appreciate this race for answers, we must smile at the fact that Jesus controls the timing of it all with his breaking of the seals. Isn't it funny how the timing of the third seal, broken around 1500 AD, released the black rider with the scales for **measuring**, which gave Satan just enough time to _nearly_ figure out the loophole before Christ's return? It's getting very close. Today scientists are making breakthroughs constantly, publishing their findings in magazines and online, trying to nail down the exact formula for how molecules, matter, energy, and the universe all fit together. As they do so, they are finding that the "quantum realm" has secrets that can change everything. Apparently, according the researchers, tapping into the quantum side of the universe is akin to unleashing true magical power, to distort reality and align events in ways that shouldn't be possible. As they get closer to figuring out the big secret, they may even be able to create miracles themselves, scientifically. Once they can do this, they will believe they have unlocked the secret and measured the heavens.

But all of it has a deadline. God only gives Satan a limited amount of time to solve the puzzle. If they can't achieve it by the time Jesus comes back, they lose. But if they can pull it off, Jesus loses. Of course, even if they did figure it out, it's not like God would come down and announce it to the world, so nobody will know whether they succeeded until the big showdown happens and Jesus comes back to earth. Let's not think that Satan hasn't been fighting all these millennia without some kind of strategy for winning!

The Jesuits and their secular gnostic offspring will most likely believe they have accomplished the Jeremiah 31:37 loophole by the time Jesus returns. They will have unlocked many secrets of the quantum (perhaps we should say "spiritual") realm and fully believe they have forced God to abandon the tribes of Israel. They won't be afraid of Jesus coming, and due to their powerful deceptions all those who aren't in the Book of Life will go along with their hubris.

In terms of timing, let's not forget that the Internet was deployed by DARPA (Defense Advanced Research Projects Agency), the United States' military science division, as a way for university researchers to share findings with each other and the military more quickly. Eventually it was expanded to home use for these same people, and the idea was to fast forward breakthroughs. But it morphed from that into a bigger plan to create a global neural network of human input, harvesting the collective consciousness of mankind. It would be indexed, sorted, searched, and studied for clues. Patterns, numbers, curves, and trends would possibly help the gnostics crack the code. And that's what Google is. It has deep ties to the military and universities to this day, along with the rest of Big Tech, which has altogether been funded and directed by DARPA.

In the end, what scientists have discovered may have been the deadline itself. A meteor stream which threatens to destroy much of the world's surface with giant impacts around the year 2030, according to current measurements. It's a hotly debated topic with many claiming it's not true, but it seems to be speeding up the timeline of Satan regardless.

2030 has become the new international goal for implementing full global weather-control systems, the implementation of a global government, massive population reduction, and more. Although we can't trust these people or their findings, the sudden obsession with 2030 suggests that the threat is real. Scientists are hurrying up their plans, and trying to solve the Jeremiah 31:37 loophole before it's too late. We'll explain how this meteor stream could fit perfectly into Revelation as well.

Lastly, we must look at earthquakes in a new light. Scientists have learned to engineer them, and may be fully able to create the very giant earthquakes we see described in Revelation. We tend to assume an earthquake is God's judgment, but that doesn't mean humans aren't (unknowingly) the ones doing the bidding. By the climax of Revelation we see that there is an earthquake bigger than any that has ever existed before, and it just so happens to open up Jerusalem for attack by Satan's army. Could this be the manufactured earthquake of the Jesuits, or some other group of Satanic scientists, believing they have the secrets of earth's foundation figured out?

8

THE TRIBULATION

We've talked about Jesus breaking of the fourth seal, unleashing the green horse and its rider, called Death. This Satanic institution, priesthood, or global movement has the divine authorization to kill 25% of the world with a variety of methods. The grave follows it. It may very well be some kind of New Age mother earth cult obsessed with population reduction, mysticism, paranormal beings, and miracles that seem to defy traditional Christian thinking. The fourth seal and the remainder of Revelation from this point will deal with **future events.**

It's unclear whether the breaking of the fifth seal interrupts the reign of Death, or follows it. When the horrific age of Death and Hades is completed, what will the world look like? It's easy to slip into "Apocalypse" thinking and assume that the whole world is unrecognizable and desolate, like in movies. But we know that only a fourth part of the world will be affected by the time that the fifth seal is broken, so it's possible that the other 75% may hardly even notice. But because each seal seems to empower Satan to reclaim and expand authority over the globe, it's more likely that the 25% who die will compel the remainder to worship Rome or the Satanic elite with new fear and enthusiasm. At the same time, this group may have an effective enough propaganda system to create the sense that there is no conspiracy behind the population reduction, and deceive the world with some other blasphemy altogether. This is one reason why the fifth seal is so fascinating:

And when he opened the fifth seal, I saw underneath the altar the souls of them that were slain for the word of God, and for the testimony which they held. And they cried with a loud voice, saying, "How long, O Lord, holy and true, do You not judge and avenge our blood on them that dwell on the earth?" Then a long white robe was given to them, and it was said to them that they should rest yet a while, until also their fellow servants and their brothers, who were about to be killed as also they were, should complete their course. (Revelation 6:9-11 EMTV)

Before we analyze the details of this passage, notice that an entire seal of the seven-sealed book is devoted to this one little scene in heaven. That is incredible. Considering that the previous ones spanned hundreds of years and massive worldwide transformations, this seems extremely minute and intimate by comparison. But what does it tell us? Remember that each seal is pre-written by God the Father in the first century already, which means that even the complaints of these martyrs was planned by God, and must happen according to prophecy. God wants there to be angry, impatient Christian martyrs in heaven!

Apparently Jesus needed to break the seal in order to authorize this interaction in heaven, placing the souls of the martyrs **under** the altar. They are not placed on the altar, as a sacrifice, but rather underneath it, as kindling. Why would Jesus put these particular martyrs there, of all places? Being under an altar doesn't sound very pleasant compared to sitting on thrones or playing harps. The poor souls were just barely killed by a horrific Satanic conspiracy, and this is their reward? Not quite. They do receive white robes, validating them and welcoming them to heaven, and they will be resting, albeit under the altar.

Perhaps they are placed as kindling because they are burning with righteous anger, loudly crying out to God, demanding to know how long God will wait to avenge their blood on the people. This speaks to their passion for justice, but also their ignorance. Despite being true saints who call God "holy and true" and are willing to die for the word of God, these martyrs aren't content. They want immediate retribution. Anyone who believes in the "Pre-Tribulation Rapture" doctrine would fit nicely into this category, assuming they can keep the faith until the bitter end. And even those who believe in a Rapture that takes place during or toward the end of the Tribulation might be impatient, wanting God to save their brethren from death and fulfill the promise to spare some believers. However, the answer they receive is not what they expect. They are told that they need to relax and wait a while, "until also their fellow servants and their brothers, who were about to be killed as also they were, should complete their course." This means that there are still Christians on the earth who haven't been killed but are about to be, and they must complete their course and be killed before God will avenge them. In other words, there is no Rapture here!

Why God orchestrates a falling away

God scripts His own strange interaction with these martyrs, seeing as this is what the fifth seal was designed to accomplish. It's another grand mystery, and hence it must be sealed. But today's Christians don't think there's any mystery at all behind it, and jump to conclusions. Praise God that His mysteries are not so easily understood! The very popularization of the incorrect Rapture theory, which says that God will immediately avenge the believers after (or while) saving them is necessary. An entire seal of the book is dedicated to it! But so is God's answer, that the remainder of the Christians need to be killed as well. If we're not trying to look for false hope, we see that it's written plainly, and not presented as a negative thing. And why would it be?

> Blessed are those who have been persecuted for righteousness' sake, for theirs is the kingdom of heaven. Blessed are you whenever they revile you, and they persecute you, and they say all kinds of evil against you falsely for my sake. _Rejoice and be exceedingly glad, for great is your reward in heaven_, for so they persecuted the prophets who were before you. (Matthew 5:10–12 EMTV)

Complaining about being killed for Jesus is totally backwards. We should be exceedingly glad, rejoicing, and happy to receive our reward in heaven. These Christians don't seem to understand that at all. It matches the current church attitude, which is a non-Biblical, entitled, worldly one. It tries to convince Christians that nothing bad will ever happen to us because God loves us. Let's be honest: if a quarter of the world—billions of people, perhaps—were killed by some fanatical Death cult running world affairs and murdering Christians in the name of some false religion, churches would preach that the end is nigh like never before! A panic and a premature declaration of an impending Rapture would sweep across countless churches. But they won't be spared. Despite the martyrs in heaven being confused (yet still faithful) back on earth we may see the fulfillment of **this** prophecy by Jesus:

> *Then they will hand you over to <u>tribulation</u> and <u>they will kill</u>*
> *<u>you</u>, and <u>you will be hated by all nations</u>, on account of my*
> *name. And <u>then many will fall away</u>, and they will <u>betray</u>*
> *<u>one another</u>, and they will <u>hate one another</u>. Then many*
> *<u>false prophets</u> will be raised up, and they will deceive many.*
> *And because lawlessness will increase, the love of many will*
> *grow cold. But <u>he who endures</u> to the end shall be saved.*
> *(Matthew 24:9-13 EMTV)*

Yes, Christ's prophecy is edifying and encouraging for all generations of believers who need to be reminded that persecution is a good thing, but we take it as an actual summary of world events and compare it to what we might see in the near future, with the fourth and fifth seals. Many so-called Christians today fit this sad description:

> *But the seed sown on stony ground is he who hears the word*
> *and <u>immediately receives it with joy</u>; yet he has no root in*
> *himself, but is short-lived. For when <u>tribulation or persecution</u>*
> *<u>comes because of the word</u>, immediately he <u>falls away</u>.*
> *(Matthew 13:20-21 EMTV)*

God doesn't want people who immediately fall away when persecution comes. He loves spiritual warriors, martyrs, and those who endure. Whether it's Satan's deception or not, people today are taught that the Rapture will protect them from all harm, and these people have no root in themselves to overcome persecution, much less rejoice when the world hates them and hands them over to be killed!

> *I know your works, that you are neither cold nor hot. I wish that you were cold or hot. Therefore, since you are lukewarm, and neither cold nor hot, I will spew you out of my mouth. Because you say, 'I am wealthy, and have become rich, and have need of nothing'--and do not know that you are wretched, miserable, poor, blind, and naked, I counsel you to buy from me gold having been tried by fire [wisdom that endured persecution], so that you may become rich; and white robes [which the martyrs receive], so that you may be clothed, and the shame of your nakedness may not appear; and eye salve, so that you may anoint your eyes, in order that you may see [the truth of God's plan]. As many as I love, I rebuke and discipline. Be zealous therefore, and repent. (Revelation 3:15-19 EMTV)*

The church today is extremely lukewarm. Almost nobody preaches tribulation or is preparing for the conspiracy to turn against us, but are rather spreading a Prosperity Gospel, where loving God means we get blessing on earth, not heaven. Others falsely preach that we can't possibly fall away once we say that Jesus is our savior, ignoring the many times that Jesus warns people to overcome and endure, and putting aside the warning about the plant that shrivels up as soon as persecution comes. Jesus wants us to be "zealous", and ready for anything. We will not be the ones rejecting him, but he will spit us out in disgust! This goes along with teachings in his Gospel:

> *Not every one that saith unto me, Lord, Lord, shall enter into the kingdom of heaven; but he that doeth the will of my Father which is in heaven. Many will say to me in that*

day, Lord, Lord, have we not prophesied in thy name? and in thy name have cast out devils? and in thy name done many wonderful works? And <u>then will I profess unto them, I never knew you: depart from me, ye that work iniquity.</u> (Matthew 7:21-23 KJV)

It is shocking, perhaps, to think that Jesus would reject anyone. But not all who call upon Jesus have been broken spiritually, reborn, and given the Spirit. These are as good as tares; fake Christians, looking like the real thing, but not producing the true crop that God desires. Many fake fairweather Christians idle along and are disgusting to Jesus, and these will be destroyed as worthless:

And whosoever shall fall on this stone [Jesus] shall be broken [convicted of sin, humbled, and ultimately redeemed]: but on whomsoever it shall fall, it will grind him to powder [in the day of judgment]. (Matthew 21:44 KJV)

And yet we can't know who is a true Christian or not, only God can. Our job is not to judge and condemn those we think are fake, but to strengthen the roots of those who are weak, and awaken them with zeal and truth. If we do our job for the Kingdom, we will receive our wages whether or not God gives increase.

In Revelation, we can presume that the falling away happened already by the time of the martyrs being under the alter, but it could be continual and ongoing. The martyrs are told that they need to wait a little longer until the rest of the believers are killed, but the book actually never follows up on this topic explicitly. This purposeful ambiguity means that those who cling to the Rapture doctrine are free to imagine that the brothers who were about to be killed "complete their course" by being caught up to heaven and spared. This vagueness is necessary in the book because, if it was any more clear, it wouldn't be possible for the heresy of Rapture to spread! Remember, God desires to sort out the good wheat from the false tares. Fairweather Christians are supposed to fall away. Additionally, while the great "falling away" will happen in large part because the church is being totally killed and no Rapture is saving them, depending on the nature of the green rider and the Death empire this apostasy may be exacerbated by the propaganda of the new priesthood as well. New discoveries, disclosures, and religions may lure away Christians or cause them to lose faith.

THE GREATEST TRIBULATION EVER, AT THE END

> *And at that time shall Michael stand up, the great prince [ruler, chief] which standeth for <u>the children of thy people</u> [the Israelites]: and there shall be <u>a time of trouble, such as never was since there was a nation even to that same time</u>: and at that time <u>thy people</u> shall be delivered, every one that shall be <u>found written in the book</u>. And many of them that sleep in the dust of the earth shall awake, some to everlasting life, and some to shame and everlasting contempt. And they that be wise shall shine as the brightness of the firmament; and they that turn many to righteousness as the stars for ever and ever. (Daniel 12:1-3 KJV)*

The "deliverance" of Daniel's people (the Israelites) will happen in a time of "trouble" greater than ever before in history. Since the church is going to be killed, it makes sense that we are not the focus of this deliverance. It may be hard to believe that there could be a time of trouble greater than the murder of the whole church, but we should not underestimate God's plan. Michael the archangel is specifically said to be involved in delivering Daniel's people, and Michael known to be the prince of the Israelites, not the churches. Remember, the seven angels of the churches are different, and in the right hand of Jesus.

It is worth noting that this passage is one of the reasons why Zionists believe that modern day Israel is a fulfillment of God's promises already. Because World War II and the Holocaust are supposedly a greater time of trouble than anything before in the history of the world, and assuming that Israel will never be persecuted like that again, it means Israel is how God chose to deliver them. Of course they seem to overlook the fact that this same prophecy describes many people rising from the dust to "everlasting life" and "everlasting contempt", and that they will shine like the stars, and turn people to righteousness. That never happened after WWII. No, the passage clearly deals with the end of the current age and the beginning of the Millennial Kingdom, where the resurrection happens and we live forever. There should be no problem with believing that the church is killed and later resurrected for the battle of Armageddon and the establishment of the Millennial Kingdom. Saying that there is a Jewish "elect" remnant that exists after us is also not controversial, since it's what Revelation clearly describes. They are the ones who get Raptured, not us.

To further explain this, we must connect the description in Daniel with the most famous passage about tribulation in the Bible, which also speaks about the end of the age and Christs' return. This is where we see a more vivid description, preceded specifically by a warning to watch for the "abomination of desolation" found in Daniel itself. Let's read what Jesus says:

> For then there shall be _great tribulation_, such as _has not been since the beginning of the world until now, nor by any means shall be_. And unless those days were cut short, no flesh would be saved; but for the _elect's sake_, those days will be _cut short_. Then if someone says to you, 'Look, here is the Christ!' or 'There!' do not believe it. For false christs and false prophets will be raised up, and they will show great signs and wonders so as to deceive, if possible, even the elect. See, I have told you in advance. Therefore if they should say to you, 'Look, He is in the desert!' do not go out; or 'Look, He is in the inner rooms!' do not believe it. For as the lightning comes out from the east and flashes to the west, so shall also be _the coming of the Son of Man_. (Matthew 24:21-26 EMTV)

There is no doubt that this passage deals with the biggest tribulation that will ever happen, and that God will cut the days short with the return of Jesus Christ to spare the elect. But he is talking to Jews regarding their precious temple that he does not care about. That's why he references the abomination of desolation, reminding them that Daniel wrote about it. Some of the prophecy must deal with the church because the events leading up to those days deal with the church's destruction, but it's purposely mingled with the fate of the Israelite elect so that it could mean multiple things. We assume it's all about the church. But keep in mind what is said to the complaining martyrs under the altar: the rest of the church must be killed. In fact, it is only logical that God begins to avenge the church after we're killed, and does not cut the days short for our sake. The "elect" is a different group of people, Israelites who are "written in the book". As we continue to study Revelation you will see exactly who this is, where they are at any given point, and how the majority of John's vision deals with **their** fate, not that of the church. Let us not be so self-centered that we assume all prophecy is about us. Zionists have no problem believing that Israel will be saved altogether, and even say that we should help protect them. They think that we will go with Jesus to protect the nation of Israel, not just an elect few. But neither of these assumptions are true in the slightest. The prophecy of Revelation can go on long after the church is killed because we do not disappear from God's mind, or fail to participate in His plan from that point forward. On the contrary! We are crucial to the completion of God's plan **after** we are killed. That's precisely why the fifth seal needs to happen: because Jesus will put our martyred souls under the altar in order to ignite the fires that begin the avenging process!

Now, no doubt the destruction of the church is a great tribulation, and in fact Revelation calls it that when it revisits the martyrs in heaven during the events of the sixth seal. That's when God prepares to avenge us. But the "greatest tribulation" only comes at the climax of God's vengeance on the earth, when the earth is many times more wicked and depraved than it is even during the reign of the fourth rider. Why does it become so wicked? Because the church is dead and absent! We can no longer oppose Satan's conspiracy! The abomination of desolation will happen only once we're gone from this earth and not able to intervene. You will see how this perfectly fits together, and leaves no room for Christians to be offended. The Rapture is not for us, but for the Israelite remnant, specially chosen and marked by God in their foreheads, who are called the "144,000 elect".

> *And one said to the man clothed in linen, which was upon the waters of the river, <u>How long shall it be to the end of these wonders</u>? And I heard the man clothed in linen, which was upon the waters of the river, when he held up his right hand and his left hand unto heaven, and sware by him that liveth for ever that it shall be for a time, times, and an half; and when he shall have accomplished to <u>scatter the power of the holy people</u> [the fleeing of the 144,000 elect after they witness the abomination of desolation], <u>all these things shall be finished</u>. (Daniel 12:6-7 KJV)*

Follow along with our study and this will not only be plausible, but inescapable.

9

GOD'S HOLY TERROR

And I beheld when he had <u>opened the sixth seal</u>, and, lo, there was a <u>great earthquake</u>; and the sun became black as sackcloth of hair, and the moon became as blood; And the stars of heaven fell unto the earth, even as a fig tree casteth her untimely figs, when she is shaken of a mighty wind. And the heaven departed as a scroll when it is rolled together; and every mountain and island were moved out of their places. And <u>the kings of the earth</u>, and the great men, and the rich men, and the chief captains, and the mighty men, and every bondman, and every free man, <u>hid themselves in the dens and in the rocks of the mountains</u>; And <u>said</u> to the mountains and rocks, Fall on us, and hide us from the face of him that sitteth on the throne, and from the wrath of the Lamb: <u>For the great day of his wrath is come; and who shall be able to stand?</u> (Revelation 6:12–17 KJV)

This is a mighty miracle by God, meant to scare the wicked Death empire which has killed 25% of the planet and so many innocent saints. And since He has just promised the martyrs that He will avenge them soon, it makes even more sense that this seal is starting to fulfill that promise, right? In a sense, yes. This could be considered the beginning of God's judgment. But the exact wording is very clever and does not say what people assume it says.

Does it say that the one who sits on the throne is appearing? Does it say that the wrath of the Lamb is happening? Does it say that "the great day of his wrath is come"? Or does it simply say that *these are the things that the men hiding under the mountains **will say** when they see the terrifying cosmic events?* These are ungodly men, guilty of murdering the church, who are scared of judgment. They are not authorities on when the Day of the Lord is. They are jumping to a conclusion and hiding in fear.

Due to God exposing only a few snippets of his playbook to the ungodly and Satanic world through Revelation, He knew that both the believers and unbelievers would become obsessed with the coming wrath of God, the fiery judgment, and other warnings. This is the manifold genius of God, because He incorporates evil men's desires and fears into his own holy plans. He allows them to rise to power just so He can show them He can topple them. How much more will He not confound the evil rulers of the world after what they've done to His church?

Think about those who are hiding under the mountains, afraid of judgment. They are evil obviously, because they would rather die than see God. Among these godless and guilty people are the greatest and the lowest of the earth, and they all seem to have the same conviction of guilt and terror. They too, just like the martyrs crying out in heaven, assume that this is the end, and that God's full judgment should happen already. Isn't that interesting? They await the vengeful wrath of God and ask the mountains to fall on them because they are certain that the end is nigh. But has it really come yet? Didn't God just barely inform the martyrs in heaven that there will be a period of waiting still? But He does not tell the people on earth the same thing! Perhaps he is setting up a doomsday ruse.

It is very possible that the remainder of the church is still alive during this period, since we are not shown them in heaven yet. Meanwhile, the survival plan, for those who are able, is to hide under the mountains, no doubt in underground labyrinths, bunker cities, fortifications, and tunnel networks. These are already in existence, and being prepared for the elite to move in and stay for years, if not decades. They were initially constructed during the Cold War as a "doomsday protocol" just as you would expect. Since then they have multiplied and become a sort of symbol of extravagance and luxury for billionaires, showing that they will be safe even if the whole world is destroyed. They will know exactly where to hide when (they think) *God is* going to avenge the church. But even there, in their own custom fortresses, they will wish for the mountains to collapse and kill them. It's a pathetic display, showing that the Satanic conspiracy is made up of cowards who think they can get away with anything, but tremble at God's warnings.

SATAN'S ANTICIPATION OF THE WRATH

Both the church and the evil world are mistaken about the timing of God's vengeance. The martyrs cry out to God and impatiently ask for retribution, while the ungodly hide and tremble at the first sign of cosmic terror. If somehow, by this point in the future, after extreme depopulation plans, world government, and gnostic technological breakthroughs, there would still be a normal government (a possibility, since it only killed a fourth part of the earth) these governments would effectively be abandoned during this terrifying period. A new civilization would be created underground, ruled by the Satanic elite of the Green Priesthood; the same ones who killed the church. They would now govern the terrified world population in their own private subterranean city states. If they truly are built to last a long time they could create their own laws and new religions, as if they were kings and gods over mankind. The Bible puts so much emphasis on the various kinds of people who all go into the mountains and underground that it's hard to deny the possibility of a whole new society forming there.

It is strange to think, but Satan may have been anticipating heavenly judgment on earth and used his own phony Cold War scare about a nuclear holocaust and "mutually assured destruction" as a pretext to construct emergency doomsday plans to begin with. He uses deceived but wealthy and well-connected servants to create emergency shelters and terrify them with the idea of nuclear bombs, and convinces governments to go along with it in the name of emergency governments, secret deals and power arrangements. Meanwhile, all of it is to ensure that his occult technocracy can survive God's judgment once the church is killed.

After all, Satan on some level knows he is trying to fulfill prophecy, he just thinks he can outsmart God with his loophole and his preparations. He knows he has a limited time to make war with the saints. He knows he is provoking God. And as researchers have pointed out upon visiting some of these underground cities, they are privately owned and policed fortresses that can house tens of thousands each; and that's just what mere journalists could discover about them! In reality this new "underworld" may be much more vast than we realize. The elite have contingency plans. Judging by the impressive and specific list of people who flee to this underworld, they may even be a trained doomsday society, made up of chosen experts, officials, military, scientists, and civilians. Perhaps the triumph of the Green Priesthood is also a way of convincing the world's elite that they have no choice but to accept them into their underworld, as priests able to do miracles or speak with spirits. The godless are easily swayed by such things.

In such an event, the owners of these fortresses will have total control over who can enter, who can leave, and who can survive within. We already know they are guilty of killing the Christians to the point of thinking this is God's revenge, so they are capable of anything! Perhaps this is exactly where God wants them, cowering in their holes. But it doesn't seem to be the end, yet.

We are not told when—or even if—this collection of great and powerful elites will fully emerge from this sanctuary. They may reside there for many years and become increasingly deranged and paranoid. They may rapidly dig and develop to the point where they don't need to live on the surface anymore. People like H.G. Wells preached about a future where society would live entirely underground back in the early 1900s already. In Dr. Strangelove, Stanley Kubrick shows a Nazi scientist excited about Doomsday because it means they can live underground and personally repopulate the planet. If even public presentations like these can flesh out the idea long ago, they may have all the resources and expertise they need to transform their havens into permanent and expanding underworld cities.

THE INTRODUCTION OF THE 144,000 ISRAELITES

> *And <u>after these things</u> I saw four angels standing on the four corners of the earth, holding the four winds of the earth, that the wind should not blow on the earth, nor on the sea, nor on any tree. And I saw another angel ascending from the east, having <u>the seal of the living God</u>: and he cried with a loud voice to the four angels, to whom it was given to hurt the earth and the sea, Saying, <u>Hurt not the earth, neither the sea, nor the trees</u>, till we have <u>sealed the servants of our God in their foreheads</u>. (Revelation 7:1-3 KJV)*

The halting of the (apparently destructive) winds and the commandment to pause is important. First of all, it directly suggests that this is not the full wrath of God, only a small taste. Secondly, to those kings and mighty people hiding under the earth it may seem there is a reprieve from God's judgment, which they were terrified of. In fact, they may be tempted to emerge in this time, and see what has happened. They may even think that they survived God's wrath! This is very important to consider, because they were just barely calling for the mountains to fall on them, and saying that the day of the Lord's wrath had come. They believe it was God's vengeance, and now it seems to be over!

> *And I heard <u>the number of them which were sealed</u>: and there were sealed <u>an hundred and forty and four thousand</u> of all the <u>tribes of the children of Israel</u>. (Revelation 7:4 KJV)*

Regardless of what the Satanic elite and their prisoners believe, what God cares about at this point is sealing and protecting a certain remnant of Israelites, called servants of God. They are not called saints. They are elect, by definition, because they were specially chosen and marked. The destruction of the world is paused specifically for this to happen, so it is no small matter. God turns His attention to Israel at this dramatic time in history, after terrifying the world's evil elite into hiding.

Objection: Downplaying the severity of the cosmic terror

Some may object by saying that the description of the heavenly events and earthquakes are too dramatic to be a mere warning, and that I am downplaying its significance. But if we look, we see that all the biggest deaths and punishments are described during the time of the seven trumpets and seven vials. Here we are still in the time of the seals, which I believe represent the building of Satan's Antichurch on earth, not its destruction and judgment. Therefore, despite the warning terrors that will seem extremely scary at the time, it won't compare to the later events. It makes more sense for the Satanic conspiracy to **expand** at this point, not shrink. Why would they expand? Because they think they have survived God's judgment, of course! And there is no church alive to stop them from doubling down on evil, confident that they weathered God's punishment and came out victorious.

There are many questions about this 144,000 elect. Have they consciously turned to God in this time of warning, or are they still ignorant? Do they know the Gospel of Jesus Christ, or do they serve the Hebrew God of Abraham, Isaac, and Jacob without knowing the Messiah? Real Christianity was killed off some time ago, and a false religion would be dominating the world or even masquerading as Christianity this whole time, like the Catholic and Orthodox Church have been. It seems very unlikely that they are Christians, especially because the angels have the seal of the living God and say they are sealing the servants of Him, not the Christ. Twelve thousand from each of the twelve Israelite tribes are sealed, totaling 144,000. From one point of view this is a very large contingent, but relative to a city of millions it is small. If they are gathered in the same place it would be even more impressive to see them all together, but they could also be scattered. Perhaps they are sealed invisibly to mankind, which would make it even more intriguing to the ungodly world when they see what happens next!

The throne room grows in population

> *After this I beheld, and, lo, <u>a great multitude, which no man could number,</u> of <u>all nations</u>, and kindreds, and people, and tongues, <u>stood</u> before the throne, and before the Lamb, clothed with white robes, and palms in their hands; And cried with a loud voice, saying, Salvation to our God which sitteth upon the throne, and unto the Lamb. (Revelation 7:9-10 KJV)*

Finally, after the protective sealing of the good Israelites, the Kingdom of Heaven explodes in population, full of saints from across the earth. John did not seem so impressed by the number of people who received the white robes before, but now he makes a special comment about how diverse and plenteous they are. Their loud praise seems to show that they are happy to be here, with a message that is about God and Christ, not the events happening in the world.

> *And one of the elders answered, saying unto me, What are these which are arrayed in white robes? and whence came they? And I said unto him, Sir, thou knowest. And he said to me, These are they <u>which came out of great tribulation</u>, and have washed their robes, and made them white in the blood of the Lamb. Therefore are they before the throne of God, and serve him day and night in his temple: and he that sitteth on the throne shall dwell among them. They shall hunger no more, neither thirst any more; neither shall the sun light on them, nor any heat. For the Lamb which is in the midst of the throne shall feed them, and shall lead them unto living fountains of waters: and God shall wipe away all tears from their eyes. (Revelation 7:13-17 KJV)*

Here we are finally told about the "great tribulation" that killed the church. They were all killed, washed in the blood of the Lamb, and are now gathered together. Perhaps many were alive during God's warning terrors, and they fled into the underground refuge only to be killed there. Perhaps they died outside of the underground shelters, from starvation, thirst, and heat, as the elder takes great care to describe how they will not hunger and thirst any more, the sun's heat won't oppress them, and God will wipe the tears from their eyes. These people truly came out of **great** tribulation, not a worrisome little period where they got spared hardship and death!

For those who assume they were Raptured up to heaven, remember that the description of the Rapture coincides with the return of Jesus Christ's appearing like lightning back on earth, the resurrection, and much more that isn't happening in the age of the sixth seal. It simply cannot be due to that.

SILENCE, AND SEVEN ANGELS RECEIVING TRUMPETS

And when he had <u>opened the seventh seal,</u> there was <u>silence in heaven</u> about the space of <u>half an hour</u>. (Revelation 8:1 KJV)

Jesus breaks the seventh seal because the 144,000 elect Israelites have been sealed, and the earth can therefore be ravaged with terror and destruction. The destructive forces had been held back until now, though they seemed eager to unleash retribution as soon as they're permitted. A major turning point has just happened, both in heaven and on earth. The events of the sixth seal began with cosmic calamity on earth and in the sky, and ends with the believers standing before the throne of God. The 144,000 elect Israelites, however, are strangely juxtaposed by both groups and their extremes. They are sealed in their foreheads by angels, but not present with God. They will be kept on earth during horrific world events, but will be protected going forward. They are not evil, nor defined as Christian believers. They are certainly distinct, and in God's eyes are servants.

However, as if to draw attention to the conspicuous peace created by holding back the four winds of destruction, we now have peaceful silence in heaven for half an hour. No singing, cries, trumpets, or commands. This is the first time we see a deliberate time period given by John about world events, despite thousands of years of history passing already. This makes it a fascinating detail, but also forces us to conclude that John has been unaware of how much earthly time has been passing in this vision. He is reporting everything he notices, but he does not notice the centuries going by. Logically, it makes sense. The whole point of the seven-sealed book is to be secretive. John only sees little clues. But now, with the seventh seal finally broken, it is as if time has begun to move forward in real time, not condensed.

By telling us about the half hour pause, God creates an important punctuation mark; a clue that what John is witnessing is in fact a linear sequence of events, not an interchangeable jumble of images and metaphors. You would never need to specify that a half hour of time passed by if the sequence was meaningless.

> And I saw _the seven angels_ which stood before God; and to
> them were given _seven trumpets_.
> (Revelation 8:2 KJV)

Logically speaking, it makes sense that these seven angels are the very same angels who had been in charge of the churches in the first chapters of Revelation; the ones Jesus was giving messages to. Now that the church is dead, their role shifts from being stewards of the churches to being the ones who call for holy vengeance and terrify the guilty Satanic world.

All of the events contained in the "age of the trumpets" (as we may call it) take place inside the "age of the seventh seal", meaning that God considers this to be the final phase of His grand strategy. There are no more seals, mysteries, or divinely ordained plans after it.

THE MYSTERY OF THE TRUMPETS AND GOLDEN CENSOR

Remember those martyrs under the altar? They cried out for vengeance, but were told to rest and wait until the rest of the Christians were killed. Now that the church is dead and the 144,000 elect are sealed, God can finally proceed with answering their prayers. As we have explained, God wants to unleash **worldwide** destruction on a collective people worthy of suffering, not try to enact individual punishments while the righteous are nearby and possibly in harm's way.

It's easy to understand the role of trumpets in this prophecy, because we need only to think about what the function of real trumpets were in the ancient world. Seals are meant to certify, protect, and hide something important, but trumpets are the opposite: they are very loud, distinct, and are meant to alert or warn people far and wide. Trumpets were used to signal something's approach. If you heard a bunch of trumpets sound all at once you might expect the arrival of an army led by a dignitary, ambassador, or king, for instance. It's no coincidence that destructive angels, the two witnesses, and Jesus will all arrive on earth during the time of the seven trumpets. Even though God's plans had been a total secret happening in the fog of history before, during the first six seals, the last seal is the unleashing of blatant signs and wonders, given to a post-church, Satanic New World Order about to receive judgment.

> *And another angel came and <u>stood at the altar</u> [where the souls of the martyrs were], having a <u>golden censer</u> [a temple incense container]; and there was given unto him <u>much incense</u>, that he should <u>offer it with the prayers of all saints</u> upon the golden altar which was before the throne. And the <u>smoke</u> of the incense, which came <u>with</u> the <u>prayers of the saints</u>, ascended up before God out of the angel's hand. And the angel took the censer, and <u>filled it with fire of the altar</u>, and <u>cast it into the earth</u>: and there were voices, and thunderings, and lightnings, and an earthquake. (Revelation 8:3-5 EMTV)*

How beautiful and poetic! As you'll recall, the prayers of the saints were already symbolized as incense earlier in Revelation:

> *And when he took the scroll, the four living creatures and the twenty-four elders fell down before the Lamb, each having a harp, and golden bowls [or vials] being*

filled with incense, which are the prayers of the saints.
(Revelation 5:8 EMTV)

The thing about incense is that it can have a pleasant odor on its own, but it's really meant to be burned in order to activate. The smoke of the incense burning is what makes it spread and fill an area. Back in chapter 5 the incense is not said to be burning yet, and no smoke is described. Here in chapter 8, however, all of the incense from the previous saints seems to be combined into a giant golden censer, lit on fire from the heat of the martyrs who had been under the altar, and presented to God as a pleasant aroma. Then, taking fire from God's own altar apparently, the angel turns and throws it to the earth, symbolizing a massive incoming destruction for the inhabitants of the earth!

This object is the combined prayer of all Christians, who want to see the world destroyed and burned with the fire. But it's no ordinary fire. It is the furious indignation of God and the martyrs, thrown to the earth as a weapon, foreshadowing what kind of fate the earth will have! Just like in a temple, the fire and smoke of the censer will fill the earth and help to purify it before Jesus comes to his kingdom.

So, putting the scene together, we understand why the golden censer scene has to happen immediately after the seven trumpets are handed to the angels. Everything we're seeing is connected to the murder of the church, the desire for revenge, the preparation of Jesus returning to earth, and the warning judgments that will terrify the wicked world. Meanwhile, the 144,000 elect Israelites are going to be spared this judgment, but witness it firsthand on earth!

So the seven angels who had the seven trumpets prepared
themselves to sound the trumpets.
(Revelation 8:6 EMTV)

Now, only after the censor is cast to the earth, can the angels sound their trumpets and fulfill in a physical, literal way what the golden censor just foreshadowed in a spiritual sense.

THE FIRST FOUR TRUMPETS

And the <u>first</u> one sounded his trumpet, and there was <u>hail and fire</u>, <u>having been mixed with blood</u>, and they were <u>thrown to the earth</u>; and a third of the earth was burned up, and a third of the trees was burned up, and all green grass was burned up. Then the <u>second</u> angel sounded his trumpet, and something like a <u>great burning mountain</u> was <u>cast into</u> the sea, and a third of the sea became blood. And a third of the living creatures in the sea died, and a third of the ships were destroyed. Then the <u>third</u> angel sounded his trumpet, and <u>a great star fell from heaven</u>, burning <u>like a torch</u>, and <u>it fell</u> on a third of the rivers and on the fountains of water. And the name of the star is called Wormwood. And a third of the waters turned into wormwood, and many men died from the waters, because they were made bitter. Then the <u>fourth</u> angel sounded his trumpet, and a third of the sun was struck, a third of the moon, and a third of the stars, so that a third of them was darkened. <u>A third of the day did not shine, and likewise the night</u>. (Revelation 8:7-12 EMTV)

In literal terms, the "golden censer" is a massive asteroid that is hurtling through space toward earth, preceded by smaller (but still giant by any modern standard) impacts that will create various effects in the atmosphere, as well as impact tectonic plates, vegetation, and the chemical composition of the oceans.

As Earth enters this asteroid field, thousands of small meteors will rain down, burning up in the atmosphere and, depending on what they're made of, seemingly be mixed with "blood". This signifies the blood of the church, contained in the golden censer that is mixed with the prayers and fire. They will burn up the vegetation because of the heat and explosions; impacts of meteors can be thousands of times more impactful than even nuclear bombs! Then a giant meteor, big enough to be like a burning mountain, will impact the sea. Another will be so bright and hot that it will be like a star, and impact a certain region where important rivers and fountains exist. The chemical fallout and debris from this meteor will poison the rivers and fountains (most likely referring to underground aquifers) and make the region's water toxic and dangerous.

The fourth trumpet event is the immediate result of the meteor stream and its burning impact on earth. With so many burning meteors streaking through the atmosphere, blowing up on the surface, burning away the vegetation, boiling the rivers, and heating up the ocean, it's only logical that a third of the sky is blacked out and obscured by water vapor, smoke, and the burning trails of the meteors!

Think about it: because the earth is a sphere and the meteor stream travels at high speed in a single direction, it's actually impossible (by nature) that the meteor stream could impact more than a third of the planet. That's why a third of the earth was burned up, a third of the sea was turned to blood, and a third of the sky is darkened. It all happens at once, and all of it affects the same portion of the planet facing the meteor stream. Let us also note that one third of the day equals eight hours. In other words, the impacts and smoke of this event will span eight time zones, which is about the full length of North America. However, it's highly unlikely that this meteor stream will impact there for reasons I will soon explain.

THE FRAGMENTATION ARGUMENT

Because Satan's conspiracy seems to realize that 2030 is the cosmic deadline for the Jeremiah 31:37 loophole, they have gone into overdrive trying to prepare for the impact of this meteor stream. On July 1st, 2020, RT.com reported[8] with a headline: *"Two asteroids to race past Earth as NASA pens deal with Space Force to bolster planetary defenses"*. The obsession with space defense against asteroids is bigger than ever before, and shows no sign of slowing down. The article reports on these two near-misses, in part, as follows:

---

[8]   https://www.rt.com/news/493453-two-asteroids-inbound-warning/
See also: https://www.cbsnews.com/news/planet-killer-mit-plans-deflect-asteroids-earth/
See also: https://www.nationalgeographic.com/science/2020/04/giant-asteroid-nasa-dart-deflection/

The close flyby couldn't have come at a better time, as the ink dried on a deal between NASA and the US Space Force to <u>combine their resources</u> to track near-Earth objects and <u>better prepare to fight off any potential impact threats</u> – be they <u>planet killers</u> or space rocks on the scale of the Chelyabinsk event.

As the old saying goes, <u>the best defense is a good offense</u>, and Earth's <u>planetary defense should be no exception</u>, as the International Astronomical Union has named <u>the first target</u> in testing our mettle against <u>space-based threats</u>.

In late 2022, NASA will conduct its <u>Double Asteroid Redirection Test mission</u>, or DART, against the newly dubbed 'Dimorphos' moonlet asteroid – which orbits the larger (524ft) asteroid known as Didymos – in the first-ever <u>asteroid deflection mission</u>, which will take place some <u>6,835,083 miles from our planet</u>.

Millions of miles away, gnostic dark scientists are already preparing weapons to be able to blow up and redirect asteroid threats. They want to negate the "golden censer" that God is sending to punish the earth. The "planet killer" asteroid may be nuked in space, fragmenting it and causing it to become the bloody hail, burning mountain, and "Wormwood" star that we see in Revelation. The Jesuits have been studying astral objects to measure the heavens, but as a bonus result they may think they can save themselves from doom with Space Force and other planetary defense initiatives. If an asteroid was dozens of kilometers wide, it would totally destroy the planet's structure; but fragmenting it could save us.

If this is the case, it ironically means that God **anticipated** their defenses when he wrote the seven-sealed book thousands of years ago, and always intended for His "planet killer" to be fragmented. Not only does this spare the planet and allow His plan to keep going, but as we will soon see, this exact fragmentation pattern is necessary for other Revelation events to make sense.

Torment of the bottomless pit

And I beheld, and heard an angel flying through the midst of heaven, saying with a loud voice, Woe, woe, woe, to the inhabiters of the earth by reason of the other voices [sounds] of the trumpet of the three angels which are yet to sound! (Revelation 8:13 KJV)

We see an angel announce to the world that the worst is yet to come. This may seem impossible, we will see that it's true. Not only is this important for reinforcing the "terror" nature of the trumpets, but it separates the first four trumpets from the last three. Once again we are given a kind of punctuation mark, making it impossible to interpret the seven trumpets as happening all at once, or being interchangeable. These are not random at all, but a very deliberate, purposeful, genius linear sequence.

Then the fifth angel sounded his trumpet, and I saw a star having fallen out of heaven, to the earth. And the key of the shaft of the bottomless pit [Greek: "abussos", or abyss] was given to him. (Revelation 9:1 EMTV)

The star has already fallen, meaning there isn't a new star falling to earth, but the same Wormwood "star" that landed on the rivers and fountains. It was said to burn "like a torch". This means that the asteroid, super hot, continues to burn intensely while on earth.

This "star" is so intensely hot that it tunnels downward, through the crust of the earth, melting and burning and sending up toxic smoke. This process opens up the so-called "bottomless pit". Once again this is a **physical** manifestation of the Bible's **spiritual** bottomless pit, which is the place of the dead, said to be the lowest place on earth, an underworld called "Sheol" in the Hebrew. In the New Testament this place of the dead is referred to as "Hades"; the same thing that was following the Death rider on the green horse. It's translated into English as "hell" sometimes, but the original concept is more like a gloomy pit that so low that it can never be escaped, and is where the cursed spirits and godless souls of the dead are sent for imprisonment.

And he opened the bottomless pit; and there arose a smoke out of the pit, <u>as the smoke of a great furnace; and <u>the sun and the air were darkened by reason of the smoke of the pit</u>. And there came out of the smoke <u>locusts</u> upon the earth: and unto them was given power, as the scorpions of the earth have power. (Revelation 9:2-3 KJV)

Now we see more clearly that the smoke of Wormwood burrowing into the earth and melting the rock and mineral is what obscures the sky. The black furnace smoke will be choking, poisonous, and terrible for anyone who breathes it. Spiritually, it may be that the dark spirits of Sheol are unleashed, having unlocked the abyss of their captivity, but it's doubtful that the humans on earth will actually see demons or spirits attacking them. Rather, the stinging, painful, and possibly paralyzing period would be explained as a natural effect of the toxic smoke. Because although these trumpets are clearly warnings sent by God, the people on earth are deceived by Satan and will be unwilling to admit it as long as there is some possibility of denying it.

And it was commanded them that they should not hurt <u>the grass</u> of the earth, neither any <u>green</u> thing, neither any <u>tree</u>; but only <u>those men which have not the seal of God in their foreheads</u>. (Revelation 9:4 KJV)

Now we see the 144,000 Israelite elect again. They are indeed on earth during the disaster, having been sealed in their foreheads and protected by God. They see the devastation, but they are not hurt by the smoke and these "locust" entities who came from the bottomless bit. This may astonish the other people in that region, if they notice that they're immune. A different question is why these locust beings are specifically told not to hurt grass, green things, and trees. Perhaps because at this point in the future, during the Satanic New World Order with their "Green" New Age religion, plant life is considered more important than human life. For decades we have already had New Age cults claiming that trees have souls, and that plants should have rights like people do. It would be ironic if the demonic tormentors are told to spare the plants and only afflict those who worship the creation more than the Creator.

And to them it was given that <u>they should not kill them</u>, but that they should be <u>tormented five months</u>: and their torment was as the torment of a scorpion, when he striketh a man. And in those days shall men <u>seek death</u>, and shall not find it; and shall <u>desire to die</u>, and <u>death shall flee from them</u>. (Revelation 9:5-6 KJV)

Another perfect irony! These killers, collectively guilty of murdering the innocent church, will desire to die, but death will flee from them! They will wish they were dead, but God doesn't let them find relief that easily. Five months of terrible agony await them.[9]

Yet there could be an even more ironic aspect to this if these future people are what is called "Transhumanists", obsessed with achieving eternal life through science. Today, the Transhumanist cult has a very clear goal of becoming like gods themselves, replacing body parts and genetically engineering themselves and their offspring to be free from disease, old age, and more. They may have developed vaccines and cures that were meant to make them immortal, but which will instead make them unable to die, even when they want to.

One <u>woe is past</u>; and, behold, <u>there come two woes more hereafter</u>. (Revelation 9:12 KJV)

Here again we see a punctuation mark, more explicit than ever: one woe is past, and two more will be hereafter. Considering we were just told about the five months of torment, it's very possible that the entire five months elapse before the next woe begins. We should also remember that a "woe" is always defined as a type of misery or affliction. Saying "woe unto" something (in this case, the inhabitors of the earth, except the 144,000) calls for them to be made miserable and mourn for their impending fate. Just as the trumpets send out a signal of something important approaching, the angel shouting "woe" to earth is the same.

---

[9]   This once again shows how time is passing more realistically in John's vision now, unlike before.

Mass death and unrepentant evil

> *And the <u>sixth</u> angel sounded, and I heard a voice from the four horns of the <u>golden altar</u> which is before God, Saying to the sixth angel which had the trumpet, Loose the four angels which are bound in <u>the great river Euphrates</u>. (Revelation 9:13-14 KJV)*

Here we see the golden altar again. The fire from this altar was added to the golden censer before it was thrown to the earth, and now a voice from there tells the angel to unleash destructive angels bound inside the Euphrates river. It may represent a sacrifice about to be made, since altars are places of sacrifice. The location gives us a major hint about which region was hit by the meteors.

The Euphrates river is actually mentioned in the second chapter of Genesis as one of the four rivers that come out of Eden. Is that why there are four angels bound there? Either way, it's fitting that God's judgment would revisit the same spot where human life first began. The "burning torch" of Wormwood probably lands on the river Euphrates and burrows down to create a bottomless pit full of toxic smoke, so it's only natural that the river itself would be turned toxic and poison the whole region's water after five months. Not to mention the cumulative effects of the burning, bloody meteorites and the burning mountain landing in the ocean! The water sources all get tainted eventually.

> *So the four angels were released, who <u>had been prepared</u> for the hour and day and month and year, so that they might kill a <u>third of mankind.</u> Now the number of the troops of the horsemen was a hundred million; I heard the number of them. …. By these three plagues <u>a third of mankind was killed</u>--from the fire and the smoke and the brimstone proceeding out of their mouths. …. But <u>the rest of mankind</u>, who were not killed by these plagues, <u>did not repent</u> from the works of their hands, that they should not <u>worship demons</u>, and idols of gold, silver, bronze, stone, and of wood, which neither are able to see nor to hear*

nor to walk. And they did not repent of their murders,
nor of their drugs, nor of their fornication or their thefts.
(Revelation 9:15-21 EMTV)

Once again we see a third of mankind affected. These angels were prepared specifically for this point in history, reinforcing the idea that this was all scripted by God long ago. If we knew which year, month, day, and hour this occurred, there might be a special significance to the people on earth. As we see, the Satanic people on earth who aren't killed by these terrors only harden their hearts and still think they can win. Why? Because to them it has all been rational: a massive asteroid that humanity saw coming years in advance was fragmented in space, finally hits earth, and people in the region start suffering and dying. No reason to panic, because they're hiding under the mountains, and at this point they don't need to worry about asteroids ever again! They continue to do all their evil as if there was no chance of being affected.

We must imagine these future Satanic conspirators and their New World Order slave kingdoms. They might even have expected this outcome, considering how feverishly they study the exact movements of asteroids and trajectories. If they believe they have unlocked the Jeremiah 31:37 loophole and gained any kind of amazing technology or gnostic power in the process, they may feel more confident than ever! If their perverse culture is an evolution of our own, they will do drugs in order to contact demons and worship them. The current New Age religion is all about connecting with spirits while in a drug-induced trance, after all. The spirits they talk to tell them to build a one world government, kill the church, and justify all their wickedness. Without a church around to protest, it can continue to spiral into total depravity, despite the warning trumpets of God.

THE LOGIC OF THE MIGHTY ANGEL IN THE SKY

And I saw another mighty angel come down from heaven,
clothed with a cloud: and a rainbow was upon his head,
and his face was as it were the sun, and his feet as pillars

of fire: And he had in his hand a little book open: and he
set his right foot upon the sea, and his left foot on the earth,
(Revelation 10:1-2 KJV)

Dear reader, behold this image! This angel is magnificent in its description, but it's so much more than that. The closer we look at his details the more it reveals about what has just taken place on the earth. In fact, this "mighty angel" is like a photograph of the devastation that the world has just experienced!

He comes down from heaven, just like the asteroids. His feet, which are said to be like "pillars of fire", perfectly match the impacts of the asteroid impacts: first, one falls into the sea, and then the second one hits the land. His body consists of giant clouds, which are being spewed upward from the boiling, fuming, smoking columns of blaze below. High above, hot vapor reaching into the upper atmosphere would create a giant rainbow around its "head", especially if the rising sun was positioned exactly where its "face" would be.

What does the rainbow symbolize? God's promise not to destroy the earth with a flood again. With the arrival of this "mighty angel" God has kept his promise, and is now destroying the earth with explosions, fire, devastation, and toxic fumes instead. It's a spectacular symbol for all the world to see. Those who survive and are not repenting of their evil will be able to witness this angel physically, even if they don't want to acknowledge what it represents!

Here we also see that the sun which was not permanently turned black in previous times. It was only obscured for a third of the day while the smoke arose from the east. It will look as if the Lord Himself is currently standing on the earth to judge mankind. He has a message for the Satanic planet that clings to evil:

and cried with a loud voice, as when a lion roars. And when
he cried out, the <u>seven thunders</u> uttered their own voices.
Now when the seven thunders spoke, I was about to write.
But I heard a voice from heaven saying, "<u>Seal up the things</u>
<u>which the seven thunders said,</u> and <u>after these things you</u>
<u>shall write.</u>" And the angel whom I saw standing on the sea

and on the land raised his right hand to heaven and swore
by Him <u>who lives forever</u> and ever, who created the <u>heaven</u>
and the things in it, the <u>earth</u> and the things in it, and the
<u>sea</u> and the things in it, that there should be <u>no more delay</u>;
but <u>in the days of the voice of the seventh angel</u>, whenever
he is about to sound his trumpet, <u>the mystery of God would
be finished</u>, as He declared to His servants the <u>prophets</u>.
(Revelation 10:3-7 EMTV)

It should be no surprise that lightning and thunder would accompany this giant disruption of the earth's atmosphere. While the sea boils from the "burning mountain" super-heating the water and the "Wormwood star" burns like a torch and opens up that smokey furnace called the bottomless pit, it's inevitable that the temperature shock would create massive thunderclaps. But like the golden censer that spiritually foreshadowed all of this destruction, this angel's arrival is anything but a "natural phenomena" in God's eyes.

The seven thunders may very well be the same seven angels who were protecting the churches, and to whom the seven trumpets were given. If their trumpets were to herald the imminent arrival of royalty, dignitaries, or armies, they have done well. We've already seen armies. Now they might be putting aside their trumpets to voice a combined pronouncement upon the earth. Shockingly, John is directly forbidden to write down the message, so we don't know what it is![10] But even though we're not told what the thunders are telling the world, we can be certain that their message will be related to the events about to unfold.

---

[10]   This is a stunning, critical fact of Revelation that destroys any interpretation that claims John was simply writing down his own feelings or thoughts in an altered state of consciousness, as some have said. He says himself that he was about to write, but he was interrupted and prevented from doing so. He is simply being a reporter, recording what he sees and hears as best as he knows how. Ever since entering the phase of the trumpets, John seems to be experiencing time's passing in a more literal way, with a more direct observation of what's actually happening on earth, to the point where he's hearing messages he isn't even supposed to record for future generations. This reinforces the idea that the seals represent a hugely secret process, but the trumpets are (mostly) blatant wonders that are supposed to be known at least to the generation who witnesses them.

Separately, the mighty angel swears that "the mystery of God" will come to completion in the days when the seventh angel is blowing his trumpet. What does this phrase about the mystery of God mean? We're given a major hint, actually: it's the mystery that the prophets were seeking answers about. This immediately narrows down the list of possibilities, since the prophets were generally only concerned with Israel's rulership, the fate of its tribes, Jerusalem, its temple, along with the earthly arrival of the Kingdom of Heaven, the resurrection of the dead, the judgment of the earth, and the reign of the Messiah. Since the first arrival of the Messiah led to rejection, crucifixion, and the delaying of his Kingdom so that the tares and the wheat could mature separately, the "mystery of God" would logically be about the fate of Israel and the Messiah.

It's worth noting that the way the angel swears by God is very creation-centric in its theme. He emphasizes how God created the heavens, the earth, and the sea, and everything within them. This is poetically appropriate, because God has seemingly ruined a third of the planet and shown that He can destroy it if He pleases. Once again this brings things full circle, just like the Euphrates river and the rainbow. This is not some random destruction with random curses and plagues, but an extremely personal message to Satan and all those who serve him, as well as to the 144,000 sealed elect who are in Israel, protected. The damned of the earth are literally doing drugs and worshiping demons during this time, fully showing that they are the tares; the counterfeit Antichurch, deceiving and conspiring with no shame.

10

CONVERSION OF JERUSALEM

*Then the voice which I heard from heaven was speaking
with me again and saying, "Go, take the little scroll <u>which
was open</u> in the hand of the angel standing on the sea and
on the land." And I went to the angel, saying to him to give
to me the little scroll. And he said to me, "Take it and <u>eat
it</u> up; and it shall make your <u>stomach bitter</u>, but it shall be
as <u>sweet as honey in your mouth</u>." Then I took the scroll
out of the angel's hand and ate it, and it was as sweet as
honey in my mouth. And when I ate it, my stomach was
made bitter. And they said to me, "You must prophesy
<u>again</u> over many peoples, nations, languages, and kings."
(Revelation 10:8-11 EMTV)*

Let's keep our train of thought coherent as we move forward,
connecting it with everything else we know. Here again we're not
told what's inside this little scroll, even though it's said to be "open", but
we can make some guesses based on the description and the context.
Being "little" means we can assume that it deals with a small, limited, or
short period of events. Being "open" and present on earth—albeit in the
hands of this gigantic angel of terror—means we can assume this is not
very secret to those who are alive at this time, and is probably related to
the cataclysm of this very same angel. Lastly, because the angel makes
a special promise about finishing the mystery of God in the days of
the seventh trumpet and will satisfy the curiosity of the prophets, it's

probably something related to Jerusalem's temple and the triumphant return of the Messiah.

Where have we seen promises related to the "last trumpet" before? In an epistle discussing none other than the resurrection of believers in the last days!

> *Now this I say, brothers, that <u>flesh and blood cannot inherit the kingdom of God</u> [disproving Zionists]; nor can corruption inherit incorruption. Behold, I tell you a <u>mystery</u> [the mystery of God?]: <u>We shall not all die</u>, but we shall all be changed-- in a moment, in the twinkling of an eye, at the <u>last trumpet</u>. For the trumpet shall sound, and <u>the dead shall be raised incorruptible</u>, and <u>we shall be changed</u>. For this corruptible must put on incorruption, and this mortal must put on immortality. So when this corruptible should put on incorruption, and this mortal should put on <u>immortality</u>, then will come to pass the word which was written: "Death was swallowed up in victory." "O <u>Death, where is your sting</u>? O <u>Hades, where is your victory</u>?" (1 Corinthians 15:50-54 EMTV)*

We know that the seventh trumpet is the last; we also know that within the seventh trumpet are contained the seven vials full of the wrath of God; and we also know explicitly that the Lord's triumphant return and the resurrection happens during the time of the vials. This once again destroys the argument that anything in Revelation is cyclical, interchangeable, or repetitive. We were just told by the mighty angel that the mysteries would be solved in the days of the seventh trumpet, not in any other period! This means the seventh trumpet must continue all the way until the total fulfillment of God's mysteries, at least as far as the prophets of Israel go, who were concerned about these things. Daniel in particular greatly desired to know, and was told to wait.

Focus: Zionism and Raptured Church Theory nullified at once

Look at the language of 1 Corinthians. Flesh and blood cannot inherit the Kingdom of God/Heaven, which means that the United Nations creating Israel after WWII cannot be fulfilling the promise of deliverance we saw in Daniel regarding the time of trouble like never before in history. After all, the people living in Israel are flesh and blood, are they not?

The only way to get around this language would be to become so Transhumanist that they literally replace their physical bodies to the point where they are no longer flesh and blood. This is exactly what gnostic dark scientists are trying to accomplish today. Who knows what will be possible as they get closer to unlocking the secrets of energy, matter and consciousness. They might become androids and think they have fulfilled the 1 Corinthians 15:50 stipulation as well. Certainly, science fiction has tried to glorify and explore the possibility, preparing humanity for the eventuality.

Also, the argument that the Rapture happens during the fifth or sixth seal is proven to be contradictory and impossible by this passage. When we respect the actual structure and divine arrangement of the book of Revelation, we see that the resurrection and our transformation happen together, and both occur only during the time of the last trumpet, not before. Therefore, the scenes in heaven that happen earlier—with the untold multitudes from all nations and tongues—cannot be showing the results of the Rapture. This should also be obvious by the emphasis on Death, which has lost its sting. Death is literally the rider of the fourth horse, and it kills the church. But it's "sting" of seemingly being victorious over Jesus Christ will be overcome by the events of the last trumpet.

Now returning to the events of Revelation, let us see whether our interpretation of the clues about these seven thunders and the little scroll are on track:

Then a reed was given to me like a rod, saying, "Rise and measure the temple of God, the altar, and those who worship in it. But leave out the outer court of the temple, and do not measure it, because it has been given to the Gentiles. And they shall trample the holy city for forty-two months. And I will give power to My two witnesses, and they shall prophesy one thousand two hundred and sixty days [forty-two months], having been clothed in sackcloth." (Revelation 11:1-3 EMTV)

Bingo! The mystery of God that was declared to the prophets is about to be fulfilled when the seventh trumpet sounds, and in anticipation of those events John is instructed to measure the temple in Jerusalem, the altar, and the worshipers. This is tremendously powerful and important. It means that even though the asteroids impacted the Near East and killed a third of the world, Jerusalem is still alive and has worshipers. But it also has Gentiles, who are apparently going to trample it for the same amount of time as the two witnesses will be around. We are not told the results of this measuring, curiously.

THE BAD NEWS OF JERUSALEM

The connections to Old Testament patterns here is uncanny, and must be respected. The two witnesses are powerful prophets, coming to Israel to preach to the ungodly people to repent and forsake their ways before God comes to destroy them. Their leadership is corrupt. They have rejected Christ, the Messiah. They are in league with the Satanic New World Order. How do we know?

- Firstly, if they were altogether Christian they would have been killed, since God said that the remainder of the Christians had to be killed soon after the fifth seal.
- Secondly, if they were Christians, they would not be worshiping in the temple. Jesus rejected the temple when he was shown it, and promised to replace it: *(John 2:19-22 KJV) Jesus answered and said unto them, Destroy this temple, and in three days I will raise it up. Then said the Jews, Forty and six years was this temple in building, and wilt thou rear it up in three days? But he spake of*

the temple of his body. When therefore he was risen from the dead, his disciples remembered that he had said this unto them; and they believed the scripture, and the word which Jesus had said.

- Thirdly, our own bodies are called the temple of the Holy Spirit, which is better than the law, freeing us from the law's bondage: *(1 Corinthians 6:19 KJV) What? know ye not that your body is the temple of the Holy Ghost which is in you, which ye have of God, and ye are not your own?*

- Fourthly, Christians are **never** supposed to sacrifice on an altar anymore, because Jesus is the eternal sacrifice for our sins: *(Hebrews 10:9-18 EMTV) Then he has said, "Behold, I have come to do your will, O God." He takes away the first [the temple and the law] in order that he may establish the second [the Kingdom guided by the Spirit]. By which will we are sanctified through the offering of the body of Jesus Christ once for all. And every priest stands ministering daily and offering repeatedly the same sacrifices, which are never able to take away sins. But he himself, having offered one sacrifice for sins forever, he sat down at the right hand of God, from that time waiting till his enemies [the Satanic conspiracy] are placed as a footstool for his feet. For by one offering he has perfected forever those who are being sanctified. But the Holy Spirit also witnesses to us; for after he had said before, "This is the covenant which I shall covenant with them after those days, says the LORD: I will put My laws on their hearts, and I will inscribe them on their minds, and their sins and their lawless deeds I shall by no means remember any longer." Now where there is remission of these, there is no longer an offering for sin.*

- Fifthly, our own bodies are a living sacrifice as we reject the pleasure and conformity of this evil, Satanic world, showing there is no need for sacrificed animals any more: *(Romans 12:1-2 KJV) I beseech you therefore, brethren, by the mercies of God, that ye present your bodies a living sacrifice, holy, acceptable unto God, which is your reasonable service. And be not conformed to this world: but be ye transformed by the renewing of your mind, that ye may prove what is that good, and acceptable, and perfect, will of God.*

- Sixthly, Christians have no holy city at all on earth, nor a temple therein. We can offer a sacrifice by praising God, confessing his name, and having thanks: *(Hebrews 13:14-15 EMTV) For* <u>*we have no permanent city*</u>*, but* <u>*we seek the one to come*</u>*. Therefore through him [Jesus] let us continually* <u>*offer up a sacrifice of praise*</u> *to God, that is, the fruit of our lips,* <u>*confessing to his name*</u>*.*

• Seventhly, real Christians worship by preaching around the world, having the Holy Spirit and the Scriptures as their guide, and God would not need to send prophets to warn us at all, because we would love to see his coming in the clouds, and await his judgment.

And more reasons besides these could be used to prove that those in the temple which John measured are not Christians, do not know the will of God, and are lost sheep without their Shepherd. This again speaks to the 144,000 Israelite elect, if we may assume that they are the ones inside the temple worshiping, because when they were sealed we were never told they were saints or Christians—only that they served God the Father. Then again, it's possible that the religion of Jerusalem is totally corrupt, hateful, and blasphemous, as it logically must be if it has denied Jesus Christ as the true Lord and Savior. Therefore the 144,000 may have nothing to do with it.

Either way, we have further evidence. The little scroll and John's measurement of the temple connect to this arrival of the prophets, which is a severe warning. Remember the function of the six trumpets thus far? Remember that the scroll tasted sweet in his mouth, but was bitter in his stomach? Obviously this gives us a hint about what was written in it. Whatever it was seemed nice at first, but then became very unpleasant once he began to "digest" or understand it. We know that John specifically does **not** measure the Gentiles, so whatever this bitterness is, it can't be about them. My best interpretation, therefore, is that John realizes that the temple is rebuilt, and feels happy about this. He sees that Jews are worshiping God within the temple, sacrifices are being made, and the holy city is intact despite the cataclysms on earth. This is all good news at first glance, and it suggests that God has been protecting Jerusalem. However, there is something deeply wrong here upon further consideration. Because these are not followers of the Messiah, they have rejected Jesus, whom John loved so much, and are totally astray, if not blasphemous. And their protection was not necessarily by God, but could have been engineered by Satan's conspiracy because they have selfish motives to keep Jerusalem and the temple around! He may realize that the two witnesses are coming to judge Israel and its partners, not praise it. Very bitter.

THE PROVOCATION OF THE WITNESSES

These are the two olive trees and the two lampstands which are standing before the Lord of the earth. And if anyone wants to harm them, fire proceeds from their mouth and devours their enemies. And if anyone wants to harm them, he must be killed in this way. These men have power to shut heaven, so that no rain falls during the days of their prophecy; and they have authority over the waters to turn them into blood, and to strike the earth with every plague, as often as they wish. (Revelation 11:4-6 EMTV)

These prophets are not named. The theory that these are Elijah and Moses is plausible, but I would offer the possibility that John himself is one of them, although he would not realize it during his vision. After all, didn't the mighty angel just barely tell him after reading the book that he would personally need to prophesy again before many peoples, languages, nations, and kings? That's exactly what these two prophets are doing in the next scene. History does not record John the disciple doing a lot of traveling and preaching after his time on Patmos, so if he were ever going to return and prophesy on earth again, it would be during this time. In fact, seeing that he was the one who had to measure the temple and the people worshiping inside, it makes even more sense. Prophets always "measure" their people in a sense. The second prophet might be Ezekiel, who was also made to eat a scroll which was sweet in his mouth (Ezekiel 3:1-3), but which is soon followed by "bitterness" (Eze 3:14) as he realizes he's going to have to condemn Israel for their ungodly stubbornness.

And when they finish their testimony [after the 42 months,
during which time the Gentiles are trampling the outer court],
the Beast who ascends out of the bottomless pit will make
war with them, and will overcome them, and will kill them.
(Revelation 11:7 EMTV)

The prophets had freedom and power to send "every plague" as often as they wish, and they obviously do exactly that, because they provoke the Beast into making war with them.

This also seems to be a victory for Satan, not God. Not only did the great leaders of the world survive the supposed day of wrath (the sixth seal) but they fragmented and deflected the "planet killer" asteroid and thus spared their precious city of Jerusalem, which Satan wants to occupy and rule. And while it's true that many people died in the process, we're told that the rest who didn't die refused to repent of their demon worship! Now, when God openly sends not one, but two prophets to do miracles and bear testimony from God, they kill them!

In light of this shocking and strange turn of events, we must once again consider the Jeremiah 31:37 loophole. If Satan and his servants truly believe they have negated the covenant of God with Israel, and can defeat all of His judgments and wrath, this would be exactly the boost of confidence they need in order to convince themselves they solved the riddle and unlocked the power. This explains why God scripts the deaths of His own prophets. He is pretending that they are weaker than Satan's "Beast" even though God obviously has supreme power (He's the one writing this future history!). God wants to trick Satan into being overconfident. It's a pattern we will see over and over again, in even more controversial ways than this!

And their corpse will lie on the street of the great city which
spiritually is called Sodom and Egypt, where also their
Lord was crucified.
(Revelation 11:8 EMTV)

Bizarrely, many scholars try to deny that the city in question is Jerusalem despite the undeniable fact that it's the only city in history where the Lord was crucified. It's the obvious, natural climax point of these world events. John just barely measured the temple there, and the prophets would naturally return to Jerusalem to judge and warn. Do they imagine that God permanently loves and supports the city, even when it was recreated by the United Nations and not Him? Even though it rejects His Messiah? We must discuss this more later.

> Then _some_ of the peoples, tribes, languages, and nations saw their corpse three-and-a-half days, and they will _not allow their corpses to be put into a tomb_. And those who dwell on the earth _rejoice_ over them, and make merry, and _give gifts_ to one another, _because_ these two prophets _tormented those who dwell on the earth_. _(Revelation 11:9-10 EMTV)_

Evidently there are some who want to properly bury these witnesses in a tomb, which is how prophets should be buried in Israel. Perhaps members of the 144,000 who listened to their message and believed. It's interesting that they have intact bodies at all. It suggests that the "war" being conducted was not carried out with excessive force and explosions, but some more personal or even mystical means. Combined with the arrival of the Beast from the bottomless pit (certainly a spiritual event with a physical aspect) and the rejoicing of mankind for several days straight seems to confirm the Jeremiah 31:37 loophole theory again, because it would seem that the Beast's victory over God's prophets confirms that the covenant is broken, and that gnostic New Age religious power has prevailed over God.

> Now after the three-and-a-half days, the _breath of life from God_ entered into them, and they stood on their feet, and _great fear_ fell on _those who were watching them_. _(Revelation 11:11 EMTV)_

God specially breathes life back into them, reviving them and allowing them to stand up. This also suggests their bodies are intact, and that they were killed by some kind of mystical power, not physical destruction. If they were killed by some kind of ritual or New Age gnostic sorcery, it could also explain why they weren't buried to begin with; people might have wanted to confirm that they were truly dead and prove to each other that the Jeremiah 31:37 loophole was a success. No doubt this is why, when they stand back up, "great fear" falls on those who were watching. It's not simply that the prophets are alive and can get revenge, but that the entire narrative of the Satanic conspiracy seems to fall apart! It means that God is still in charge of the world, and that the Beast is not all-powerful! It has far-reaching implications about the fate of everyone who took part in killing the church and partaking in the Satanic covenant.

> *And I heard a loud voice from heaven saying to them, "Come up here." And they <u>went up to heaven in a cloud</u>, and <u>their enemies watched them</u>. (Revelation 11:12 EMTV)*

God makes sure that the whole world watches as the witnesses ascend up to heaven. The fact that they do not avenge their own deaths or cast more plagues upon the people must be a very unnerving and unsettling sign to them. It means God has something much bigger and more devastating in store, which will show that those who defy Him are totally powerless to stop Him.

> *<u>In that day</u> there was a <u>great earthquake, and a tenth of the city fell</u>, and <u>seven thousand</u> men were <u>killed</u>. And <u>the rest became fearful</u> and <u>gave glory to the God of heaven</u>. (Revelation 11:13 EMTV)*

At first glance, when compared to everything else we've seen already, this almost seems like a mediocre event. A big earthquake happens and 10% of Jerusalem is destroyed, killing a measly 7,000 men? How does that compare to stars falling to earth, bottomless pits being opened, and giant angels standing with pillars of fire for feet? A third of humanity was killed by the Euphrates river and they only hardened their hearts and refuse to repent! But now a tiny portion of one city collapses and a small number of men die, and this is what strikes fear into their hearts? This is what changes their mind and compels them to give glory to the God of heaven? It makes no sense. That is, it makes no sense without the Jeremiah 31:37 loophole as the backdrop.

We must ask: which part of the city was destroyed exactly? Which 7,000 men were killed? Depending on the answer it could change everything. Those who remain might get the "message" loud and clear! For example, the earthquake may destroy the underground bunkers and fortresses of the Satanic elite high priests who combined their gnostic rituals to kill the two witnesses. Or what if it exclusively killed only the governing/legislative body of Jerusalem? What if it simply collapsed the defense grid and its generals and military leaders, leaving the city totally vulnerable to invasion? Whatever it is, it has a transformative effect on everyone in the city, to the point where they finally give glory to God! Amen!

THE HEART OF THE SATANIC CONSPIRACY DEMOLISHED

The second woe is past; and, behold, <u>the third woe cometh quickly.</u>
(Revelation 11:14 KJV)

To recap, the sixth trumpet (called the second woe) was devastating and powerful. It included the killing of a third of the earth's population via the river Euphrates, the "mighty angel" appearing, the two witnesses plaguing the world, the war with the Beast from the bottomless pit, and the earthquake that destroys a tenth of the city and kills 7,000. The culmination of these events finally "converts" the city in question, which is undoubtedly Jerusalem.

Is Jersualem evil during this future time period? Were they part of the Satanic New World Order? Is that why they're spiritually Sodom and Egypt? Is that why they didn't let the bodies of the prophets be buried, and why they gave gifts? Just how significant is Jerusalem to this future Satanic world empire? The answer is right in front of us in the next verse:

> *And the seventh angel sounded; and there were great voices in heaven, saying, The kingdoms of this world are become the kingdoms of our Lord, and of his Christ; and he shall reign for ever and ever. (Revelation 11:15 KJV)*

Jerusalem is at the very heart of the entire Satanic world empire at this point in the future, and their conversion is enough to flip control of the world into God's hands, spiritually speaking. We talked about this passage in the introduction of the book. It's the moment in Revelation where Satan officially stops being the "ruler of this world" and must find another way to regain power. Bible scholars have tragically overlooked the connection between the city's conversion and the rest of Revelation, even though everything so far has been leading up to this critical point, and everything afterwards is the aftermath of it!

Perhaps it is because we are self-centered people, and we suppose that the church and our own salvation is the only thing God cares about in history anymore. But with this view in mind, we accept that our place is in heaven during these events, and God's priority is taking back his holy city from Satan and saving an elect remnant (144,000 Israelites) to fulfill his ancient prophecies to Israel, serve as the firstfruits of the Millennial Kingdom, and so much more. All seven of the seals have been about Satan gaining worldly power, and all six of the trumpets so far have been about warning the world (and Jerusalem) about the impending arrival of judgment and God's reclamation. That's why the Jeremiah 31:37 loophole is so pivotal, because it creates a very real and legitimate (though ultimately hopeless) possibility for how Satan and his servants could destroy the covenant between God and Israel, and therefore Satan could occupy the holy city and be worshiped as if he were God, which is his ultimate fantasy. For God to disprove their loophole and show that He is still in control of the city, killing 7,000 powerful men who believe they are immune to God's wrath, is extremely important and worth celebrating. Look at how happy the elders are:

> *And the four and twenty elders, which sat before God on their seats, fell upon their faces, and worshipped God,*

Saying, We give thee thanks, O Lord God Almighty, which art, and wast, and art to come; because thou hast taken to thee thy great power, and hast reigned. And the nations were angry, and thy wrath is come, and the time of the dead, that they should be judged, and that thou shouldest give reward unto thy servants the prophets, and to the saints, and them that fear thy name, small and great; and shouldest destroy them which destroy the earth. And the temple of God was opened in heaven, and there was seen in his temple the ark of his testament: and there were lightnings, and voices, and thunderings, and an earthquake, and great hail. (Revelation 11:16-19 KJV)

This passage has confused many interpreters because it boldly speaks about things that haven't happened yet in the text as if they were already in the past. But this misunderstanding is easily solved. The sounding of the seventh trumpet has just barely happened, and we know it is the final phase of God's plan. The mighty angel promised that the mysteries of God would be fulfilled in the days of the seventh trumpet. Therefore it's appropriate to begin celebrating the arrival of these **inevitable** outcomes as if they are as good as complete. The elders don't need to wait for the events to unfold on earth.

The heart of the Satanic New World Order has been demolished, because the people of its capital city have turned to God and will serve him. Satan is rejected. Even the Beast that came from the bottomless pit is presumably rejected, if we can imagine it to be some kind of presence people were aware of. Meanwhile, we have to assume that the rest of the world has gone from celebrating the death of the two prophets to being dismayed that they were deceived by Satan's gnostic experts and their false promises of supremacy over God!

11

HEAVENLY HISTORY

While many scholars assume that chapter 12 of Revelation is a diversion from the main topic, or a restart point of some kind, it's actually deeply tied to the logic of the seventh trumpet and the preceding events. In fact it is central to revealing the "mystery of God" that the mighty angel promised would be uncovered!

We've seen how the seven seals of God's top-secret strategy book have been broken by Jesus Christ, building up the conspiratorial empire of Satan on earth, persecuting the true church while creating a false "tares" church trying to replace it. Then, with the breaking of the seventh seal, we have seen six trumpets terrorizing the ungodly world after the death of the church, avenging them as the martyrs called for. Ultimately, this holy terror and vengeance won back the city of Jerusalem from Satan. Spiritual control of Jerusalem is the final objective of both Satan and God during this phase of world events. Thanks to the Jeremiah 31:37 loophole, Satan and his gnostic agents convince themselves that they can undo the covenant of God with Israel, but the final events of the sixth trumpet have reversed that thinking, "converting" the evil city of Jerusalem back to God's control. During the time of the seven trumpets the 144,000 Israelite elect have been watching and learning. However, despite all of this, the people of this city have no proper understanding of how badly they were deceived by Satan, and what they should believe in instead. They fear God and glorify Him, but they are totally ignorant about the truth.

We must remember that the church is dead at this point, and these people were deceived by gnostic myths and false religion until now. Therefore, it is only natural that God would find a way to educate them on what's really been going on in the world while they were ignorant, leading all the way back to the prophetic arrival of the Jewish Messiah, ancient Rome, and the unexpected nature of how the Kingdom of Heaven was established. We don't know what the two witnesses said to these people, but we know that they did not believe them until after their resurrection and the earthquake that killed 7,000 key people in the city. What happens next is their education by the heavens themselves:

> And *there appeared a great wonder in heaven*; a woman clothed with the sun, and the moon under her feet, and upon her head a crown of twelve stars: (Revelation 12:1 KJV)

This is not a personal vision of John's, but a great wonder appearing in the sky for all the inhabitants of Jerusalem to witness. It's a visible miracle happening after the seventh trumpet is blown, in linear sequence after the conversion of Jerusalem. This is the method by which God will teach them on the nature of the Beast they have been allied with for so long, ultimately leading to a lesson on how to identify and reject the "Mark of the Beast".

God wants to show them the history of the church, God's protection of it, and the role of Satan in persecuting it. Many people in Jerusalem will be under the impression that God did not love Christians, and they will realize for the first time that Jesus really is the Messiah and that the church was his. Among these, there will be people who lie about being Jews, who will now realize that Satan was deceiving them, and have their eyes opened to the amazing truth, which is why Jesus said this to the churches:

> Behold, I will make them of the *synagogue of Satan*, which *say they are Jews, and are not, but do lie*; behold, I will make them to come and worship

before thy feet, and to <u>know that I have loved thee</u>.
(Revelation 3:9 KJV)"

The history of Satan's conspiracy shows us that it is managed by deeply deceived authorities who are blinded and fueled by the "spirit of antichrist". Christ's promise to show fake Jews (whoever they are) that he loved the church is even more mystifying in this context. It means that there may be a deep history of impostor Jews from the first century until today, and raises questions about their role in the creation of the evil Kabbalah, the formation of Satanic groups like Los Alumbrados, their evolution into the Jesuits, and more. Whoever this "synagogue of Satan" may be historically, or in the future, it's important to God that they are taught to respect and honor the church before the end of the world, to the point where they will come and worship at the feet of the angel in charge of the church he's speaking to in that verse, or perhaps even the saints themselves.

THE BEAST SYSTEM

The heavenly history lesson teaches the newly converted Jerusalem about the Beast system. Most of it is straightforward. We have extensively discussed the significance of the war in heaven (Rev 12:7-12) and the fact that Satan is sent to earth, but it may not be obvious how this matches up with the breaking of the first four seals. Indeed, the seals establish Satan's empire on earth, but here we see the same process from a different angle—one specifically leading to the "Mark of the Beast" global system which God hates so fervently.

> *And the dragon [Satan] was wroth with <u>the woman</u> [faithful*
> *Messianic Jews and their converts], and went to make war*
> *with the remnant of her seed [the early church], which keep the*
> *commandments of God, and have <u>the testimony of Jesus Christ</u>.*
> *(Revelation 12:17 KJV)*

The testimony of Jesus Christ is what Satan hates most. He wants to erase the knowledge, suppress it, corrupt it, distort it, kill it, and control it. That's the Beast system in a nutshell. It's not about creating one religion, or having one plan of attack, but having as many avenues as possible to detract from the true Gospel. Why? Because every time somebody is saved they receive the Holy Spirit and become a member of the Kingdom of Heaven, which is the greatest threat on earth to him. Look at how Jesus describes it:

> "The wind *blows where it wills*, and *you hear* its sound, but *you do not know* from where it comes and where it goes. *So is everyone* who has been *born of the Spirit*." *(John 3:8 EMTV)*

Christians have their own will, and mental liberty. They are immune to the control of Satan and the propaganda of the world. Not only that, but wherever we go, people hear us. They can't anticipate us, can't stop us, and can't stop others from listening to us. If Satan were not made the ruler of the earth and given extra power with the breaking of the first four seals we would have converted it a long time ago. But as you'll recall, God doesn't want to have the godly and ungodly mixed together like wheat and tares when the Day of the Lord comes. Therefore, the church must be suppressed and eventually killed, clearing the battle path. That's why the meteor strikes and devastation of Revelation happens at all: there are no Christians caught in the crossfire and the 144,000 are sealed and safe!

The Beast system begins when Satan gives his throne, power, and authority to Rome, which is the same kingdom as Daniel's fourth "beast". It gets wounded to death, but then comes back thanks to Satan reviving it with the Antichurch of the universal Roman (catholic) system. This is the first Beast. It makes war with the true church and prevails, killing them and forcing populations to convert to the Satanic Roman religious empire,

> If *any man have an ear, let him hear*. He that leadeth into captivity [forced conversion, conquest] shall go into captivity: he that killeth with the sword [persecution, Inquisitions] must be killed with the

sword. Here is the patience and the faith of the saints. (Revelation 13:9-10 KJV)

This verse is placed directly after the description of the first beast, as if to give a major hint to Christians that the Roman Catholic system is evil. As we saw with the rider of the white horse, starting with Constantine, their goal is to "conquer". When you conquer something, you also lead it into captivity. It becomes your captive, your slave. Catholicism has forcibly converted every major population who has ever identified with it, unlike the preaching of the Gospel which saves individuals and sets them apart from the world. The "universal" part of that Beast church system is about universal conquest by Satan, plain and simple.

UNHOLY MIRACLES AND SPIRITUAL CAPTIVITY

Eventually the first Beast weakens and diminishes. Rome is collapsing, and the Roman expansion to the East (the Byzantine empire, as it's called) is left carrying the traditions and glory on their own. However, the second Beast, which has two horns which appear to be like a lamb (Christian) arrives to save Satan's Beast system from collapse:

And I beheld another beast coming up <u>out of the earth</u> [referencing Europe's land conquests on behalf of the Vatican, the Holy Roman Empire, the rider of the red horse]; and he had two horns like a lamb [seemingly Christian], and he spake as a dragon [Satanic blasphemy]. And he exerciseth <u>all the power of the first beast before</u> him, and causeth the earth and them which dwell therein to <u>worship the first</u> beast, whose deadly wound was healed [Roman imperialism]. And he doeth great wonders, so that he <u>maketh fire come down from heaven on the earth in the sight of men</u>, And <u>deceiveth</u> them that dwell on the earth <u>by the means of those miracles</u> which he had power to do <u>in the sight of</u> the beast; saying to them that dwell on the earth, that they should make an image

to the beast, which had the wound by a sword, and did live.
(Revelation 13:11-14 KJV)

A few mysteries present themselves here. This description has led many scholars astray in interpreting the second Beast. When we recognize that this second Beast represents the Middle Ages and the shared dominance of the Catholic and Orthodox churches, we can make sense of these "great wonders" it has the power to do. Although not appreciated by modern people—and perhaps even mocked by evangelical Christians who wish to ignore the rhetoric of the false churches—there was a long period of history where magic, demons, and miracles were popularized and able to mystify humanity into accepting the need for Catholic priesthoods and special orders such as the Rosicrucians, Knights of Malta, and the infamous Dominican Order who caused so much bloodshed in the name of stamping out heresy. We think of demonic possession, exorcism, dragons, knights, and wizards as all lumped together into old mythology, but the Bible puts a much different spin on this period of superstition and radical religious zeal. For one, it specifies that this institution had the power to make fire come down from heaven to earth "in the sight of men" and could do wonders "in the sight of the Beast". This is very strange wording, but very deliberate.

What it means is that the Satanic powers behind these twin church empires were able to conjure up delusional visions in the eyes of those who were under their spell, causing them to see fire fall from heaven. It's not that priests could actually call down fire like the old prophets of God, but that they could make fellow Catholics or Orthodox believers see visions as if it were happening. If you think this is not still a part of their culture today, you are mistaken:

> *At the Fatima apparition site, on October 13, 1917, 70,000 people witnessed the sun appear to fall from the sky. These eyewitnesses said that they watched as the sun fell from heaven toward the crowd and then returned to its normal position in the sky. Many thought this was signaling the end of the world and were sure they would perish. Here is a brief recount of the events at Fatima:*

Just when it seemed that the ball of fire would fall upon and destroy them, the miracle ceased and the sun resumed its normal place in the sky, shining forth as peacefully as ever. When the people arose from the ground, cries of astonishment were heard on all sides. Their clothes, which had been soaking wet and muddy, now were clean and dry. Many of the sick and crippled had been cured of their afflictions.

The Miracle of the Sun is a common, albeit fantastic, event at many apparition sites. At dozens of locations, literally millions have reported the sun miracle. It happened before a crowd of 100,000 in Puerto Rico on April 23, 1991, which was the 38th anniversary of the apparitions there. It happened again in the Philippines on March 5, 1993, in front of a crowd of 300,000. In El Cajas, Ecuador 120,000 pilgrims were in attendance when the Miracle of the Sun occurred there in the late 1980s.

This is a small portion of a wonderful book called "Queen of All" by Jim Tetlow, Roger Oakland, and Brad Myers. It explores the notion of apparition sites, usually centered around a statue of a woman the Catholic Church claims represents the Virgin Mary. The pilgrims all come to worship her and see miracles, and their faith is apparently rewarded with miracles. As you can see, these are recent events, not some distant age. The book's claims are backed up by legitimate news sources and research, and it would behoove the reader to inspect it yourself. The unbelievable claims of these millions of Catholics and Orthodox witnessing miracles is not so hard to believe when we read Revelation 13's description of the second Beast. The fact that these events mostly happen in Latin or Eastern European countries, where the Catholic or Orthodox churches are dominant, is no coincidence. The second Beast only has power to do these miracles in the eyes of its own people. This keeps them enslaved, captive, and desperately believing. The same goes for demon possessions, exorcisms, stigmata, apparitions, and much more. To the people trapped in this Beast system of unholy deception and bondage, such miracles are worth infinitely more than rational arguments or preaching. It has been around since the rise of the second Beast over a thousand years ago, and continues to cause the earth to worship the first Beast: Rome.

We must consider: with deceiving powers like these, how likely is it that this same Satanic institution can change its stripes to become New Age and perform more miracles for the world? Even without gnostic technology breakthroughs and true magic power, the death of the church will lead to a massive consolidation of power by the Vatican and the rise of a priesthood able to do these miracles without skeptical Protestants or evangelicals in the way.

TRIBUTE TO THE BEAST, FOREVER

Even with the first two Beasts clarified in this way, it may be extremely difficult to guess what the "image of the Beast" could be. In order to see it clearly, we must be able to deconstruct and expose the lies of our own world system, because we are unknowingly living in the image of the Beast ourselves today.

> … *saying to them that dwell on the earth*, that *they* should make an image [recreation] to the *beast, which had the wound by a sword, and did live. And he had power to give life unto the image* of the beast, that the image of the beast should both *speak*, and *cause* that as many as would not *worship the image* of the beast [recreated Greco-Roman imperialism] *should be* killed. *(Revelation 13:14-15 KJV)*

Where in history have we seen a passionate manmade revivalism movement of Greco-Roman government, literature, philosophy, architecture, frescos, sculptures, temples, and education? Put simply, the image of the Beast begins with the Italian Renaissance and has continued to this day. By the 1400s Rome had become little more than an Italian city in Europe, filled with ruins that its people did not understand or appreciate, despite having the Vatican inside it as its own city state. As for New Rome (Constantinople), it was conquered by the invading Muslims in 1453 and became part of their Ottoman Empire.

This forced its religious scholars to abandon the region and transport all of their precious ancient Greco-Roman texts, artwork, and artifacts northward to eastern Europe, where it filtered into the Holy Roman Empire and fueled a desire to bring back the old glory days of the first Beast, whose wound was healed.

> The _intellectual basis_ of the Renaissance was its version of _humanism_, derived from the concept of _Roman Humanitas_ and the rediscovery of classical _Greek_ philosophy, such as that of Protagoras, who said that _"Man is the measure of all things."_ This new thinking became manifest in art, architecture, politics, science and literature. _(Wikipedia's page on Renaissance)_

It is undeniable that Europe reinvented itself in the image of ancient Rome and Greece after the medieval period, transitioning to a whole new era of politics, education, art, science, and religious attitudes. And although Wikipedia correctly points out "Humanism" was behind it on a surface level, the Bible tells us the real truth: that Satan was orchestrating the whole thing in order to get the world to worship him. But notice they do not worship the first Beast, even though the image is modeled after it: rather, they worship the image itself, as a new thing.

Outwardly, the Renaissance was a rejection of the Catholic Church, superstition, spirituality, and even the old pagan gods of Rome and Greece, despite being modeled after these classical cultures. That's because the mission of the second Beast (Catholic/Orthodox) was not to be worshiped itself, or to make people worship the first Beast, but to direct mankind to worship the image itself, which he caused them to make. It does not care whether people worship the Pope, or give honor to Constantine, but would rather have mankind reject "Christianity" altogether and simply recreate a new kind of Rome. That's why the second Beast "gives life" to the image and causes it to speak. It represents how the Vatican/Orthodox religions fueled the Renaissance intellectually with the ancient treasures of the Byzantine archives, funded it with its new Spanish/Jewish secret societies under its command thanks to Ignatius Loyola, and pursued "science" (gnosticism) as much as possible to transform the world and create the illusion of progress. We today have the Olympics and countless sports teams playing out meaningless feats of athleticism in arenas for our entertainment, just like the Greeks and Romans. Our society is modeled after theirs. Our cultural landmarks are taken from them, but without their pagan religion. We are an atheist, Humanist copy; an image of the Beast. And who secretly organizes and empowers this image? The second Beast, which has the power to cause our society to "speak" as if it had an intelligent mind of its own. This means that the Vatican's Jesuits have the command over the rhetoric of the entire Renaissance and its more evil sibling, the Counter-Reformation. Intellectually, the Jesuits have been the masters of propaganda, psychology, and covert influence since their formation, multiplying into Freemasons, Illuminati, and much more.

PROTESTANTISM AND HUMANISM

There was a shared disgust between Protestant and Humanists in the wake of the medieval Catholic empire's genocidal Inquisitions against truth. Both sides were disgusted with the oppression and ignorance, but they had different conclusions. Protestants wanted to either "reform" the Catholic Church (like Martin Luther tried), or split off and be independent from its iron grip. Humanists on the other hand wanted to destroy Christianity altogether, and replace it with the idea that mankind didn't need god or religion. This "debate" continued for hundreds of years, and continues to this day. Humanists are so tired of being unable to vanquish religion that they've begun to praise it for having a placebo effect, or saying that its byproducts of community, personal responsibility, and irrational hope may be necessary, even if God is not. Of course, Satan is happy to keep religion as long as its doctrine is false and the real God is not involved.

But what about the statement that the second Beast would "cause that as many as would not worship the image of the beast should be killed"? How has that proven to be accurate, historically? Well, it's extremely easy to answer if we maintain the same level of literality as the rest of heavenly history lesson so far. It's not literally true that every person who does not worship the image of the Beast is murdered by the second Beast, just as it is not literally true that the "woman" of the early church was hidden from persecution for only 42 months, or that the whole world ever consciously worshiped Satan at all. These are expressions used in the heavenly history lesson to make a point about how evil and far-reaching the Satanic conspiracy has been since Jesus established the church. There's no reason to suddenly shift to a hyper-literal interpretation at this moment in the passage. Broadly speaking, on a symbolic and general level, it is very true that the Renaissance (the image) led to the systematic destruction of those who would not conform to its new ideologies. How? With bloody "revolutions" led by the Jesuits and their international gnostic spy network. The French Revolution is today famous for its guillotines, where Protestant aristocracy were beheaded in public view without trial or mercy, simply because they did not conform to the image: they were not a Humanist Democratic Republic!

The verse does not say that everyone who does not worship the image is killed, or even that anyone kills them. It only says that the second Beast causes the demonizing of the non-conforming nation/government/group/institution/people to become severe enough that the world believes they "should be killed". And indeed, that is the propaganda ever since. Those who do not abide by the Renaissance principles of Democratic elections and a Republic form of authority are castigated, villainized, and condemned to the point where it is eventually overthrown and its monarchs are killed in public as if this were a cause for celebration. Humanist "self-governance" is a Satanic joke, as he knows very well that without religion he can guide the thinking of the masses and trick them into anything, one step at a time. Christians are the only exception to this, which is why (true) Christian monarchies are the most hated and violently attacked form of government ever since the Renaissance.

The British Empire's fake Christianity is of no threat to the Jesuits, since they controlled it completely, along with the Freemasons who operated out of there, and the self-identifying Jewish Socialists of Europe. On the other hand, the reign of Otto von Bismarck (a Lutheran monarchist who hated the Vatican's grip on Europe) and his "Kulturkampf" (culture war against the Pope and the Jesuits) in the late

1800s was so effective at exposing and countering the Jesuit conspiracy that the Jesuits were ultimately exiled from Germany, and subsequently used their international network to orchestrate both World War I and II against Germany in retaliation, hoping to permanently erase the existence of Germany and level it to the ground. But they did not wage war openly while Otto von Bismarck was alive, which would have allowed him to fight back and spread his own message; no, that would be too obvious and risky. Instead, they waited until he died of natural causes, demonized Germany in as many ways as possible, and created the most convoluted pretense possible for how Germany would become destroyed during a so-called "World War" that was really a Satanic power grab from every angle imaginable. Then, after WWI, they spent decades setting up their own so-called Jewish Socialist menace, installed their own puppet of Adolf Hitler (who had a concordat with the Pope) and orchestrated the biggest coordinated attack in human history, genociding millions of innocent Jews, Christians, Catholics from one angle or another, reducing Europe to a shell of its former self, traumatized and unable to believe in a God who would allow such carnage.

We have already spoken about how this period allegedly ties into the Daniel prophecy about "deliverance" and Israel's creation by the United Nations. Jesuit-controlled Britain had captured the land of Palestine during World War I and generously donated it to the United Nations specifically so that they could create a homeland for the self-proclaimed Jews after WWII. How much of this was a planned operation based on hoaxes and lies only God knows. However, suffice it to say that it is an example of a nation that did not worship the image of the Beast, and which led to the second Beast causing the world to turn against it, and believe that it "should be killed".

Likewise, America was founded by Jesuits and Freemasons in a bloody Revolution, recreating the image of the Beast like no other. Despite the sincere hopes of many American Christians throughout the centuries, America was always a puppet of the second Beast, mirroring the Humanist Democratic Republic. This supposedly independent nation outwardly emphasized the separation of church and state, but as millions of ignorant Catholics and their conniving priests filtered in there was no hope of escaping the clutches of Papacy. The struggle of true Christians to leverage this doomed system of government to steer the nation towards God has failed. In truth it was never possible. The only thing that resulted was a blasphemous pretense of Christian veneer, placating the Christian voters and lulling them into a false belief that they are living in a Christian nation, not controlled by the Vatican, Freemasons, or any other organization of the gnostic Satanic conspiracy. Meanwhile, what has America been doing around the world ever since those World Wars? Overthrowing governments big and small who do not conform to the Renaissance model of Humanist Democratic Republics. They demonize monarchies, religious governments, dictatorships, saying that their leaders should be killed. They are joined in this effort by many countries, including Canada, Britain, and many European states. The United Nations is the global face of this movement, serving as a trans-national, globalist vehicle for undermining any truly sovereign state.

THE LOGIC OF THE MARK OF THE BEAST

And he <u>causes</u> all, small and great, rich and poor, free and bond, that they should receive marks on their <u>right hand</u>, or on their <u>foreheads</u>, and that no one may buy or sell except he that has <u>the mark</u>, <u>the name</u> of the beast, or the <u>number of his name</u>. Here is wisdom. Let him that has understanding <u>calculate the number</u> of the beast, for it is <u>the number of man</u> [Greek: "anthropos"]--<u>his number is 666</u>. (Revelation 13:16-18 EMTV)

The Greek word "anthropos" does not refer to a single individual male, nor does it refer to "man" as a gender. It is instead the broadest possible term for humanity itself, which is why "**anthropo**logy" is the study of humans, and why being "mis**anthro**pic" means being averse to humans altogether. In Hebrew logic, the number 6 represents the **number of man** because man was created on the sixth day of creation.

When we look at the verse in the light of these terms and facts, it should be clear that the number 666 is none other than Humanism itself.

Humanism is an ideology entirely centered on human supremacy, from beginning to end. It leaves no room for God. The wise are supposed to count (analyze) the "number of his name" (Humanism) with the knowledge that it's the "number of man" (6), and thus realize that the core identity of the Mark of the Beast is godlessness, atheism, and Humanism. As Wikipedia pointed out, *"the intellectual basis of the Renaissance was its version of humanism, derived from the concept of Roman Humanitas and the rediscovery [thanks to the influx of Orthodox/Byzantine literature] of classical Greek philosophy, such as that of Protagoras, who said that "Man is the measure of all things."*

But for as amazing and revolutionary as this realization is, we cannot lose sight of the bigger picture. This mark is specifically supposed to be put into the right hand, or the forehead. How does that work? It's very simple. When we stop being hyper-literal and take it on the same broad spiritual message as the rest of the heavenly history lesson, we see that the right hand is not literal, but represents a person's strength and their actions. We have already seen the importance of the right hand over and over in Revelation. Jesus holds the seven stars in his right hand; God the Father keeps the seven-sealed book in his right hand. There is an ancient and almost universal understanding that a man's right hand is his dominant one, his powerful side, and the hand that symbolizes control. If you receive the Humanist mark of 666 in your right hand, it means that you have dedicated your strength, control, and actions (we might call it lifestyle) to Humanism. Likewise, the forehead is not literal either, but represents a man's mind, the center of his thinking, the place of greatest concentrated will and intention. We see that the 144,000 Israelite elect were sealed with the seal of God in their foreheads, showing that they are devoted to God in their minds.

But still we have not solved the riddle completely. What about buying and selling? Surely this must be a personal, literal statement about common transactions in a capitalist society, right? Wrong. Despite talking about the great and the small, the rich and the poor, and so on, this is the natural evolution of the world order born out of the Renaissance and the black rider's conquest. The Jesuits and their

Los Alumbrados "Enlightenment" ushered in an age of international banking, finance, trade, and standardization under a handful of elite Satanic families. Any nation—whether big or small, free or enslaved, rich or poor—who did not subscribe to one of the Beast's preferred ideologies would be spurned by this global financial conspiracy to the point of not being able to participate on the world marketplace. This is precisely what sanctions and tariffs are used for: punishing countries who don't play along with the agenda of the international banking cartel. They might subsist on a basic internal economy and a handful of partnerships, but these are always being targeted and disrupted by the gnostic, Satanic intelligence agencies and their minions.

When the Muslim leader of Libya, Muammar Gaddafi, tried to organize a new independent currency for his fellow African nations, backed with gold, the international banking system mobilized their propaganda machine to say that he "should be killed" and sent their revolutionaries to do the job. Within two years there was a NATO-led uprising in the name of "freedom". Of course, the Libyans themselves enjoyed free education and almost free gasoline at the time, but this was not free enough for the international banking system. This is but one of countless governments who have been forced into submission by the image of the Beast, which demands to be worshiped.

Finally, let us acknowledge that Humanism is not the only path to economic participation in this Satanic conspiracy. The Bible says that there is a mark, a name, and a number, and that all three are separately viable. The plain mark of the Beast may be direct conspiratorial allegiance of a nation's leadership with Rome or its international systems, like Catholics and Orthodox countries have enjoyed for centuries without violent upheavals by Satan's forces; the name might be more similar to America, having the (false) term of Democratic Republic, which gives credibility to the idea that there is no conspiracy controlling the world. The number, which represents a purging of God and a secularization of society and government, is the least conspicuous and most subtle. Every nation's leadership which does not devote itself to one of these three with its "right hand" (strength) or its "forehead" (intellect) is doomed.

THE HISTORY LESSON IN TOTALITY

For a reminder, let us look again at the circumstances leading up to this amazing history lesson God gives future converted Jerusalem: they were deceived into practicing anti-Christian religions, most likely secularized and atheist for the most part, but also worshiping in a temple contrary to the Gospel. Because they conformed to Satan's conspiracy they were left alone, and in fact protected by the Beast that came from the bottomless pit to make war with the two witnesses. They celebrated when the two witnesses were killed, and did not let them get buried in a tomb properly. They were terrified when they came back to life, and finally began to fear God and give glory to Him when the earthquake hit and destroyed a tenth of the city, killing 7,000.

The lesson teaches them about the history of Christianity, Satan's war against them, and the evolution of the Antichurch empire that has unfolded in so many interesting ways. Ultimately, they are warned about the Mark of the Beast, which is simply the conformity to Satan's Beast system of anti-Christian, godless, and generally Renaissance-style government. This lesson would not take very long if God has a way of getting the point across, and as we will very soon see, it is followed up by very clear and undeniable warnings about anyone who still accepts the Mark of the Beast from that point forward. God wants to make sure that these people of converted Jerusalem never slide backward into Satanic conformity again. They are now His, and by extension, the kingdoms of this world are His.

Objection: What about a literal microchip or mark?

This point is worth considering, but is not as important as traditional fears would insist. We are saints, born again, filled with the Holy Spirit, sealed and sanctified by the blood of Jesus Christ, set apart from the world, and living in the grace of God Almighty. A lousy microchip could never undo that, even if the Satanic elite use all of their gnostic technological powers to try to make it a reality. Evil people are the most deceived about what makes a person saved, and so they think a physical mark can undo what God has done. That is not the case. More and more, the world is racing toward some kind of literal fulfillment of this passage in Revelation, but they themselves are hopelessly ignorant. The lesson for Christians remains the same: fear God, serve Christ, and reject the world. A good rule of thumb has always been whether the world hates you, as they hated Christ. If you reject a microchip and the world says you will be stripped of your money, fired from your job, brought to court, or handed over to die, accept the outcome. Millions of Christians through the millennia have been tortured, raped, slandered and killed for nothing more than loving Jesus Christ and refusing to deny his word. Their families and children paid the price as well. To join their ranks would be a great honor we should celebrate, not fear.

> And _fear not them which kill the body,_ but are not able to kill the soul: but rather _fear Him which is able to destroy both soul and body in hell._ Are not two sparrows sold for a farthing? and one of them shall not fall on the ground without your Father. But the very hairs of your head are all numbered. _Fear ye not_ therefore, ye are of more value than many sparrows. Whosoever therefore shall confess me before men, him will I confess also before my Father which is in heaven. But _whosoever shall deny me before men, him will I also deny before my Father which is in heaven._
> (Matthew 10:28-33 KJV)

We cannot be tricked into hell. The mark and its placement in your right hand or forehead represents a devotion of your actions and mind to the Beast, not some magical implant or system. God will not condemn you for being forced into something, just as we today are all born into the image of the Beast, but are not loyal to it, but rather to the Kingdom of Heaven and the arrival of God's reign on earth. If you have an opportunity to reject such a thing, you can reject it and testify that it is against your religion, because it is.

12

HARVEST SEASON

THE RETURN OF JESUS FOR HIS FIRSTFRUITS

> *And I saw, and behold, <u>the Lamb standing on Mount Zion</u>, and with him one hundred and forty-four thousand, having <u>his name</u> and the name of <u>his Father</u> having been <u>written on their foreheads</u>. (Revelation 14:1 EMTV)*

After the heavenly history lesson is complete and the people of the newly-converted Jerusalem understand the history of the Beast system, Jesus Christ himself returns to Mount Zion and congregates with the 144,000 Israelite elect. Not only do they have the seal of the Father in their forehead, but now they also have the seal of the Son; they are proper Christians, worshiping their Messiah.

Once again I will remind the reader that the trumpets have been heralding the return of Christ for this very remnant the whole time. It is only after the 144,000 Israelite elect are sealed that the trumpets were allowed to sound, because a holy portion of Israel was required to witness the devastation of the earth and be redeemed as the first members of the impending Millennial Kingdom.

And I heard <u>a voice</u> from heaven, like the voice of many waters, and like the voice of loud thunder. And the voice which I heard was as of harpists playing on their harps. And they sang a <u>new song</u> before the throne, and before the four living creatures, and the elders; and <u>no one was able to learn that song except the hundred and forty-four thousand</u> who had been <u>redeemed from the earth</u>. These are those who were not defiled with women, for they are virgins. These are those who <u>follow the Lamb wherever he may go</u>. These were <u>redeemed by Jesus</u> from among men, <u>firstfruits</u> to God and to the Lamb. And no guile was found in their mouth, for they are blameless. (Revelation 14:2-5 EMTV)

The Bible places a great deal of emphasis on these 144,000 elect, but scholars struggle to consider that they could be a new group of post-church believers, living in Israel at the time of God's vengeance upon the earth. Their description leave no room for us to conflate it with our current church, however. They were specially chosen from the twelve tribes of Israel, not the Gentiles or any other group; they were marked with the seal of the Father only at first, but then with the seal of Jesus after the cataclysm, the two witnesses, the earthquake, and the heavenly history lesson; the Bible even goes as far as to say that they are blameless, redeemed by Jesus himself from the earth (showing that they were on earth this whole time), serve as firstfruits (of the Millennial Kingdom that is about to appear, not of the Kingdom of Heaven that has been reigning since Christ's first appearance), not defiled by women, have no guile in them, and now they learn a special song that no one was able to learn except them. We know the exact history of this group, and they are unique. The four winds of destruction were held back to allow them to be sealed initially, which is a unique period in the future, impossible to confuse with any other group. We should all celebrate this future people, who will fulfill so many prophecies given to the prophets; they are the people prophesied about so frequently in the ancient "mystery of God" descriptions to Isaiah, Jeremiah, Ezekiel, Daniel, and Jesus himself. Perhaps we, the saints, are the ones who are playing those harps in heaven for these elect's new song.

The wording might suggests that the 144,000 are now dead and stand in heaven for this song, but I will suggest that they learn the new song directly from Jesus on the earthly Mount Zion, in Jerusalem; probably in the Third Temple itself. The music provided by heaven and the presence of Jesus on earth would indicate a powerful bridge has been created between the two realms, in the holiest place on earth. This new group is being taught, lifted up, and encouraged to sing, and their voices are being heard spiritually in heaven as if they are there, because on some level the two places are merging here. We already know that the prayers of the saints were symbolized in heaven as vials full of incense, if not harps as well, thanks to Rev 5:8. Who is to say that the new song of these firstfruits is not specially presented before the throne of God in this blessed hour?

There are better reasons yet why these 144,000 cannot be dead at this point. First of all, nothing has killed them. Secondly, they are chosen to participate in the unveiling of the mystery of God, and many important prophecies will converge upon them after this point.

THE GOSPEL PREACHED WORLDWIDE ONE LAST TIME

And I saw another <u>angel fly</u> in the midst of heaven, having the <u>everlasting gospel to preach</u> unto them that <u>dwell on the earth</u>, and to every nation, and kindred, and tongue, and people, (Revelation 14:6 KJV)

Now that Jesus has returned to earth to meet and teach his chosen people, the time for harvest has come. But as we know already, there will be two harvests: one for the righteous, and one for the wicked. The wheat must be gathered up to heaven, and the tares must be bundled together to be burned. To that end, an angel flies across the world preaching the everlasting Gospel to every single nation, people, language, and culture. Despite today's church being dead for a while at this point, God is not willing to let even a single person be destroyed in his wrath who could have been saved if they had heard the promise of redemption through Christ.

> *Saying with a loud voice, <u>Fear God, and give glory</u> to him; for the <u>hour of his judgment is come</u>: and worship him <u>that made</u> heaven, and earth, and the sea, and the fountains of waters. (Revelation 14:7 KJV)*

Notice that the gospel this angel preaches is about fearing and glorifying God. This is the same thing we were told about those who were converted in Jerusalem after the earthquake that killed 7,000 men. They feared and gave glory to God. Why? Because the hour of his judgment is finally arriving. This proves that the evil men who were hiding under the mountains in Rev 6:16-17 were mistaken when they said, *"Fall on us, and hide us from the face of him that sitteth on the throne, and from the wrath of the Lamb: for the great day of his wrath is come; and who shall be able to stand?"* What they experienced was nothing but a hint of the true hour of judgment. We should also notice that there is special emphasis put on God being the one who created the universe, because the "666" Humanist/Atheist ideology of Satan is entirely about denying this reality, which especially provokes God.

> *And there followed another angel, saying, <u>Babylon is fallen</u>, is fallen, <u>that great city</u>, because <u>she made all nations drink</u> of the <u>wine</u> of the <u>wrath of her fornication</u>. (Revelation 14:8 KJV)*

We will discuss this at length in the next chapter. But for now, let's consider that the city in question is not literally called Babylon, but is compared to it by God. It is known for spiritually fornicating, and this provokes God. This surely has something to do with the "mystery of God" that has troubled the prophets and raised so many questions throughout the millennia. This second angel's warning is given to the same people who just barely heard the Gospel being preached to them, elaborating on the promise of God's hour of judgment.

And the third angel followed them, saying with a loud voice, <u>If any man worship the beast and his image, and receive his mark in his forehead, or in his hand, the same shall drink of the wine of the wrath of God</u>, which is poured out without mixture into the cup of his indignation; and he shall be <u>tormented with fire and brimstone</u> in the presence of the holy angels, and in the presence of the Lamb: And <u>the smoke of their torment ascendeth up for ever and ever:</u> and <u>they have no rest day nor night</u>, who worship the beast and <u>his image</u>, and whosoever <u>receiveth the mark</u> of his name. Here is the patience of the saints: here are they that keep the commandments of God, and the faith of Jesus. And I heard a voice from heaven saying unto me, Write, <u>Blessed are the dead which die in the Lord from henceforth</u>: Yea, saith the Spirit, that they may rest from their labours; and their works do follow them. (Revelation 14:9-13 KJV)

The third angel drives the point home clearly for those who still haven't figured it out: all those who wish to avoid eternal damnation and fiery torment must fear God alone and give up their lives in exchange for salvation. John is specially told to write down that those who die in the Lord **from this point on** will be blessed, just to make the point unmistakable. That's because it is only at this point, after witnessing the cataclysms on the earth, the plagues of the two witnesses, and having had the Gospel preached to them directly by angels, that the ultimate punishment is promised for those who continue to stubbornly reject God: eternal torment in the Lake of Fire. Until now the Mark of the Beast (Humanism/Atheism, and false Christianity) has been accepted by mankind out of ignorance, deception, and the Satanic conspiracy's effectiveness at demonizing the true church. But that time is past. In this miraculous final phase of God's plan, faith is no longer about believing whether God exists or the Bible is true, but its deeper and older meaning, which is whether a person is willing to sacrifice their life with confidence that God's promises are true. There will certainly be some kind of Satanic counter-message to this divine warning happening around the world, and people who turn to God will be mercilessly killed, if not tortured, for taking God's side at this last hour. This is exactly what God wants, because he doesn't want even one Christian to remain in the crossfire of what's about to come.

THE SPIRITUAL CALL TO BEGIN THE HARVEST

> *And I looked, and behold a white cloud, and upon the cloud one sat like unto the Son of man [Jesus Christ], having on his head a golden crown [eternal dominion], and in his hand a sharp sickle. And another angel came out of the temple, crying with a loud voice to him that sat on the cloud, <u>Thrust in thy sickle, and reap: for the time is come for thee to reap; for the harvest of the earth is ripe.</u> And he that sat on the cloud thrust in his sickle on the earth; and the earth was reaped. And another angel came out of the temple which is in heaven, he also having a sharp sickle. And another angel came out from the altar, which had <u>power over fire</u>; and cried with a loud cry to him that had the sharp sickle, saying, <u>Thrust in thy sharp sickle, and gather the clusters of the vine of the earth; for her grapes are fully ripe.</u> And the angel thrust in his sickle into the earth, and gathered the vine of the earth, and cast it into <u>the great winepress of the wrath of God.</u> And the winepress was trodden <u>without the city,</u> and <u>blood came out</u> of the winepress, even unto the horse bridles, by the space of a thousand and six hundred furlongs. (Revelation 14:14-20 KJV)*

Just as the heavenly breaking of the seals and the golden censer signaled future events on earth, these two harvests take place before the physical manifestations start to unfold on earth. The two harvests represent the eventual killing of all believers who decide to listen to the three angels, giving up their lives for eternal salvation, and on the other hand the destruction of all those who reject the Gospel and take the Mark of the Beast after this point, believing in whatever gnostic cult reigns over their minds and promises victory over God.

But he said, Nay; lest while ye gather up the tares, ye root
up also the wheat with them. Let both grow together until
the harvest: and in the time of harvest I will say to the
reapers, <u>Gather ye together first the tares</u>, and <u>bind them in
bundles</u> to burn them: but gather the wheat <u>into my barn</u>.
(Matthew 13:29-30 KJV)

Obviously there is a shift in metaphors here, as the final reaping is about "grapes" and Jesus' teaching was about "tares" and "wheat", but the point remains the same: two different harvests, which can only take place when the crops are fully ripe. In this critical teaching by Jesus, the "barn" could represent Jerusalem and the 144,000 elect who are now with him, or it could represent heaven as the destination for all those new believers who are giving up their lives.

THE VIALS AND THE NEW ARRIVALS

And I saw another sign in heaven, great and
marvellous, seven angels having the seven <u>last
plagues</u>; for in them is <u>filled up</u> the <u>wrath of God</u>.
(Revelation 15:1 KJV)

Notice that these are the "last plagues", the final ones. They are in no way repeating what has already happened. It is not a different perspective of the same subject. To further emphasize this, the metaphor has been changed once again, and for a very good reason: these vials represent a stockpile of holy anger God has been keeping for millennia. Whereas the seals were a top-secret strategy for quietly building up Satan's power on earth with mysterious processes, and the trumpets are an open terrorizing of the evil world, warning about what is about to come, in order to convert Jerusalem from Satan's grip, these vials are the ultimate release of God's built up indignation, judgment, and condemnation on the ungodly, without danger of collateral damage. He has been holding back his wrath this whole time because the wheat and the tares were still somewhat mixed together, at least in some regions of the world.

(2) And I saw as it were a sea of glass mingled with fire: and them that had <u>gotten the victory</u> over <u>the beast</u> [Satanic Roman spiritual imperialism], and over his <u>image</u> [the secular Renaissance], and over his <u>mark</u> [ungodly devotion to false causes], and over the <u>number of his name</u> [Humanism/ Atheism], stand on the sea of glass, having the harps of God.

The new arrivals have come up to heaven after being killed on earth. They were killed because they rejected the Beast system after the three angels preached to the entire world in every language. They are called victorious as a result.

(3) And they sing the <u>song of Moses</u> the servant of God, and the song of <u>the Lamb,</u> saying, Great and marvellous are thy works, Lord God Almighty; just and true are thy ways, thou King of saints. <u>Who shall not fear thee</u>, O Lord, and <u>glorify thy name</u>? for thou only art holy: for all nations shall come and worship before thee; for <u>thy judgments are made manifest</u>.

They celebrate both Moses and Jesus, recognizing the history of the covenant God has made with humanity, not just God. Presumably, this means the three angels taught them enough to appreciate how enduring God's patience has been toward humanity and Israel in particular. They love that His judgments are manifesting themselves finally.

And <u>after that</u> I looked, and, behold, the temple of the <u>tabernacle of the testimony in heaven</u> was opened: And the seven angels [the same ones who oversaw the churches and had the trumpets?] came out of <u>the temple</u>, having the seven plagues, clothed in pure and white linen, and having their breasts girded with golden girdles. And one of the four beasts gave unto the seven angels seven golden vials full of the wrath of God, who liveth for ever and ever. And the temple was filled with smoke from the glory of God, and from his power; and no man was able to enter into the temple,

till the seven plagues of the seven angels were fulfilled.
(Revelation 15:5-8 KJV)

Let's look at the timing first. Only after the singing of the new arrivals does the tabernacle (not the temple) open, perhaps signaling that the believers are allowed to enter and worship in the tabernacle until the temple is not being filled with the smoke of God's glory. The angels with the seven plagues and the new golden girdles come out of the temple. They receive the vials full of wrath. Presumably, after the seven plagues are fulfilled, the believers can return to the temple, which is preferable to the tabernacle.

Wrath poured out on the Beast's adherents

Then I heard a loud voice from the temple telling the seven angels, "Go and pour out on the earth the seven bowls of the wrath of God." So the first angel went and poured out his bowl on the earth, and harmful and painful sores came upon the people who bore the mark of the beast and worshiped its image.
(Revelation 16:1-2 ESV)

Clearly there are still people on earth devoted to the Beast system, but we don't know how many. We can't go by the heavenly history lesson, because it symbolically exaggerates many elements to make its point and turns thousands of years of abstract history into abstract little vignettes. So while it says that everyone on earth worshiped the Beast, it also portrays Jesus Christ as being a newborn child when he was taken up to heaven. Jesus was a grown man, and not every culture and individual on the planet was inducted into the Beast system. This does not discredit the history lesson, because God is simplifying and characterizing history the way that He sees it; or at least the way He wants those people to see it. Of course it's also possible that literally everybody outside of Jerusalem is now a subject of the Beast, since the angels preached and gave them a clear choice.

More plagues are poured out, killing everything in the sea and making it and the rivers and fountains like putrified blood. Angels praise this because the people are guilty of shedding the blood of saints and prophets; specifically, they find it fitting that they now have blood to drink, meaning this will presumably have a major impact on life going forward. In literal terms it may be the contaminating effect of the meteors continuing to spread; the process of turning the water into "blood" may be gradual or sped up, affecting more and more people with the collapse of the ocean's ecosystem and all the ramifications.

> *And the fourth angel poured out his vial upon the sun; and power was given unto him to scorch men with fire. And men were scorched with great heat, and blasphemed the name of God, which hath power over these plagues: and they repented not to give him glory. (Revelation 16:8-9 KJV)*

The ozone layer of the earth may be badly damaged by the raining down of all the meteors and the rising smoke of the bottomless pit. If so, it only makes sense that sunlight would burn people badly in the regions affected.

> *Then the fifth one poured out his bowl on <u>the throne of the Beast</u>, and <u>his kingdom</u> became <u>darkened</u>; and they gnawed their tongues from the pain. They blasphemed the God of heaven because of <u>their pains and their ulcers</u>, and they did not repent of their works. (Revelation 16:10-11 EMTV)*

This sounds like a culmination of many effects in our interpretation. If the location of the kingdom of the Beast remains southern Europe and Italy, it would be near the middle of the cataclysm that devastated a third of the planet. The darkness could be from toxic smoke, which would still be flying up from the hole in the earth, perhaps now descending back to earth as a massive shroud of toxic smog, blocking the light. Volcanic eruptions tend to have this effect, and the chemical composition of the meteor that's burning up could make it even worse. The pain seems to be mostly due to the existing sores and agonies.

CLEARING THE PATH FOR EVIL

> *Then the sixth one poured out his bowl on the great river Euphrates, and its water dried up, so that the way of the kings from the east might be prepared. (Revelation 16:12 EMTV)*

Here we see the Euphrates river mentioned by name yet again, reminding us of the ongoing effects of the "burning torch" meteor that landed there. But where is "there" exactly? The river itself is the largest in the region, beginning in Turkey and flowing all the way down to the Persian Gulf, through Syria and Iraq. Well, because the river is "dried up", this tells us it must be northward, closer to Turkey. I believe this is the location for several reasons.

For one, God probably still considers Turkey to be part of the "Beast kingdom" geographically, if not the location of Satan's throne. Remember Rev 2:13, where Jesus says *"even in those days wherein Antipas was my faithful martyr, who was slain among you, <u>where Satan dwelleth</u>."* This message was sent to the church in Pergamum, which is located inside ancient Greece, which is modern day Turkey. None of it is coincidence. The pouring out of darkness on the throne of the Beast would logically correlate with the drying out of the Euphrates river, which is where Jesus said Satan's throne was. The themes converge. Remember that Constantine the Great officially changed the capital of the Roman empire from Rome in Italy to Constantinople, Greece, which is today's Istanbul, Turkey. The Beast's throne and kingdom is now dark from the smoke; the Euphrates river starts here, and is now dried up, making way for the "kings of the east". We will talk about them more later.

> *And I saw <u>three unclean spirits</u> like frogs come out of the mouth of the <u>dragon</u>, and out of the mouth of the <u>beast</u>, and out of the mouth of the <u>false prophet</u>. For <u>they are the spirits</u>*

of devils, working <u>miracles</u>, which go forth unto the kings of the earth and of the whole world, <u>to gather them to the battle of that great day of God Almighty</u>. Behold, I come as a thief. Blessed is <u>he that watcheth</u>, and keepeth his garments, lest he walk naked, and they see his shame. And he <u>gathered them together</u> into a place called in the Hebrew tongue <u>Armageddon</u>. (Revelation 16:13–16 KJV)

What an incredible turn of events! As with the sixth seal and the sixth trumpet, the sixth vial is a major escalation compared to the five before it. Not only is the throne and kingdom of the Beast darkened and in agony, but the river Euphrates dries up completely, and now this. The unclean spirits are described as being like frogs for some reason, but otherwise they are admitted to be the spirits of devils, able to work miracles and convince the world powers to unite in battle against the Lord Jesus Christ. Much like how the Beast from the bottomless pit rose up to attack the two witnesses after they inflicted so much suffering on the world, it seems that Satan has once again been provoked and empowered to make war against God's people. This time their target will be the converted Jerusalem itself.

But who are these characters? We know that the dragon was called Satan in the heavenly vision, and we might assume that the Beast here is the Pope of the Vatican or some earthly religious emperor, but then we also have the False Prophet being introduced. Whoever this is, they are suddenly equal to Satan and the Beast in this respect at least! Obviously many major changes have been happening on earth that John was not able to see or record. This only makes sense. The world was unrepentant after being scorched by fire, and cursed God. They have the Mark of the Beast and are hellbound anyway. Or perhaps not, in their imagination. Remember the Jeremiah 31:37 loophole:

Thus saith the LORD; If heaven above can be measured, and the foundations of the earth searched out beneath, I will also cast off all the seed of Israel for all that they have done, saith the LORD.
(Jeremiah 31:37 KJV)

If the gnostic Satanist scientist-priests ruling the world have gotten any closer to achieving this goal, they might believe they succeeded once again. Simply consider the obvious: the False Prophet (who may be the only visible character of the three powers) can send out spirit devils to perform actual miracles in front of the kings and powers of the world, not just illusions or tricks, there would be immense eagerness to follow the new religion. Perhaps they can heal wounds, make people immune to the choking black smoke in the air, give people immense speed and stamina, or something more directly destructive. Perhaps they can infuse souls into androids, fulfilling the Transhumanist dream. There are dozens of major feats that would convince the world to join the cause of this False Prophet. And if my interpretation is correct, this False Prophet is the same "Man of Sin" talked about by Paul regarding the last days, who is entirely different than the fictional Antichrist that first century Jewish believers had heard about. We'll get to why it's important to distinguish these terms later.

Curiously, Jesus Christ decides to give a special blessing if we watch for this. Perhaps this was John's addition alone, reminding the reader because he felt that readers would be prematurely guessing when this would happen, or perhaps he felt the Spirit compelling him to write it down at this point specifically for reasons beyond even his understanding. Either way, it is striking. Not only are we reminded that Jesus will come like a thief in the night, but we (or whoever is reading it in the future) are told that we will be blessed if we watch and don't let ourselves be naked and shameful. It's most likely a sort of warning for perseverance for all church generations not to jump to conclusions and begin behaving shamefully because they believe the prophecy is either being fulfilled in their lifetime or will never happen. But I find it extra intriguing because Jesus is already on earth according to chapter 14: he showed up on Mount Zion with the 144,000 Israelite elect, singing a new song. How can Jesus show up like a thief in the night when he's already in the most obvious place in the world, waiting? This paradox might be why John was moved to write it in this exact verse.

The "battle of the great day of God Almighty" is going to take place at "Armageddon", thought of as the Megiddo Valley in Israel. Tourism in modern Israel even advertises the place where it should happen, to attract evangelical believers interested in seeing the place where the armies will muster. This does not prove that it's the correct location, but it makes sense. What matters more is that we're finally witnessing the most important prophetic climax of the entire Bible, known generally as the Day of the Lord. This is where all of Israel's hopes have rested since the first prophets: in the final showdown between the evil world and the Messiah who is to deliver them and establish his kingdom on earth. It's the harvest, the treading of the winepress of the wrath of God, and so much more. It is the day we should all be excited for, and the day we will be looking forward to while we're in heaven, eager to come back down to earth with Christ.

13

MOTHER OF HARLOTS

And the seventh angel poured out his vial into the air; and there came a great voice <u>out of the temple of heaven, from the throne, saying, It is done</u>.
(Revelation 16:17 KJV)

We know there is only one entity who could be on the throne in the temple of heaven, and when He says "it is done" there is no other answer. However, nothing has happened yet. The vial was poured out into the air, but no events unfolded on earth. By this simple declaration, therefore, we have a confirmation of our whole method of approaching interpretation: first an event occurs in heaven, signifying what must happen on earth, and then it is immediately treated by those in heaven as if it is already accomplished, irreversible and fated to play out. This happens over and over again, with the breaking of the seals in heaven unleashing the riders on earth; the golden censer being thrown into the earth signifying the impending meteor strikes; the conversion of Jerusalem's inhabitants signifying the capture of all the world's kingdoms; the harvests and treading of the winepress leading to the plagues being poured out. Here, the pouring out of the final vial of wrath does not seem to accomplish anything just yet, but God already declares "it is done". It means there is no stopping it now.

And there were voices, and thunders, and lightnings; and there was a <u>great earthquake</u>, such as was not <u>since</u>

men were upon the earth, so mighty an earthquake, and
so great. And the great city was divided into three parts,
and the cities of the nations fell: and great Babylon came
in remembrance before God, to give unto her the cup of the
wine of the fierceness of his wrath. And every island fled
away, and the mountains were not found. And there fell
upon men a great hail out of heaven, every stone about the
weight of a talent: and men blasphemed God because of the
plague of the hail; for the plague thereof was exceeding great.
(Revelation 16:18-21 KJV)

Unlike the scary cosmic events of the sixth seal, which sent the men of the earth to hide under mountains and declare that it was the Day of the Lord, we now see true devastation with world-changing results when the real day approaches. Never before in history has there been an earthquake as powerful as this. Cities around the world will be ruined, and Babylon itself will be split into three parts. This is extremely important. The "hail" that is so exceedingly great may be the result of the earthquake itself, as human structures and the mountains which somehow "were not found" could suddenly be airborne, hurled through the skies. All that stone has to go somewhere, right? The more devastated the world becomes, the more the False Prophet will no doubt consolidate his grip on their minds, convincing them of the need to kill Jesus and destroy Jerusalem to save the planet.

Babylon itself has been only mentioned once so far, a while ago, as the second angel flying through the sky was warning the world about how it was doomed. Now we see that Babylon "came in remembrance" of God, to give "her" the cup of the "wine of the fierceness of his wrath". These are obviously very old and enduring symbols throughout prophecy, but that only further magnifies this ultimate climax of world history about to happen. Everything before this was a "shadow fulfillment" as scholars call it, or a rehearsal for this final conclusion. For some reason, God has chosen not to remember Babylon until now, but has been storing up his wrath like wine in his cup. She will have to drink that cup. When we see the description of "her" it will be clear how fitting this punishment is, since she has been "drunk" on the blood of the saints, and caused kings to "drink" of her fornication, acting like the biggest whore in the world.

Babylon, the home of evil, doomed for destruction

Let's look at a psalm that contrasts Babylon and Jerusalem:

> By the rivers of Babylon, there we sat down, yea, we wept, when we remembered Zion. We hanged our harps upon the willows in the midst thereof. For there they that carried us away captive required of us a song; and they that wasted us required of us mirth, saying, Sing us one of the songs of Zion. How shall we sing the LORD'S song in a strange land? _If I forget thee, O Jerusalem, let my right hand forget her cunning_. If I do not remember thee, let my tongue cleave to the roof of my mouth; if I prefer not Jerusalem above my chief joy. Remember, O LORD, the children of Edom in the day of Jerusalem; who said, Rase [destroy] it, rase it, even to the foundation thereof. O daughter of _Babylon, who art to be destroyed_; happy shall he be, that rewardeth thee as thou hast served us. Happy shall he be, that taketh and dasheth thy little ones against the stones. _(Psalms 137:1-9 KJV)_

This psalm shows us the emotional contrast between Babylon and Jerusalem. Ever since the early accounts of Genesis, where Nimrod commanded the building of the tower of Babylon (Babel) shortly after Noah's flood, Babylon has been a symbol of worldly power and gnostic forbidden arts. God personally disrupted their language and scattered them across the world in order to prevent them from accomplishing everything they wanted.

"Neo-Babylon" is the term historians use for its later revival, over a thousand years later, around 600 BC when Nebuchadnezzar defeated Israel and took them captive. By destroying Solomon's Temple and forcing the captured Jews to live within their pagan society as a class of captive citizens, Babylon not only served as a symbol of united global evil, but the biggest symbol of God's punishment against His people if they stray too far. Strangely, this punishment comes in the form of seduction away from God rather than outright oppression and slavery like in ancient Egypt. Notice how the psalm talks about the danger of **forgetting** Jerusalem while sitting by the river Euphrates. That is a very unusual risk. It talks about being invited to sing and be happy, too. Jewish scribes were allowed to mingle their Judaic religious beliefs with the religion of the Babylonians—which is considered spiritual fornication by God. This all leads to the devout prophet Daniel talking to King Nebuchadnezzar, predicting the fall of the empire and the succession of other kingdoms that will take over until the time of the Messiah and the eternal kingdom.

Considering how the Euphrates river has already taken center stage repeatedly in Revelation, it might be tempting to look at modern enemies of Israel along the Euphrates river as "Babylon"; countries like Syria and Iraq. Anyone supporting these nations could also be accused of defying God and helping Babylon, such as the United Nations, which is openly modeled after the original tower of Babel concept in their own admission. This interpretation helps explain the obsession with toppling the anti-Israeli governments and killing their leaders among Neocon Zionists, who believe they are fulfilling the deliverance of Israel and ushering in the construction of the Third Temple and the return of the Messiah. Others have given up on a literal fulfillment, and see only themes, archetypes, and an eternal struggle to protect Israel and secure the holy land for themselves, with the role of "Messiah" fitting anyone who does their part to save Israel and aid them. Either way, we have a massive Satanic deception surrounding the topic.

JERUSALEM'S ROLE IN THE POST-CHURCH WORLD

The destruction of the (true) church by Satan's conspiracy will change the landscape of the religious-political world and remove the influence of real Christianity from inside governments and institutions worldwide. Most likely, all false churches within the Beast system will thrive and maintain the illusion that Christianity is alive and well, though perhaps with a new twist of environmental extremism, or some other heresy. Their unchallenged blasphemy and corruption will taint the image of Jesus in ways that are impossible to fulfill today, thanks to the resistance of real Christians within their organizations and at the grassroots level. We have no way of knowing how quickly or thoroughly nations will change as a result of the true church dying, but if the true Christians were killed as a result of some enormous wedge issue that exposes and divides the real ones from the false ones, it could explain a power shift happening at the same time. It could be a "Mark of the Beast" project engineered by Satan's servants to make that prophecy literal, instead of just spiritual. Whatever the issue is, it's likely that the survivors of the so-called "church" and the evil world leaders will unite in a New World Order system. In this framework, the question becomes what Israel's role will be. Will they be complicit? Will they defend the true church? Do they have blood on their hands?

Satan knows that Jerusalem is the prize, and thanks to the Jeremiah 31:37 loophole, his gnostic conspirators will believe that they can take it over forever and resist God's attempts to take it back. As we have seen, that leads to the two witnesses, the earthquake, and the realization that this loophole was unsuccessful. But before that point comes, in their arrogance, they will build a temple (which John measures) and the Beast itself will rise up to stop the witnesses, showing an alliance of some kind, since the Beast does not go on to destroy the city, but only the witnesses. The Third Temple will therefore need to be constructed in a time when Israel is protected by the Beast, and likely positioned as the backbone of the New World Order's economy. The ambitious Zionist agenda of today morphs into a lust for world dominance, fulfilling in their minds the promise of God to establish Zion as the divinely protected Kingdom of Heaven, ruling the nations. Therefore, in this future post-church world, the city of Babylon found in Revelation is none other than Jerusalem itself, creating the ultimate paradox. After all, how can Babylon and Jerusalem be the same? Isn't Babylon supposed to be destroyed, but Jerusalem saved?

If we remember the massive angel swearing that the "mystery of God" would be resolved in the days of the seventh trumpet, we see that God Himself acknowledges the magnitude of the enigma. But at the same time, logically, this means Babylon cannot be something obvious like the United Nations, because otherwise it would not be mysterious, which is how Revelation characterizes it. It must be surprising and controversial, despite also fulfilling ancient prophecies that have been studied by dozens of generations.

Let's remember the big picture. Jesus Christ talks to his churches in the first few chapters, showing that they are his only concern. He gives no message whatsoever to Israel or Jerusalem as a people, but rather warns Christians to watch out for the "synagogue of Satan" which claim to be Jews but are lying. And since Jesus is the Messiah of the real Jews, and Savior of all nations, it is impossible to suggest that anyone complicit in the death of the church can be in any way holy or blessed by God. The Judaism of the post-church world must be wayward at best, if not complicit.

> For the Father judgeth no man, but hath committed <u>all judgment</u> unto the Son: That <u>all men should honour the Son</u>, even as they honour the Father. <u>He that honoureth not the Son honoureth not the Father</u> which hath sent him. Verily, verily, I say unto you, He that heareth my word, and believeth on him that sent me, hath everlasting life, and shall not come into condemnation; but is passed from death unto life. (John 5:22-24 KJV)

We already know that everyone who denies Jesus Christ is deceived by the spirit of antichrist, so it's impossible for any religion, including Judaism, to be legitimate if they don't honor Jesus as Lord. In the post-church world this will be even more obvious. Revelation is a commentary on the fate of the Christian church from the first century until the end of the world. In particular, it revolves around our struggle against Satan's deceptive, blasphemous conspiracy on earth. It shows how we are falsely accused and killed for speaking the truth, just as Jesus himself was. Once the church is totally killed, however, the focus shifts to the 144,000 Israelite elect, who are destined to fulfill some of the oldest and biggest promises of the Bible. This holy remnant is met by Jesus on Mount Zion, merging end time Israel and Christian promises.

For "Babylon" to come into God's remembrance means that the city is going to be held accountable for all of its past sins, blasphemies, arrogance, and wicked dealings, even though it was tolerated until now. This contradicts the myth that God is constantly judging and punishing nations for things they do from day to day. For an unknown period of time, since perhaps before the death of the church, Jerusalem has been controlled by fake Jews and the synagogue of Satan, leading it into the most evil conspiracy in history. The offensiveness of this final period will be far beyond even ancient blasphemy, because these people had the church of Christ as an example. If there was any doubt, just look at how God calls Jerusalem Sodom and Egypt, connecting it with the only city in history where the Lord was crucified:

> And their dead bodies shall lie in the street of the great city, which _spiritually_ is called Sodom and Egypt, _where also our Lord was crucified_.
> (Revelation 11:8 KJV)

If God considers Jerusalem to be Sodom and Egypt, it means He will want to destroy it the way He did with those ancient evils. Sodom was known for constant wickedness and perversion, while Egypt was known for enslaving the Israelites and not letting them go. Why would God equate the Jewish homeland to Egypt? It's another paradox. It speaks to the deeper Satanic deception. By creating his own version of Jerusalem, Satan can lure in the Jews and enslave them to his Beast system, rewarding them with riches and protection as he seeks the Jeremiah 31:37 loophole, which is his chance to divorce Israel from God!

We should praise God for wanting to destroy this future Babylon, but we must be careful to see the layers of prophecy coming into view. The judgment and destruction of Jerusalem is not a simple affair. It will tie into the "abomination of desolation", the "Man of Sin", the Rapture, the resurrection, and of course the battle of Armageddon.

SYNAGOGUE OF SATAN, IN TOTAL POWER

Then one of the seven angels having the seven bowls came and spoke with me, saying, "Come, I will show you the judgment of the great harlot who <u>sits on many waters</u>, with whom the <u>kings</u> of the earth <u>committed fornication</u>, and those dwelling on the earth became <u>drunk from the wine of her fornication</u>." And he led me away in spirit, into a deserted place. And I saw a woman <u>sitting on</u> a scarlet beast being filled with names of <u>blasphemy</u>, having seven heads and ten horns. (Revelation 17:1-3 EMTV)

And the woman which thou sawest is that great city, which <u>reigneth over</u> the kings of the earth. (Revelation 17:18 KJV)

The most important thing about this city is its relationships. Women are not considered symbols of strength; instead, they are defined by their relationships and sexual activity with men. In other words, this future city is not a military superpower of the world, but needs others to protect it and do its bidding for her. This makes sense when we notice that she sits on the Beast; she can be weak, but it is strong and carries her like a queen. God finds "her" relationships repulsive, sinful, and improper. This already points us to Jerusalem, because that's the only city God really cares about keeping pure. He has always wanted His city to be holy, like a virgin for its Messiah, or a perfect bride. On the other hand, it means Satan's ultimate goal would have to involve defiling it, fornicating with it, and blaspheming with it as much as possible in order to mock, provoke, and tempt God. This in turn heightens our Jeremiah 31:37 view, because that verse says God will reject Israel specifically for all that it has done, not just a general rejection. The more guilty Jerusalem is, the more God will have no choice but to honor his own promise and forsake it.

Fornication is a perfect metaphor for what goes on with this city. World leaders partner with it and have indecent arrangements with it; their "fornication" becomes a "wine" that the whole world gets "drunk" on. This is another way of saying it is involved in alliances and conspiracies with various nations that result in global deception. The fact that she sits comfortably on the Beast shows that it has a particular relationship with Rome's final incarnation, which looks to be similar to the first one we saw, but now scarlet colored and not wounded and healed. This could be the Beast that came out of the bottomless pit and waged war against the two witnesses. If so, we would expect it to be a dark gnostic sect or movement that controls world elites and religious views. The city rules over the kings of the earth, but not in some distant past. It has power in the period John is witnessing, in our future. This means it's not necessarily commenting on our current day's powers, or some eternal city that always reigns. Very likely its rise to this triumphant position will be connected with the death of the church and the ensuing corruption of the world, because it is drunk on the blood of the Christian martyrs themselves:

> *And the woman was clothed in purple and scarlet, gilded with gold and precious stones and pearls, having in her hand a golden cup being filled with abominations and the filthiness of the fornication of the earth. And on her forehead a name was written: MYSTERY, BABYLON THE GREAT, THE MOTHER OF HARLOTS AND OF THE ABOMINATIONS OF THE EARTH. I saw the woman, <u>drunk with the blood of the saints</u> and with the <u>blood of the martyrs of Jesus</u>. And when I saw her, I marveled with great amazement. (Revelation 17:4-6 EMTV)*

Notice first that John is amazed by this woman and her nature. This reinforces the fact that John does not know what he is describing in this vision. He is not holding back any information, and he is not making it up himself. This is not some intellectual exercise, combining his own ideas of prophecy and "remixing" the promises of the old prophets or disciples. This is not a book simply influenced by the apocryphal Book of Enoch or John's own musings. This should be obvious when we remember what Peter said about prophecy:

> *knowing this first of all, that no prophecy of Scripture comes from someone's own interpretation. For no prophecy was ever produced by the will of man, but men spoke from God as they were carried along by the Holy Spirit. (2 Peter 1:20-21 ESV)*

As for the description of the woman, we see that she is rich, arrogant, and drunk on the blood of saints and martyrs. When we keep in mind that this is a description of a future city, having world power and reigning over kings, it has far-reaching implications about our own future. This city not only tastes the blood of the (true) Christians, but drinks so much of our blood and enjoys it so much that "she" gets drunk by it. And this is no wonder: if the fake Jews belonging to the synagogue of Satan, who will run this future Jerusalem, managed to kill the church and get away with it, they would feel like they had defeated the gospel of Jesus, whom they consider to be an accursed false Messiah! Thus, it is also no wonder that she is so deeply hated in God's eyes. The first descriptor in her name is "mystery", making it indisputable that something about her is paradoxical, enigmatic, and hard to believe. Calling Jerusalem "Babylon the Great" and the "mother" of harlots and abominations seems to imply a long lineage tracing back to the Tower of Babel, but it does not necessarily have to do with the past or present. It could be entirely about the future version of Jerusalem yet to manifest, which conspires (fornicates) with the world leaders to eliminate the Christian church and get drunk on their blood. This fornication produces abominations and harlots, in the sense that it will convince world leaders that they should go along with the Satanic NWO agenda and have no fear of God. In our current day, despite so much horrific evil and conspiracy already, the existence of the church is holding back the worst extremes because Christians are quick to raise awareness and objections to wicked plans when we see them. Just imagine how many abominations will be birthed by the whoring and fornicating of world leaders after we're gone! And as we have seen many times already in Revelation, the lack of fear toward God is something He takes very seriously. Getting drunk on the blood of the saints speaks to a total arrogance.

THE BEAST AGAINST JESUS AND HIS 144,000 ELECT

> But the angel said to me, "Why did you marvel? I will tell you the mystery of the woman and of the Beast carrying her, which has the seven heads and the ten horns. The Beast which you saw _was_ [existed before], and _is not_ [does not currently exist], and is _about to_ ascend out of the bottomless pit [rise to power again] and _go to_ perdition [be destroyed]. And those who dwell on the earth shall marvel, _whose name is not written_ in the Book of Life from the foundation of the world, _when they see_ the Beast that was, and is not, and shall be present. (Revelation 17:7-8 EMTV)

This is not as complicated as it first seems. Rome was the fourth Beast kingdom in Daniel's vision, predicted to last until the end of the world. Therefore, we know that Rome will be the great ruling power until the end, no matter how many versions and rebirths it must undergo. And it has had a very diverse history! Even when it seems to go away, it is promised to come back.

Remember that in the heavenly history lesson we see that Rome gets a fatal wound and should have died, but is revived in power by Satan giving it his power, "healing" it and causing the world to be amazed. From there it reinvents itself and is reinvented as the Antichurch, splitting into Catholic and Orthodox and gaining new powers over time. Then the Italian Renaissance reinvents Roman power again, except with a secular Humanist guise. Taken all together, this is the Beast that "was". But by the time John is being shown the great whore, that Beast system seems to be gone. There are many reasons the Beast could appear to be gone, but we also see that she is still sitting on it. This creates a paradox, which is why the angel calls it a mystery. However, it's not so impossible to understand if we remember that Jerusalem itself is fraudulent and run by fake Jews belonging to the synagogue of Satan. Israel was created by the United Nations via Jesuit conspiracy, and has been under their protection and guidance ever since, duping evangelical Christians into the theological view that modern Israel is sacred and must be protected at all costs. We've discussed how this ties into the Neocon agenda. If the modern "Beast" of neo-Roman influence becomes interchangeable with secret societies, Jesuit proxies, and impostor Judaism, it's very appropriate to say that the Whore can be riding the Beast even while the Beast (antichristian Roman imperial power) seems to be invisible or missing. In place of outward Roman Catholic and Orthodox religions there may be New Age mysticism or some branch of paranormal science cults. The "image of the Beast" means that Satan does not need the veneer of Christian religion to carry out his Beast system.

As for the version of the Beast that ascends out of the bottomless pit and goes into perdition, it could be many things. It seems to have already popped up temporarily to kill the two witnesses, and perhaps gone away again. We will remind the reader how unlikely it is for the average person in the future to recognize any of these prophetic events for what they are, just as we today are not recognizing the Beast, the Mark, and so many other things in Revelation. It may be that, in the time of the False Prophet, after Jesus returns to Mount Zion with the 144,000 and the wrath of God is poured out on the planet, the Beast that is about to rise is the same as the False Prophet itself, exploiting the hatred and misery of world leaders as he unites them in a crusade against Jesus. Whether they would acknowledge the reality of Christ's return or not is another matter.

> *Here is the mind which has wisdom: The <u>seven heads are seven mountains</u> on which <u>the woman sits</u>. And there are [additionally] seven kings. Five have fallen, <u>one is</u> [the False Prophet], and the other has <u>not yet come</u> [the Man of Sin]. And whenever he [the Man of Sin] comes, he must abide for a <u>short time</u>. And <u>the Beast which was, and is not, is also an eighth</u>, and is of the seven, and <u>is going</u> to perdition. And the*

ten horns which you saw are ten [conspirator] kings who <u>not</u> <u>yet</u> have received a kingdom, but they receive authority <u>as</u> <u>kings</u> for <u>one hour with the Beast</u>. These have <u>one purpose</u>, and they will give their power and authority to the Beast. These will <u>make war with the Lamb</u>, and <u>the Lamb will</u> <u>conquer them</u>, for He is Lord of lords and King of kings; and <u>those who are with Him are called, and elect, and faithful</u>." (Revelation 17:9-14 EMTV)

Then he said to me, "The waters which you saw, <u>where the</u> <u>harlot sits</u>, are peoples, multitudes, nations, and languages. (Revelation 17:15 EMTV)

How can the Whore city be simultaneously sitting on many nations and languages, but also sitting on the Beast that does not exist, and on seven mountains? The answer is that her "seat" is a symbol of her power source, or the geopolitical and spiritual arrangements she enjoys. Just as Jesus said that he knew where Satan's "seat" or "throne" was, and Satan gave his "seat" to the Beast, and the angel poured out a vial of wrath on the "seat" of the Beast to fill its kingdom with darkness, this city has a "seat" that is abstract and not meant to be taken so literally. Jerusalem's "seat" is distributed among the nations. It has no true source of power, but rather makes conspiratorial arrangements with various world leaders, nations, peoples, and languages. It is responsible for their wealth, their luxury, and the Satanic triumph over the church, so it only makes sense that a description of her seat would be so complicated. This is different from how a proper kingdom operates, having a throne and a spiritual being in charge of it.

At the time of this description, immediately before the destruction of Jerusalem by the armies of the False Prophet, there have been five kings before, perhaps symbolizing the four riders of Rome's amazing blasphemous history, and somebody else we wouldn't recognize today. The sixth is the False Prophet, currently leading the world against Jesus and, seemingly, united in spirit and body with the Beast itself. The seventh is the Man of Sin, who will create the abomination of desolation, and who must abide for a short time, perhaps being another embodiment of the Beast.

Interestingly, the ten kings who conspire to attack Jesus and the 144,000 do not have power yet, but they will be empowered. This could mean that the False Prophet has to forge new alliances, looking in unusual places to raise up military leaders purely for this one task; this explains why they only have power for one hour. That one hour is the assault on Jerusalem.

> *And the ten horns [temporary leaders] which you saw, and the Beast, these will <u>hate the harlot</u>, and will make her <u>desolated</u> and <u>naked</u>, and will <u>eat her flesh</u>, and will <u>burn her</u> up with fire. For <u>God</u> has put it into their hearts to fulfill <u>His purpose</u>, to be of one mind, and to give their kingdom to the Beast, <u>until the words of God are fulfilled</u>." (Revelation 17:16-17 EMTV)*

Now we begin to see the convergence of the narratives. After all, weren't we just told that the ten horns had "one purpose" and were going to make war with the Lamb and his elect? But suddenly they are attacking the harlot of Babylon! Considering that they only have power for one hour and for this one purpose, these are not separate goals. So how is it possible that they will destroy "Babylon" and make her "desolate", and yet be against Jesus Christ, who presumably hates Babylon just as much? Only by realizing that Jerusalem is Babylon, and that this conspiracy is being sent to destroy Zion, where Christ is waiting with his 144,000 elect.

A CONTINUATION OF ISAIAH'S WARNING

John's language of **Babylon** being desolate, stripped naked, having its flesh eaten, and being burned with fire is not accidental. It is a reference to judgments that were reserved for **Jerusalem** in the prophetic warnings of Isaiah, hundreds of years before the Neo-Babylonian reign of Nebuchadnezzar and the supposed injustice against Jerusalem in the days of Daniel:

> *The vision of Isaiah the son of Amoz, which he saw <u>concerning Judah and Jerusalem</u> in the days of Uzziah, Jotham, Ahaz, and Hezekiah, kings of Judah.*

This is the first verse of Isaiah, explicitly saying that what follows is about Judah and Jerusalem, not anybody else. See for yourself how God feels about Jerusalem and think about how it compares to future "Babylon" in Revelation:

> *Hear, O heavens, and give ear, O earth: for the LORD hath spoken, I have nourished and brought up children, and <u>they have rebelled against me</u>. The ox knoweth his owner, and the ass his master's crib: <u>but Israel doth not know</u>, my people doth not consider. Ah <u>sinful nation</u>, a people laden with iniquity, a <u>seed of evildoers</u>, children that are <u>corrupters</u>: they have <u>forsaken the LORD</u>, they have <u>provoked the Holy One of Israel</u> unto <u>anger</u>, they are gone away backward. Why should ye be stricken [corrected] any more? <u>ye will revolt more and more</u>: <u>the whole head is sick</u>, and the whole heart faint. <u>From the sole of the foot even unto the head there is no soundness in it</u>; but wounds, and bruises, and putrifying sores: they have not been closed, neither bound up, neither mollified with ointment. <u>Your country is desolate, your cities are burned with fire</u>: your land, strangers <u>devour it</u> in your presence, and it is <u>desolate</u>, as overthrown by strangers. And the <u>daughter of Zion</u> is left as a cottage in a vineyard, as a lodge in a garden of cucumbers, as <u>a besieged city</u>. (Isaiah 1:1-8 KJV)*

It is the same language. Stripped naked, desolate, burned, and eaten, because in God's eyes the entire project of Judaism has been a failure and can no longer be corrected with small reminders and punishments. It is beyond healing, hopeless from head to toe, even before He can send the

Messiah to try. Therefore He engineers a plan to keep them ignorant and send a Messiah whom they will reject, and changes the plan to be a covenant for all mankind, not just Israel.

We see that the 144,000 remnant of Israelites is also prophesied immediately after, showing that God will not abandon the people themselves altogether:

> *Except the LORD of hosts had <u>left unto us a very small</u> <u>remnant</u> [the 144,000], <u>we should have been as Sodom</u>, and we should have been like unto Gomorrah. (Isaiah 1:9 KJV)*

Considering that God calls Jerusalem (the city where the Lord was crucified) "Sodom" in Revelation, we know that His feelings about the city have not changed since this time. From Isaiah until the end of the world, He sees the city as Sodom, needing destruction. Jerusalem is altogether beyond redemption and cannot be pleasing to God, destroying the Christian Zionist narrative. Jesus himself mourned for the city because it rejected him, and would not hear him:

> *O <u>Jerusalem</u>, Jerusalem, <u>thou that killest the prophets</u>, and <u>stonest them which are sent unto thee</u>, how often would I have gathered thy children together, even as a hen gathereth her chickens under her wings, and ye would not! Behold, your house is left unto you <u>desolate</u>. For I say unto you, <u>Ye shall not see me henceforth, till ye shall say,</u> <u>Blessed is he that cometh in the name of the Lord</u> [when the two witnesses ascend, and the earthquake kills the 7,000 men, and the heavenly history lesson is complete]. (Matthew 23:37-39 KJV)*

In John's gospel account we actually see a direct reference to Isaiah because of this mystery of God hardening the hearts of the Jews:

> *Though he had done so many signs before them, <u>they still did</u> <u>not believe</u> in him, so that the word spoken by the <u>prophet</u> <u>Isaiah</u> might be fulfilled: "Lord, who has believed what he heard from us, and to whom has the arm of the Lord*

been revealed?" Therefore they could not believe. For again Isaiah said [in Isaiah 6:10], "He has blinded their eyes and hardened their heart, lest they see with their eyes, and understand with their heart, and turn, and I would heal them." Isaiah said these things because he saw his glory and spoke of him. Nevertheless, many even of the authorities believed in him, but for fear of the Pharisees they did not confess it [condemning themselves], so that they would not be put out of the synagogue; for they loved the glory that comes from man more than the glory that comes from God. (John 12:37–43 ESV)

John—who writes Revelation—recognizes the importance of Isaiah's warning about how God **refused to allow** Judah to understand the truth about His Messiah. Even those who secretly believe in Christ are too afraid of the Jewish leadership to confess it, and therefore they will be accursed and rejected by God, since confessing Jesus is an absolute requirement for salvation. They loved the glory of men more than the glory of God. But let's look at the bigger context of Isaiah John is quoting, to make the point even more clear:

And he [God] said [to Isaiah], "Go, and say to this people: "'Keep on hearing, but do not understand; keep on seeing, but do not perceive.' Make the heart of this people dull, and their ears heavy, and blind their eyes; lest they see with their eyes, and hear with their ears, and understand with their hearts, and turn and be healed." Then I [Isaiah] said, "How long, O Lord?" And he said: "Until cities lie waste without inhabitant, and houses without people, and the land is a desolate waste, and the LORD removes people far away, and the forsaken places are many in the midst of the land. And though a tenth remain in it, it will be burned again, like a terebinth or an oak, whose stump remains when it is felled." The holy seed is its stump. (Isaiah 6:9–13 ESV)

Considering that Isaiah himself asks the question, we know that the timing here is of the utmost importance. Just as Daniel wanted to know about the time of deliverance, Isaiah is aching to know how long God will blind the Jews and hold back their understanding. The shocking answer is that it will continue until the land of Jerusalem is totally desolate and destroyed, and only a small remnant remains like a stump after the tree is cut down, called the "holy seed". This did not happen in the days of Jesus, and neither did it when the great "Jewish diaspora" after 70 AD happened. If it had, we would expect their eyes to be opened and their understanding to be restored, leading them to Jesus Christ. But the practitioners of Judaism who were so attached to the Second Temple in 70 AD were falsely trying to maintain the Jewish law, rejecting Jesus. When they were scattered around the world they did not turn to Jesus. Doing so would have been the correct path, and proof that Isaiah's warning was fulfilled. Instead they became even more perverse in their thinking and created new branches of Judaism that eventually led to more extreme mysticism, subversion, and anti-Christian sentiment. They only became more blinded, in other words. This has never been reversed, and self-proclaimed Jews still hate and disrespect Jesus in their teachings. Some believed, perhaps, that the "holy seed" being spoken of was the Jewish bloodline itself, and that Isaiah's prophecy was fulfilled in the sense that it pointed away from Jesus and towards some kind of world conspiracy to overthrow governments and restore Zion themselves.

As for why God would deal so harshly with His own people for thousands of years, we must go back to the first chapters of Isaiah. He's tired of their falseness, their arrogance, and their lack of true understanding:

> *Hear the word of the LORD, ye rulers of Sodom; give ear unto the law of our God, ye people of Gomorrah. To what purpose is the multitude of your sacrifices unto me? saith the LORD: I am full of the burnt offerings of rams, and the fat of fed beasts; …. Bring no more vain oblations; incense is an abomination unto me; …. it is iniquity, even the solemn meeting. Your new moons and your appointed*

feasts my soul hateth: they are a trouble unto me; I am weary to bear them. And when ye spread forth your hands, I will hide mine eyes from you: yea, when ye make many prayers, I will not hear: your hands are full of blood. (Isaiah 1:10-15 KJV)

This is not simply an archetypal reminder to Jewish leaders to consider. The great purpose of it is to establish the "mystery of God" that will be fulfilled only in the days of the seventh trumpet. Jerusalem is so worthless to God that He calls it Sodom, both in Isaiah and in Revelation. It has not changed. He also calls Jerusalem a whore in Isaiah already:

How is the faithful city become an harlot! it was full of judgment; righteousness lodged in it; but now murderers. (Isaiah 1:21 KJV)

God decides to relieve His grief by using His own enemies to do the job, purging the city of its evil and leaving nothing behind but the small remnant:

Therefore the Lord declares, the LORD of hosts, the Mighty One of Israel: "Ah, I will get relief from my enemies and avenge myself on my foes. I will turn my hand against you and will smelt away your dross as with lye and remove all your alloy. (Isaiah 1:24-25 ESV)

Anyone who still thinks that God values Jerusalem inherently is mistaken, and has not understood what Jesus himself taught:

And think not to say within yourselves, We have Abraham to our father: for I say unto you, that God is able of these stones to raise up children unto Abraham. And now also the axe is laid unto the root of the trees [tradition, dogma, institutional religion]: therefore every tree [belief] which bringeth not forth good fruit is hewn down, and cast into the fire. (Matthew 3:9-10 KJV)

"HIS HAND IS STRETCHED OUT STILL"

There is a phrase in Isaiah which is repeated many times when discussing the fullness of God's judgment against the Jews and the rest of the world: "His hand is stretched out still". God reaches His hand out to destroy the wicked and save the righteous. Reaching out is a metaphor for interference in the ways of the world. It's scattered throughout the book, crossing over many different prophecies about kingdoms, tying together into a theme of condemning the proud and sparing the meek. It speaks to how relentless and unwavering God is in this particular strategy. He is not willing to reverse His purpose:

> *This is the <u>purpose</u> that is purposed upon the whole earth;*
> *and this is the <u>hand that is stretched out</u> upon <u>all the nations</u>.*
> *For Jehovah of hosts hath purposed, and who shall annul it?*
> *and his hand is stretched out, and who shall turn it back?*
> *(Isaiah 14:26-27 ASV)*

Amazingly, Isaiah also receives some of the most clear and profound descriptions of Jesus Christ and his ministry, but even then it is characterized by being rejected, punished, misunderstood, and abused:

> *Behold, <u>my servant</u> [Jesus Christ] shall act wisely; he shall*
> *be high and lifted up [crucified], and shall be exalted. As*
> *many were astonished at you— his appearance was so*
> *marred, beyond human semblance, and his form beyond*
> *that of the children of mankind— so shall he sprinkle [with*
> *his blood] <u>many nations</u>. Kings shall shut their mouths*
> *because of him, for that which has not been told them they*
> *see, and that which they have not heard they understand.*
> *(Isaiah 52:13-15 ESV)*

> *He was <u>despised and rejected by men</u>, a man of sorrows and*
> *acquainted with grief; and as <u>one from whom men hide their</u>*
> *<u>faces</u> he was despised, and <u>we</u> [children of Israel] <u>esteemed</u>*
> *<u>him not</u>. Surely he has borne our griefs and carried our*

sorrows; yet <u>we esteemed him stricken, smitten by God</u>, and afflicted. But <u>he was pierced for our transgressions</u>; he was crushed for our iniquities; upon him was the chastisement that brought us peace, and <u>with his wounds we are healed</u>. All we like sheep have <u>gone astray</u>; we have turned— every one—to <u>his own way</u>; and the LORD has laid on him the iniquity of us all. He was <u>oppressed</u>, and he was <u>afflicted</u>, yet he opened not his mouth; like <u>a lamb</u> that is led to the slaughter, and like a sheep that before its shearers is silent, so he opened not his mouth. By oppression and judgment he was taken away; and as for his generation, who considered that <u>he was cut off</u> [killed] <u>out of the land of the living</u>, stricken for the transgression of <u>my people?</u> (Isaiah 53:3-8 ESV)

Much more could be said about how God's plan to blind His own people until the Millennial Kingdom could be cited and explained. The book is massive and full of important promises connecting the downfall of kingdoms with the redemption of Zion and the remnant. For now, let us understand that God's plan has never been a failure or a mistake. The Jewish people of Isaiah's day, and those today, are not being **allowed** to see Jesus for who he truly is. This is God's judgment, His hand outstretched over the world, and who can turn it away? Let us rather praise God and thank Him for extending His promises to us, even though we will be destroyed by Satan and the corrupt Jerusalem will become drunk on our blood.

THE TRAGIC IRONIES PILE UP

After these things I saw another angel coming down out of heaven, having <u>great authority</u>; and the earth was <u>lightened with his glory</u>. And he cried with a <u>mighty voice</u>, saying, Fallen, fallen is Babylon the great, and is become <u>a habitation of demons</u>, and a hold of <u>every unclean spirit</u>, and a hold of every unclean and hateful bird. (Revelation 18:1-2 ASV)

This angel is so mighty and impressive that we may guess it is an archangel. If so, it would probably be Michael, referred to by Daniel as the prince of the Israelites. Jerusalem ought to be his jurisdiction, after all, and he would be eager to see its corrupt form destroyed so that it can be restored with the reign of Jesus and the Millennial Kingdom. Either way, we see that the future is discussed as if it were already the past: Babylon is fallen, not "is about to fall". This is because heavenly decrees of God are irreversible, and thus already considered to be done. The seventh vial was poured out, breaking Jerusalem into three parts and opening it up for invasion by the Satanic army. The city is doomed.

Not only that, but there is a specific focus here on demonic prevalence. Every unclean spirit and demon will be gathered there. This is perfect, because God wants to destroy them all at once, not allow them to scatter or hide. The harvests require that everything is bundled together!

As we continue to realize the implications of this paradox, let's turn to Jeremiah, who explores the same contradiction we're about to see unfold. He was active during the time of the Neo-Babylonian empire, and so compares Jerusalem and Babylon himself:

> *We would have healed Babylon, but she is not healed: forsake her, and let us go every one into his own country: for her judgment reacheth unto heaven, and is lifted up even to the skies. The LORD hath brought forth our righteousness: come, and let us declare in Zion the work of the LORD our God.* (Jeremiah 51:9-10 KJV)

> *The violence done to me and to my flesh be upon Babylon, shall the inhabitant of Zion say; and my blood upon the inhabitants of Chaldea, shall Jerusalem say.* (Jeremiah 51:35 KJV)

> *My people, go ye out of the midst of her, and deliver ye every man his soul from the fierce anger of the LORD.* (Jeremiah 51:45 KJV)

God's remnant are supposed to flee "Babylon". In Jeremiah's day this was literally the Neo-Babylonian empire holding the Jews captive, but by the end of the world Jerusalem becomes Babylon itself. This is not new or controversial, either. The Apostle Peter labeled the holy city "Babylon" in his epistles: *The church that is at Babylon, elected together with you, saluteth you; and so doth Marcus my son. (1 Peter 5:13 KJV).* Therefore, Jeremiah's prophetic warning easily doubles as an end-time message to the final flock of believers, who are supposed to flee Jerusalem because God is about to destroy it. He could not "heal" it, as we already know from Isaiah's description. We see that the violence done to Jerusalem and Zion should be inflicted upon Babylon; this is a perfect description of what will happen, but one that paradoxically happens to the same city! Sadly, by the end, Jerusalem is so blind that it has become the thing it hates the most. Those who are in the city and listen to God are supposed to flee, not defend it. It's good to abandon it, because its destruction is holy. The destruction of Jerusalem does not represent the completion of the Jeremiah 31:37 loophole or the abandonment of Israel, but rather God's purging of its sins, which must happen. It seems doubtful that the people of that day will realize this.

> And *I will turn my hand* [of destruction] upon thee [Jerusalem], and *purely purge away* thy dross, and take away all thy tin: And I will restore thy judges as at the first, and thy counsellors as at the beginning: *afterward* thou shalt be called, *The city of righteousness*, the faithful city. *Zion shall be redeemed with judgment*, and her converts with righteousness. And *the destruction of the transgressors and of the sinners shall be together*, and they that forsake the LORD shall be consumed. (Isaiah 1:25-28 KJV)

Zion is redeemed by being destroyed and purged. But the sinners and transgressors will be destroyed also, in the same conflagration of war known as the Day of the Lord. God lures in all of the Satanic conspiracy, allows them to raze Babylon to the ground for Him and declare victory, and then hits them with the full power of His own army, led by Jesus Christ. This fulfillment requires an even greater paradox and controversy, which we will explore later.

> *For all nations have drunk of the wine of the wrath of her fornication, and the kings of the earth have committed fornication with her, and the merchants of the earth are waxed rich through the abundance of her delicacies. And I heard another voice from heaven, saying, Come out of her, my people, that ye be not partakers of her sins, and that ye receive not of her plagues. (Revelation 18:3–4 KJV)*

So we see another parallel of Isaiah and Revelation. The holy people should flee and spare themselves the punishment of Babylon. The 144,000 are not supposed to be hurt, and hopefully will be safe in the Third Temple with Jesus, singing the song only they can learn. The remainder of Jerusalem will fear God and want to glorify Him, but will most likely ignore these warnings and try to defend the city and overcome the Beast at the doorstep.

> *For her sins have reached unto heaven, and God hath remembered her iniquities [before being converted]. Reward her even as she rewarded you, and double unto her double according to her works: in the cup which she hath filled fill to her double. How much she hath glorified herself, and lived deliciously, so much torment and sorrow give her: for she saith in her heart, I sit a queen, and am no widow, and shall see no sorrow. Therefore shall her plagues come in one day, death, and mourning, and famine; and she shall be utterly burned with fire: for strong is the Lord God who judgeth her. (Revelation 18:5–8 KJV)*

Tragically, Satanic Jerusalem has glorified itself, lived luxuriously, and believes that it is not even a widow—meaning it does not care about the death of Jesus Christ, its rightful husband. God will not abide this. The city cannot simply have Jesus now, in their fallen state, without being totally purged and burned to the ground first. It does not deserve Jesus, and God will not forget its sins so easily. We might notice a parallel to how sinners must die in Christ and be reborn spiritually, not simply convert on an intellectual level. Isaiah said the blindness will continue until the city is annihilated. Only the 144,000 elect are chosen to have the honor of his protection and guarantee of safety, and the rest may even believe in God but not receive the same protection.

A REMINDER OF ITS ROLE AS ECONOMIC QUEEN

> "The kings of the earth [New World Order elite] who committed fornication [conspiracy] and lived luxuriously with her [Jerusalem] shall weep and mourn over her, when they see the smoke of her burning, standing from afar on account of the fear of her torment, saying, 'Alas, alas, that great city Babylon, that mighty city! Because in one hour your judgment came.' "And the merchants of the earth shall weep and mourn over her, for no one buys their merchandise anymore: merchandise of gold and silver, precious stones and pearls, …. and bodies and souls of men. (Revelation 18:9–13 EMTV)

The elite stay far away from Jerusalem, not interested in waging war and destroying her. This is because the "kings of the earth" described here are **not** the same ten "horns" that have temporary power from the Beast. Those kings are only given kingdoms for one hour in order to destroy Jerusalem. The regular rulers are mostly interested in getting rich and continuing their New World Order conspiracy. They are heartbroken and hate the destruction. If they indeed implement their "Mark of the Beast" digital world finance system, it will be headquartered in Israel, using their technology. The destruction of Israel means the destruction of the whole post-church world economy. Somehow they were even able to buy and sell the souls of men, implying that the New Age gnostic power may actually result in mysticism and soul slavery. The level of demonic activity could be that bad; allowing evil spirits to possess men perhaps.

> *"And they [the merchants] threw dust on their heads and were crying out, weeping and sorrowing, and saying, 'Alas, alas, that great city, by which all who had ships on the sea became rich by her wealth! Because in one hour she was laid waste.' "Rejoice over her, O heaven, and you saints and apostles and prophets, because God has pronounced judgment for you against her!" (Revelation 18:19-20 EMTV)*

Here we have a good reminder that the city is considered guilty of attacking the saints, apostles, and prophets. This rules out America, Britain, and many other countries. Jesus said that Jerusalem itself was the one who killed prophets, and here we see the confirmation.

> *and the light of a lamp shall shine no more at all in thee; and the voice of the bridegroom and of the bride shall be heard no more at all in thee: for thy merchants were the princes of the earth; for with thy sorcery [drugs, magic] were all the nations deceived. And in her was found the blood of prophets and of saints, and of all that have been slain upon the earth. (Revelation 18:23-24 ASV)*

We know that this commentary by the angel takes place immediately before the city's destruction, and so it would have to include all of the events leading up to that point of final judgment. This means that, in addition to the guilt brought up by Isaiah and earlier prophets, and the commentary made by Jesus about how it kills the prophets, the city may be indicted for its involvement in future events like the reign of Death on the green horse, and much more, depending on Jerusalem's potential involvement with bloody conspiracies.

14

MARRIAGE SUPPER

BEGUN TO REIGN

After the lesson on Babylon/Jerusalem provided by the angel, John sees the heavens rejoicing. Once again, people in heaven talk about future events as if they were already in the past:

> *After these things* I heard as it were a loud voice of a great
> multitude in heaven, saying, "Hallelujah! Salvation and
> glory and power belong to our God! For true and righteous
> are His judgments, for He has *judged* the great harlot who
> *corrupted the earth* with her fornication; and He has *avenged*
> *the blood of His servants* shed by her hand." And a second one
> said, "Hallelujah! *Her smoke goes up forever and ever!*" And
> the twenty-four elders and the four living beings fell down
> and worshipped God who sits on the throne, saying, "Amen!
> Hallelujah!" Then a voice came from the throne, saying,
> "Praise our God, all His servants and those who fear Him,
> both small and great!" (Revelation 19:1-5 EMTV)

On a spiritual level these things are guaranteed and destined to occur. Not only is God's word impossible to contradict, but these events are still part of the seventh seal broken by Jesus, and God's immutable plan for the world. The judgment is therefore the equivalent of the actual event. It is only our flawed human minds that create room for doubt once God has spoken; but those in heaven have no such illusions, and so they celebrate as soon as they see what is declared by God as if it were done already. "Babylon", the corrupt version of Jerusalem operated by a Satanic elite, will be destroyed to the point where its smoke goes up forever, and it will never be found again. The vengeance that the Christian martyrs called for back in the fifth seal is finally enacted.

> *And I heard, as it were, the voice of a great multitude, and like the sound of many waters, and like the sound of mighty thunders, saying, "Hallelujah! For the Lord God Almighty has begun to reign! (Revelation 19:6 EMTV)*

According to the heavens, it is only at this point that the Lord has "begun" to reign on earth. Jesus is still in Jerusalem on Mount Zion, waiting for the harvest to be complete and the winepress to be treaded. In literal earthly terms, the earthquake that killed 7,000 men may have been as recent as a few months. The seven vials might be poured out rapidly, and the False Prophet might quickly respond to the plagues by gathering his new "kings" to assault Jerusalem as the traditional ruling class watches in horror. The biggest earthquake in history splits the city into three parts, and Satan's army is ready to invade. The Lord has "begun to reign" in the sense that Jesus is present on earth and coordinating world events to orchestrate the Day of the Lord.

BRIDAL PURIFICATION

Ancient Hebrew tradition and law regarding marriage worked differently than today. Marriage began when a girl accepted a man as her husband and her father signs a legal contract for them. This could be done many years before they are even mature adults, binding them as a married couple long before they hit puberty or can consummate their relationship sexually. Child brides were normal, but consummation was a different story. Burdensome requirements for the husband can be stipulated in the contract before consummation was allowed, such as paying the father a certain amount of money, called the dowry. This can take years and allows the girl to grow up while the man works to satisfy the demands of her father. Joseph and Mary were married, but were not having sex. They were waiting to consummate when God gave her a child and created the controversy around a secret virgin impregnation, and Joseph considered divorcing her privately. There are many great commentaries on how this parallels God's covenants and Messianic promises, but for now let's remember that purification and being washed (immersed in water) is part of the bridal ceremonies. Baptism symbolizes this being done spiritually, as the church is the bride of Christ and therefore must be washed, but remember that it also symbolizes our death and rebirth. Dying and being washed pure are the same thing.

> *Let us rejoice and be <u>exceedingly glad</u>, and let us give Him glory, for the <u>wedding of the Lamb</u> has come, and <u>His wife has prepared herself</u>."*
> *(Revelation 19:7 EMTV)*

Here the paradox becomes perfect. The heavens are exceedingly glad that Jerusalem is going to be destroyed, and consider it to be a bridal preparation. They know Zion must be redeemed by judgment. All evil spirits, conspirators, and Satanic followers, including the False Prophet and some manifestation of the Beast itself, will gather themselves together in one place and attempt to destroy God's people, His city, and the Messiah together. It will make perfect sense to these evil people because they will again believe in the Jeremiah 31:37 loophole being fulfilled. They think they can destroy Israel and Christ, and that the giant earthquake that divided the city into three parts is proof that God has abandoned his covenant! Little do they know that God considers the city to be nothing more than Babylon until it is destroyed.

> *And to her it was granted that she should be dressed in fine linen, bright and pure, for <u>the fine linen is the righteous deeds of the saints</u>. Then he said to me, "Write: '<u>Blessed are those who are invited to the marriage supper</u> of the Lamb!'*

"And he said to me, "These are the true words of God."
(Revelation 19:8-9 EMTV)

The city will be erased, stripped naked, eaten, burned, and demolished, but it will afterward be clothed in the "fine linen" of saints doing righteous deeds. The smoldering ruins of Jerusalem will be considered perfect and pure by God, because no amount of architecture, temples, sacrifices, gold, or glorious earthly things are pleasant to Him anymore. We know this from Isaiah, where he promised to never heal them again until they were utterly destroyed.

> *For <u>Jerusalem is ruined</u>, and Judah is fallen; because <u>their tongue and their doings are against Jehovah, to provoke</u> the eyes of his glory. The show of their countenance doth witness against them; and they declare their sin <u>as Sodom</u>, they hide it not. Woe unto their soul! for they have done evil unto themselves. (Isaiah 3:8-9 ASV)*

God's righteous hatred of Jerusalem's worldly glory cannot be overstated. He despises the arrogance, the splendor, and the harlotry of the ungodly city, and promises to strip it all away and reduce it to nothing.

> *Moreover Jehovah said, Because the daughters of Zion are haughty, and walk with outstretched necks and wanton eyes, walking and mincing as they go, and making a tinkling with their feet; therefore the Lord will smite with a scab the crown of the head of the daughters of Zion, and Jehovah will lay bare their secret parts. In that day the Lord will take away the beauty of their anklets, and the cauls, and the crescents; the pendants.... <u>Thy men shall fall by the sword</u>, and thy mighty in the war. And her gates shall lament and mourn; and <u>she shall be desolate and sit upon the ground</u>. (Isaiah 3:16-26 ASV)*

> *<u>In that day</u> [the Day of the Lord, the Marriage Supper, the Battle of Armageddon, the Rapture, the First Resurrection]*

shall the branch of Jehovah [Jesus Christ and his followers] be beautiful and glorious, and the fruit of the land shall be excellent and comely for them that are escaped of Israel. And it shall come to pass, that he that is left in Zion, and he that remaineth in Jerusalem, shall be called holy, even every one that is written among the living in Jerusalem; when the Lord shall have washed away the filth of the daughters of Zion, and shall have purged the blood of Jerusalem from the midst thereof, by the spirit of justice, and by the spirit of burning. And Jehovah will create over the whole habitation of mount Zion, and over her assemblies, a cloud and smoke by day, and the shining of a flaming fire by night; for over all the glory shall be spread a covering. And there shall be a pavilion for a shade in the day-time from the heat, and for a refuge and for a covert from storm and from rain. (Isaiah 4:2-6 ASV)

God wants nothing more than to "wash away the filth" of Zion, and "purge the blood" of Jerusalem with "justice" and "burning". It perfectly teaches how God can redeem His city by destroying its excesses and worldly glory, reducing it to nothing but a pure, clean, and simple restart point. The "cloud of smoke" and "flaming fire" which God will create has the same double-meaning and beautiful paradox within it: the **same** fires and smoke that are going to rise up eternally from "Babylon" to show its judgment in Revelation are here characterized as a "covering" and a beautiful cloud of smoke in the day, and a shining flame at night.

So we see that the "washing" is part of the bridal preparation; washing the city with fire, war, and desolation. God wants no reminders of her evil past and harlotry with the kings of men, or its Satanic covenant.

THE ABOMINATION OF DESOLATION

As we saw in both Isaiah and Revelation, believers who escape Babylon/Jerusalem will be blessed, and those who return and remain will be called holy. This "holy seed" and "very small remnant" will remain like a stump of a tree that is cut down once Jerusalem is wiped out by Satan's forces. They are called to flee, not to defend the doomed city. But this creates problems for our narrative. First, we are told that the 144,000 Israelite elect will follow wherever Jesus goes, and Jesus is still on Mount Zion, presumably in the Third Temple; so unless he leaves, they cannot possibly flee. Secondly, if they do stay with Jesus, how is it possible that they will avoid being killed when the city is made desolate and utterly destroyed? These questions require us to pay very close attention to multiple scattered accounts of the final confrontation.

As a warning to the reader, what this hypothesis is about to explore is such an extreme, radical, controversial possibility that it will be guaranteed to offend at first glance. I ask that the reader bears in mind the celebratory event in heaven as evidence that God and the heavens see things very differently than we do today, due to our flawed preconceptions and their total confidence in God's plan. At no point in this narrative does God ever lose, and yet it must seem like God has lost entirely in order for various prophecies to be fulfilled. Jesus was put in full control over the world after his ascension, breaking the seals of the book in order to allow Satan to rise to power and eventually remove the church from this earth. This final battle is the climax of Satan's power on earth. Satan does not believe he struggles in vain. But much like with Christ's paradoxical victory on the cross, God will once again allow Satan to believe he has won, when in reality he has only sealed his own doom and given God a perfect opportunity to fulfill His mysteries.

> *and to give you who are being afflicted rest along with us <u>at the revelation of the Lord Jesus from heaven with his mighty angels, in flaming fire, inflicting vengeance on those who do not know God</u>, and on those who do not obey the gospel of our Lord Jesus Christ. These shall pay a penalty—<u>eternal destruction</u> from the presence of the Lord and from the glory of his might, <u>whenever he comes, in that day</u>, to be glorified among his saints and to be marveled among all those having believed, because our testimony among you was believed. (2 Thessalonians 1:7-12 EMTV)*

Now, brothers, <u>concerning the coming of our Lord Jesus Christ</u> and <u>our gathering together to him</u>, we beseech you, not to be quickly shaken from your mind, nor be disturbed, neither by spirit nor by word nor by letter, as if from us, as though the day of Christ has come. Let no one deceive you by any means; for <u>that day will not come unless the falling away comes first</u>, and <u>the man of sin is unveiled</u>, the son of perdition, who <u>opposes and exalts himself above all that is called God, or every object of worship, so that he sits as God in the temple of God, showing himself that he is God</u>. Do you not remember that while I was still with you, I was telling you these things? And now you know that which is restraining, that <u>he may be revealed in his own time</u>. For the mystery of lawlessness is already at work; only He who now restrains will continue until <u>one comes out of the midst</u>. And then <u>the lawless one will be unveiled</u>—whom the Lord will consume with the breath of his [Jesus'] mouth, and will <u>destroy by the brightness of his coming</u>—whose coming [the Man of Sin's coming] is according to the <u>working of Satan</u>, with <u>all power, signs, and lying wonders</u>, and in <u>all deception</u> of unrighteousness among those who perish, because they did not receive the love of the truth, that they might be saved. And because of this, <u>God will send them strong delusion</u>, in order for them to <u>believe the lie</u>, so that <u>they all might be damned who did not believe the truth</u>, but delighted in unrighteousness. (2 Thessalonians 2:1-12 EMTV)

Clearly there must be a major "falling away" before Jesus can come back, and the Man of Sin must also be revealed. This means there can be no imminent or unexpected return, although we don't know what day these things will happen. But this Man of Sin is not the Antichrist, because that figure is a myth. The Man of Sin is not content with being compared to Christ, who is below God the Father as a servant, exalted through his obedience; worse, he opposes God Himself and exalts himself above God and everything that is worshiped in the universe!

He will show himself to be **God,** not Christ! That's why he will sit in the throne of the Third Temple as if he were God, which not even Jesus Christ would do. This wicked man will step out of the "midst" and deceive the world with wonders, powers, and signs. These miracles won't be trickery, but appear to be total victory over Christ. Not only that, but God Himself will actually **help** this Man of Sin by sending a strong delusion over the people, so that everyone who is not devoted to Jesus will fall for the lie. Certainly, whatever this Man of Sin does, it will involve an event that could only be described as blasphemous if not impossible for a believer to accept, unless he had total faith in God's master plan.

This will lead to the Abomination of Desolation, which Daniel prophesied and Jesus himself warned about. Although we're never told in Revelation when this abomination occurs, we can see the connections lining up:

"Therefore when you see the 'abomination of desolation,' spoken of through Daniel the prophet, standing in the holy place [the Third Temple]" (whoever reads, let him understand), then let those who are in Judea [the 144,000 elect and anyone else willing to listen] flee upon the mountains. Let the one on the housetop not go down to take the things out of his house. And let the one in the field not turn back to take his clothes. But woe to those women who are pregnant, and to the women nursing a baby in those days! But pray that your flight may not take place in winter, nor on the Sabbath. For then there shall be great tribulation, such as has not been since the beginning of the world until now, nor by any means shall be. And unless those days were cut short, no flesh would be saved; but for the elect's sake, those days will be cut short [by the Rapture of the 144,000 elect]. Then if someone says to you, 'Look, here is the Christ!' or 'There!' do not believe it. For false christs and false prophets will be raised up, and they will show great signs and wonders so as to deceive, if possible, even the elect. See, I have told you in advance. Therefore if they should say

181

to you, 'Look, He is in the desert!' do not go out; or 'Look, He is in the inner rooms!' do not believe it. For <u>as the lightning comes out from the east and flashes to the west, so shall also be the coming of the Son of Man</u>. For wherever the carcass may be, there the eagles will be gathered together. (Matthew 24:15-28 EMTV)

Jesus directly references the Abomination of Desolation written about by Daniel, so let's go there next. But before that, let's acknowledge that most people believe Daniel's prophecy was already fulfilled when Jesus was crucified. This doesn't make sense for many reasons, especially as we see how many different accounts discuss the same time period:

While I was speaking and praying, confessing my sin and the sin of <u>my people Israel</u>, and presenting <u>my plea</u> before the LORD my God for <u>the holy hill</u> [Zion] of my God, while I was speaking in prayer, the man Gabriel, whom I had seen in the vision at the first, came to me in swift flight at the time of the evening sacrifice. He made me understand, speaking with me and saying, "O Daniel, I have now come out to give you insight and understanding. At the beginning of your <u>pleas for mercy</u> [for Jerusalem, which God has already decided is doomed] a word went out, and I have come to tell it to you, <u>for you are greatly loved</u> [and therefore deserve to know the tragic reality]. Therefore consider the word and understand the vision. "<u>Seventy weeks</u> are decreed about <u>your people</u> [godly Israelites] and <u>your holy city</u> [Jerusalem, considered "Babylon" by God], to <u>finish the transgression</u> [Satanic destruction], to put <u>an end to sin</u>, and to <u>atone for iniquity</u> [of "Babylon"], to <u>bring in everlasting righteousness</u> [Millennial Kingdom and resurrection], to <u>seal both vision</u> [revelation] and <u>prophet</u> [False Prophet, or perhaps "prophecy"], and to <u>anoint a most holy place</u> [the purged Jerusalem]. (Daniel 9:20-24 ESV, English Standard Version)

This clearly has never happened yet; everlasting righteousness doesn't exist for the holy city and Daniel's people today. They continue in vast majority to reject Jesus Christ, their Messiah. "Babylon" is yet to be destroyed, and therefore Jerusalem's sins are not atoned for. The transgression of Satan's assault has not even begun. Remember, Daniel was specifically praying to God about his people and Jerusalem's Mount Zion. The discussion is about **those** things, not some abstract theology or change of topic. That's why Gabriel was quickly sent to put a stop to Daniel's plea: because God loves Daniel greatly, but what he's asking for is totally impossible. There will be no mercy for Jerusalem. We already know from Isaiah that the city must be destroyed before it can be redeemed. The city which Daniel loves so much is the same city God hates. Therefore God is provoked to respond quickly, because He does not like to see his servant Daniel making pleas for a place that is already doomed to utter desolation. Daniel doesn't understand that Jerusalem is considered Sodom in God's eyes and must be burned down.

> *Know therefore and understand that <u>from the going out of the word to restore and build Jerusalem</u> [after the earthquake that destroys 10% of the city and kills 7,000] to the <u>coming of an anointed one, a prince</u> [Jesus on Mount Zion with the 144,000], there shall be seven weeks. Then for sixty-two weeks <u>it shall be built again</u> with squares and moat, <u>but in a troubled time</u> [as the city is hit with the biggest earthquake in history, dividing it into thirds, and Satan besieges the city in war]. And after the sixty-two weeks, an anointed one [Jesus Christ] shall be <u>cut off</u> [Hebrew: "karath", meaning consumed or destroyed] and shall <u>have nothing</u> [Hebrew: "ayin", meaning not exist]. And the people of <u>the prince who is to come</u> [the Man of Sin] shall <u>destroy the city and the sanctuary</u>. Its end shall come with a flood [of war], and <u>to the end there shall be war</u> [as some believers try to defend Jerusalem]. <u>Desolations are decreed</u> [meaning Daniel's plea is not feasible]. And he [the Man of Sin] shall make a <u>strong covenant</u> [the great delusion] <u>with many</u> [not just the 144,000] for one week, and for half of the week he*

shall put an end to sacrifice and offering. And on the wing
of abominations shall come one who makes desolate, until the
decreed end [Christ's vengeance from heaven in glory with
his army] is poured out on the desolator."
(Daniel 9:25-27 ESV)

It may seem completely blasphemous and impossible to consider that Jesus would come back to earth and be "killed" again, but it makes perfect sense when we consider the full strategy God is using to allow Satan to believe he has won and fulfilled the Jeremiah 31:37 loophole, among other things. There would be no greater proof of Satan's triumph than destroying Jesus again, erasing him from existence in the middle of his own temple, in front of his own people. People assume that Jesus cannot come back to earth unless it is in the clouds, but that's not true. The Bible doesn't forbid Jesus from returning—it only promises that he will eventually return again in the clouds like he ascended. The "**Second Coming**" tradition term is misleading, therefore. His triumphant return in the clouds could just as well be his third coming. This is why it's so beautiful that Satan himself misunderstands the prophecy and will think he has won. Jesus won't truly die, of course, but it will signify to his followers that they need run and wait for his triumphant return in the clouds. God frequently warns those final believers to flee the city and **not** try to defend Jesus, or prevent the Abomination of Desolation.

For Satan to believe he has achieved the Jeremiah 31:37 loophole once again and attained victory over Christ and God's covenant with Israel, the "victory" must be even more convincing than killing the two witnesses. This could be extra convincing if the False Prophet, the demons, and the gnostic cultists have all been predicting these things. The giant earthquake and the apparent defeat of everything God holds sacred will certainly convince the Satanic conspiracy that they have managed to beat God Himself, which will lead to the Man of Sin stepping up into the role of God in the temple. This perfectly completes the "Babylon" metaphor, since it will be like Nimrod or the ancient Babylonian god-kings who believed they could surpass God and do anything they wanted with no fear.

As for the "death" of Jesus, it's very possible that his body will not be harmed at all, but that being "cut off" will mean vanishing instead. As the text describes, he won't even exist… on earth, that is. We know that in his resurrected body Jesus could teleport from place to place, or hide his identity from anyone he chose. He's not at all limited to mortal logic. It might look to everyone as if Jesus was eradicated by the Man of Sin's power, but in fact it would be God's plan to allow Satan to take credit and celebrate prematurely. The supposed death of Jesus in the temple will be the "Abomination of Desolation" that triggers the warning to flee Jerusalem. The "strong delusion" will be completed here as well, and the Man of Sin will truly believe he is above God and sit on the throne, making a deal with many about his new false religion and need to be worshiped. Evidently, the sacrifices and temple offerings will even be allowed to continue for half a week, although they will be offered to the Man of Sin himself, since he will sit on the throne as if he is God! When he betrays this new covenant, he will hope to ensnare the elect and have them all put to death horribly. One would hope that he cuts the week short **because** so many God-fearing people will think better of it and flee the city, knowing that Jesus is still alive and the Man of Sin is nothing but a pathetic loser waiting to be destroyed. The wrath and cruelty of the Man of Sin when he does decide to attack and destroy will become the greatest tribulation in human history. We can certainly hope that the holy people will be long gone and on the run when that happens.

TIMING OF CHRIST'S RETURN

Many shall purify themselves and make themselves white and be refined [by converting to Christ and being killed], but the wicked shall act wickedly. And none of the wicked shall understand, but <u>those who are wise shall understand</u> [that God's covenant is intact, that Christ did not truly die, and that he will come back in glory with his army]. And from <u>the time that the regular burnt offering is taken away</u> [due to some disaster perhaps?] and <u>the abomination that makes desolate is set up</u> [the Man of Sin taking the throne as God],

there shall be 1,290 days [3.5 years]. <u>Blessed is he who waits</u>
<u>and arrives at the 1,335 days</u> [45 days later].
(Daniel 12:10-12 ESV)

This is intended for the 144,000 elect to track, not us. They will literally be reading Daniel and can count the days from the time that the burnt offering is taken away. At that point they can expect the abomination of desolation to be set up in three and a half years. They will want to stay with Jesus and only flee the city once the abomination of desolation occurs, and at that point they will have 45 days to flee and escape the greatest tribulation. But anyone who listens to the warning and wants to flee in advance could theoretically just leave and wait for the right time to return, abandoning the city. The "blessing" that will be given to those who wait and arrive at the 1,335 days will be the "Marriage Supper" this chapter is focused on:

And he saith unto me, Write, <u>Blessed are they which are</u>
<u>called unto the marriage supper of the Lamb</u>. And he saith
unto me, These are the true sayings of God.
(Revelation 19:9 KJV)

THE RAPTURE-RESURRECTION CONNECTION

Now this I say, brothers, that flesh and blood cannot inherit
the kingdom of God; nor can corruption inherit incorruption.
Behold, I tell you a mystery: <u>We shall not all die, but we shall</u>
<u>all be changed</u>—in a moment, in the twinkling of an eye,
<u>at the last trumpet</u>. For the <u>trumpet shall sound, and the</u>
<u>dead shall be raised incorruptible, and we shall be changed</u>.
(1 Corinthians 15:50-52 EMTV)

The 144,000 must flee for 45 days upon seeing the Abomination of Desolation, but after this they will be gathered in the clouds with Jesus, after the "last trumpet". This is how God will cut short the days and protect them. We know that the 144,000 must go where Jesus is, so it's fitting that when Jesus returns in the clouds that's where they will be gathered. Meanwhile, the Man of Sin (acting as God) will have his own "christs" who deceive and lure. They may lure confused, scared believers into torture or demonic agony if they aren't sure if the Jeremiah 31:37 loophole has been fulfilled or not. Whatever the tribulation looks like, Jesus told us it would be the worst in history.

> *Immediately after the tribulation of those days* shall the sun be darkened, and the moon shall not give her light, and the stars shall fall from heaven, and the powers of the heavens shall be shaken: And *then shall appear the sign of the Son of man in heaven:* and then shall *all the tribes of the earth mourn,* and *they shall see the Son of man coming in the clouds of heaven with power and great glory* [this, as opposed to the modest form he will take on Mount Zion]. And he shall send his angels *with a great sound of a trumpet* [the last trumpet], and *they shall gather together his elect from the four winds, from one end of heaven to the other.* (Matthew 24:29–31 KJV)

This is perfectly logical. After the tribulation we have a final trumpet, because the trumpet itself is the signal to cut the days short and signal the angels to gather the elect. It coincides with Jesus coming in the clouds, as lightning flashes from east to the west, and the earth will mourn.

> And at that time shall Michael stand up, the great prince which standeth for the children of thy people: and there shall be *a time of trouble* [tribulation], *such as never was since there was a nation even to that same time* [the same time Jesus was describing]: and *at that time thy people* [Israelites] *shall be delivered,* every one that shall be found written in the book [the elect]. And *many of them that sleep in the dust of the earth shall awake, some to everlasting life* [the first resurrection], *and some to shame and everlasting contempt* [the second resurrection]. And they that be wise shall *shine as the brightness of the firmament* [receive new spiritual

bodies]; and they that turn many to righteousness as the stars
for ever and ever.
(Daniel 12:1-3 KJV)

Notice that this cannot be any of the past resurrections or miracles that brought people back from the dead, such as the incidents found in the New Testament. Simply ask yourself: was their resurrection to everlasting life? Did they shine like stars for ever and ever? The answer is no. Those who were brought back from the dead, like Lazarus or those after Christ's crucifixion, died again. This passage speaks of everlasting life to some, and everlasting shame to others; it has not happened. God is therefore telling Daniel that the salvation of the Israelites is going to correspond with the first resurrection and eternal life in new spiritual bodies that never die. The language of shining bodies is not random or coincidental, but a very real fact of what the resurrection will look like:

> *So also is the resurrection of the dead. The body is sown*
> *in corruption, it is raised in incorruption. It is sown in*
> *dishonor, it is raised in glory. It is sown in weakness, it*
> *is raised in power. It is sown a natural body, it is raised*
> *a spiritual body. There is a natural body, and there is a*
> *spiritual body. (1 Corinthians 15:42-44 EMTV)*

And before this, Paul tells us about how the resurrection will happen in a certain order at Christ's coming, not as a separate event:

> *For since by man came death, by man came also the*
> *resurrection of the dead. For as in Adam all die, even so*
> *in Christ shall all be made alive. But every man in his*
> *own order: Christ the firstfruits; afterward they that are*
> *Christ's at his coming. Then cometh the end, when he shall*
> *have delivered up the kingdom to God, even the Father;*
> *when he shall have put down all rule and all authority and*
> *power. For he must reign, till he hath put all enemies under*
> *his feet. The last enemy that shall be destroyed is death.*
> *(1 Corinthians 15:21-26 KJV)*

Thus we know that the following things must coincide together:

- The greatest tribulation in history ending suddenly
- The days being cut short for the sake of the elect
- Israelites being delivered (who are written in the book)
- Christ's return in the clouds
- The gathering up of the elect to the clouds, to be with Christ
- Transformation of those who remain at Christ's return
- The first resurrection

And when we continue to read Revelation, we will see that this all coincides with the battle of the Lord's hosts against Satan's armies at Jerusalem.

15

THY KINGDOM COME

GATHERING AND FEASTING FOR A MARRIAGE SUPPER

And I saw heaven opened, and behold a white horse; and he that sat upon him was called Faithful and True, and in righteousness he doth <u>judge and make war</u>. His eyes were as a flame of fire, and on his head were many crowns; and he had a name written, that no man knew, but he himself. And he was clothed with a vesture dipped in blood: and his name is called The Word of God. And <u>the armies which were in heaven followed him</u> upon white horses, clothed in fine linen, white and clean. (Revelation 19:11-14 KJV)

The Lord's appearing in the heavens comes immediately after the angel tells John about the Marriage Supper being a blessed event for everyone who attends. The destruction of the Satanic forces will be the Marriage Supper itself, and the armies who come down from heaven with him are participating in that feast. There is good reason to believe that army will consist of the resurrected saints who will spiritually rise up from the dust of the earth, be given new bodies, and rise to him first. But soon after, the 144,000 Israelite elect are also going to be gathered up as well, because they will all be together in the air as he prepares to descend:

> *Now we do not want you to be uninformed, brothers, concerning those who have died, lest you be sorrowful as those who have no hope. For if we believe that Jesus died and rose again, thus also God will <u>bring with him those who die in Jesus</u> [meaning, all the dead Christians]. For this we say to you by the word of the Lord, that <u>we who are alive and remain until the coming of the Lord</u> [the 144,000 elect] shall by no means precede those who are dead. Because the Lord himself shall descend from heaven with a word of command, with the voice of an archangel, and with <u>the trumpet of God</u> [the last trumpet], and <u>the dead in Christ shall rise first</u>. Then <u>we who are alive and remain</u> [the 144,000 remnant] <u>shall be caught up together with them</u> [all caught up together] <u>in the clouds</u> to <u>meet the Lord in the air</u>. And thus <u>we shall always be with the Lord</u>. So then comfort one another with these words.* (1 Thessalonians 4:13-18 EMTV)

This is the Day of the Lord, when Jesus Christ returns in his fully glory, ready to make war and judge the world once and for all, destroying evil and saving the innocent. It is called the Marriage Supper because the slaughter of the Satanic wicked conspiracy will be like a wonderful feast, and the "wine" that is served with this feast will be their blood, squeezed from the winepress of God's wrath:

> *And out of his mouth goeth a sharp sword, that with it he should smite the nations: and <u>he shall rule them with a rod of iron</u>: and he <u>treadeth the winepress of the fierceness and wrath of Almighty God</u>.* (Revelation 19:15 KJV)

Amen! We saw the metaphor of the winepress introduced much earlier, in Rev 14:20, when the two harvests were spiritually being foreshadowed in the heavens, but now the actual fulfillment is happening. "Babylon" is ruined and desolate, the merchants of the earth will be heartbroken by the loss of their New World Order economic hub, and the Man of Sin and his armies are now going to mourn when they realize that they have failed yet again to sabotage the covenant of God using the Jeremiah 31:37 loophole, despite "killing" Jesus in the temple and setting up their abomination. In truth they were given a strong delusion to believe such a thing, and now they realize it is totally hopeless, and will have no hope of fighting back, because we will all have spiritual bodies, incapable of dying.

> *And he hath on his vesture and on his thigh a name written, KING OF KINGS, AND LORD OF LORDS. And I saw an angel standing in the sun; and he cried with a loud voice, saying to all the fowls that fly in the midst of heaven [the transformed 144,000 and the resurrected saints, all gathered together in the air with Jesus], Come and gather yourselves together unto the supper of the great God; That ye may eat the flesh of kings, and the flesh of captains, and the flesh of mighty men, and the flesh of horses, and of them that sit on them, and the flesh of all men, both free and bond, both small and great. (Revelation 19:16–18 KJV)*

Clearly these "birds" are not animals. The angel told John that those who attend the Marriage Supper will be blessed, and it won't be mere fowls who receive this eternal blessing by God. Rather, it's a poetic way to picture all of us in the sky together, clustered and gathered like a terrifying vision to the evil ones below, eager to consume them with holy retribution for all of their lies and sin.

> *And I saw the beast, and the kings of the earth [the ten temporary ones that were given power by the Beast, at least], and their armies, gathered together to make war against him that sat on the horse, and against his army. And the beast was taken, and with him the false prophet that wrought miracles before him [because they are merged into one person?], with*

which he deceived them that had received the mark of the beast, and them that worshipped his image. These <u>both were cast alive into a lake of fire burning with brimstone</u>. And the remnant were slain with the sword of him that sat upon the horse, which sword proceeded out of his mouth: and <u>all the fowls were filled with their flesh</u> [satisfaction of vengeance]. (Revelation 19:19-21 KJV)

It is clear that Jesus himself will be responsible for the death of many if not most of Satan's army here. The role of Christ's accompanying army is not clear, but obviously we will be happy to contribute in whatever way we can. Ultimately the result is the same: the Beast and the False Prophet—now seemingly joined—are taken and thrown into a lake of fire together, alive. This speaks to a supernatural, yet physical, person. We'll see later that they never perish, but continue to burn there forever. Does the False Prophet merge with the Beast to become the Man of Sin? Revelation never uses the term "Man of Sin" and so we are left to apply Paul's label to a character in John's account. I can think of no better candidate than this False Prophet, because he happens to share the same fate as the Beast, implying they are somehow equal and the same. There will probably be an actual "lake of fire" on earth at this point, perhaps in the "bottomless pit" that was opened up by Wormwood. The bottomless pit is indeed a spiritual abode that has root in the Old Testament, but as with so many things in prophecy, there is ultimately a physical and spiritual hybridization, so that they form a powerful symbolic reality, equal parts literal, metaphorical, and spiritual.

THE KINGDOM ESTABLISHED ON THE RUINED EARTH

And I saw an angel come down from heaven, having the key of the bottomless pit and a great chain in his hand. And he laid hold on the dragon, that old serpent, which is the Devil, and Satan, and bound him a thousand years, And cast him into the bottomless pit, and shut him up, and set a seal upon him, <u>that he should deceive</u>

> *the nations no more, till the thousand years should be*
> *fulfilled: and after that he must be loosed a little season.*
> *(Revelation 20:1-3 KJV)*

Once again we see that any premature, short-sighted interpretations of Bible scholars falls apart as the timeline of Revelation goes on. The idea that the Beast and False Prophet could be cast into the lake of fire forever, but that Satan himself is only bound for a thousand years and then has to return, destroys any view that tries to equate the Millennial Kingdom with eternal paradise, or heaven itself being the final destination of believers. Satan is going to be released again, and will be allowed to deceive the nations once more after the thousand years.

> *And I saw thrones, and they [the "fowls" who were at the*
> *Marriage Supper] sat on them, and judgment [to rule the*
> *world] was given to [1] them, and [2] the souls of those*
> *who had been beheaded on account of the testimony of Jesus,*
> *and [3] on account of the word of God, and [4] those who*
> *had not worshipped the Beast or [5] his image, and [6]*
> *they did not receive the mark on their forehead or [7] on*
> *their hand. And they [all seven groups] came to life and*
> *reigned with Christ for the thousand years. But the rest*
> *of the dead [everyone not in those seven groups] did not*
> *come to life until the thousand years were finished. This*
> *[the seven groups] is the first resurrection. Blessed and holy*
> *is he that has part in the first resurrection. Over these the*
> *second death has no power, but they shall be priests of God*
> *and of Christ, and shall reign with him for a thousand years.*
> *(Revelation 20:4-6 EMTV)*

The First Resurrection takes place at the same time as the Lord's return, the Marriage Supper, and the establishment of the Millennial Kingdom on earth. We have shown that this single day will merge many of the greatest prophecies in the Bible at once. We will return to the question of the "Second Resurrection" and "Second Death" in the next chapter, but for now it's important to realize that the world will be ruled by Christians and enemies of the Beast system. We were already told (in Rev 13:8) that everyone who was not written in the Book of Life of the Lamb will worship the Beast, so this narrows down the possibilities. Essentially, all those who Christ chose and deemed worthy will be rewarded with power and judgment in the thousand years of reigning, and this then confers added benefits by making them immune to the Second Death.

There are more important prophecies regarding this Kingdom. One of the most vivid and direct is the prophet Joel's description of the Day of the Lord and the things that will happen before (blood, fire, pillars of smoke, sun being darkened, moon being blood) and afterward (pouring out God's spirit and giving believers prophecy and visions):

> *Blow ye the trumpet in Zion, and sound an alarm in my holy mountain: let all the inhabitants of the land tremble: for <u>the day of the LORD cometh</u>, for it is nigh at hand; …. (2:28-32) And it shall come to pass <u>afterward</u> [after the Day of the Lord], that <u>I will pour out my spirit upon all flesh; and your sons and your daughters shall prophesy, your old men shall dream dreams, your young men shall see visions</u> [in the Millennial Kingdom, with the First Resurrection]: And also upon the servants and upon the handmaids <u>in those days</u> will I pour out my spirit. And I will shew wonders in the heavens and in the earth, <u>blood, and fire, and pillars of smoke</u> [the trumpet terrors of Revelation]. The sun shall be turned into darkness, and the moon into blood, <u>before</u> the great and the terrible day of the LORD come. And it shall come to pass, that whosoever shall call on the name of the LORD shall be delivered [from God's wrath]: for <u>in mount Zion and in Jerusalem</u> [not the scattered church] shall be deliverance, as the LORD hath said, and <u>in the remnant</u> [the 144,000] <u>whom the LORD shall call</u>. (Joel 2:1 KJV)*

Although Peter, speaking with the Holy Spirit, refers to this prophecy (in Acts 2:14-22) to explain the behavior of the saints who received the Spirit, there is no reason to believe this prophecy was fulfilled **in its entirety** back then already. Like so many prophecies that began with Jesus and the disciples, it is only a taste of what is to come. A much greater pouring out of the spirit will happen in the Millennial Kingdom, when Zion will literally and geographically be the destination of all those who want to learn about God. It is not a contradiction, but a final and ultimate fulfillment in addition to the sneak preview that began 2,000 years ago. In the final time, Satan will be locked up, the Beast system will be gone, and the Millennial Kingdom's inhabitants will need the full pouring out of the Spirit in order to reign and manage the world from Jerusalem quickly and efficiently. Our visions and prophetic dreams will help us govern.

LOGIC OF THE MILLENNIAL KINDGOM

Most Christians can't even begin to imagine what the Millennial Kingdom will look or feel like. We rarely consider Jesus to be the fierce KING OF KINGS who will come down physically to this planet in order to rule our **actual** world system with a rod of iron, rebuking the real nations and setting things straight with judgment. We forget how even at the beginning of Revelation, before the vision of the future, Jesus is depicted as having white hair, fire-filled eyes, and a sharp sword coming out of his mouth. He is not like he was on earth (except when transfigured). The sword represents the sharp, dangerous, powerful, and precise Word of God, which divides all things and is quick and ready to destroy evil. If you don't like that imagery, you don't like the reality of Jesus Christ alive today.

Many Christians would be shocked or even disgusted if they suddenly were invited to slaughter the wicked armies of Satan, even though they are pure evil and the opportunity is offered by God Himself in the Day of the Lord. Christians today either believe we should already be fighting and warring with guns and armies (which is not true), or they are so sensitive and peace-loving that they can't even enjoy the thought of Satanic armies being killed. The heavens rejoice greatly when it happens, so why aren't we excited about it? I wonder if there are some Christians who will go to heaven but refuse to partake in the Marriage Supper, and miss out on the blessings. How can these Christians sit on thrones and reign over a plagued, desolate, bloody planet for a thousand years straight? It's true that we should be kind, loving, tender, and forgiving to people in our lifetime, but it's for the purpose of showing the difference between the evil world and the church, and the righteousness within us. We can't be gullible about the ungodly world or think that it should be spared. We are not supposed to love the present world or be friends with it:

> *Ye adulterers and adulteresses, know ye not that the friendship of the world is enmity with God?* <u>*whosoever therefore will be a friend of the world is the enemy of God*</u>. *(James 4:4 KJV)*

God knows that this world is ruled by a Satanic antichrist conspiracy of men and false gods, so why don't we rejoice at the thought of his taking it back from them once and for all? Yes, he loved humanity enough to send the Messiah and offer salvation, but that is very different from loving a world system that **rejects** His beautiful Chosen One and tries to deceive and kill His precious church. Our suffering, tribulation, and oppression in this life is supposed to teach us how to be good and understanding rulers in the Millennial Kingdom, which is why we will keep our memories when we come back. When Jesus talks about the meek "inheriting the earth" in his famous sermon he is talking directly about the Millennial Kingdom period, where we literally are given control over this planet as if we were inheriting land, the same way that royalty always have.

The logic is simple, but only if we remember how the world used to work before our Humanist "image of the Beast" system. The king owned all the land, and he placed people in charge of managing it for him, in exchange for loyalty against his enemies. His heir inherits all of it, including the authority to punish, the subjects living on his land, and the obligation to maintain it. Nobles were allowed to manage and tend the land on the king's behalf, as land*lords*. Lords grew up being pampered and spoiled most of the time, which made them unfit to rule in a godly way. They were taught well by their tutors, but they lacked the common sense, humility, and suffering of daily life that creates values. They didn't know the importance of caring for the poor, for example. They've never been hungry, so they don't realize what hunger truly means. They can't sympathize with inequality. That's why **our** suffering and tribulation is so important, and why God has allowed Satan to control the world as its lord, persecuting us. He's preparing us for that position of future responsibility, because we should be humble and meek, charitable and graceful, not greedy and ambitious, or proud. We should be eager to serve God and realize that everything we have depends on Him. That's why we will be placed on thrones, ruling not only men, but angels (1 Cor 6:1-3). Jesus is the KING OF KINGS, but he is in heaven breaking the seals and orchestrating events from above, not on earth taking his rightful reign; he's leaving that to the "nobility" of Satan and his angels, or false gods. Revelation describes how that will eventually change, so that Jesus is reigning on earth and we will join him.

We should be excited about this prospect, because we should care about this world and the treatment of its people. Escaping to heaven when we die is certainly a nice period of rest, but it's not our final destination. Our destiny is to return to this very same earth and rule these very same people around us (if they survive)! Therefore, the Resurrection is not some eternal paradise in the clouds, but a new life on this planet, which is currently being ruined in front of our eyes. Satan is destroying our inheritance. The Satanic elites are bent on polluting the planet while pretending to be its greatest champion with the "green movement".

God wants people who can weigh complex matters and settle things without needing to resort to a cumbersome system of laws like in the Old Testament. The laws of God should be written in our hearts, forever. During the thousand years we will be in power, but not arrogantly. We will be diligent, productive, and help decide how the affairs of the world should operate. We'll be learning, communicating, dealing justice, showing leadership, and enjoying fellowship. We will no doubt help to rebuild the world and use our incredible access to Christ and the angels to do fascinating things. But such things are not even contemplated by today's church, much less fantasized about as an exciting promise. These are not new ideas, however. They all relate back to the older expectations of the Messiah's Kingdom, and older yet to the Garden of Eden and the initial hope of Adam to be a son of God who would tend the garden and have authority and empowerment over the animals and the land. The Millennial Kingdom will still have the curse of Adam, meaning it will require work unless we simply provide everything through miracles and power. The desolate and ruined world will come to us for guidance, hope, and teaching. In this life we are sheep in the midst of wolves (Mat 10:16), learning how to obey and serve, as if to train our spirit for the great task that lay ahead.

This is why our present age of comfort is not good. We are being deliberately lulled into sleep and tranquilized by the Satanic empire, so that we will lose the strength and lessons that come from struggling. We are pacified by our lack of oppression, and numbed to the Satanic conspiracy around us by deception and distraction. We do not weigh the utter horror of our world. We ignore the injustices and blasphemy for the most part, and want to stay comfortable and lukewarm. But the more comfortable and safe we feel, the more danger we are in:

> "I know your works, that you are neither cold nor hot. _I wish that you were cold or hot_. Therefore, _since you are lukewarm_, and neither cold nor hot, _I will spew you out of my mouth_ [reject with disgust]. Because _you say_, 'I am wealthy, and have become rich, and have _need of nothing_'—and do not know that _you are wretched, miserable, poor, blind, and naked_, I counsel you to _buy from me_ [trade one for the other] _gold_ [wisdom and righteousness] _having been tried by fire_ [of intense persecution], so that you may _become rich_ [in zeal and spirit]; and _white robes_ [untainted purity], so that you may be clothed [honorable], and _the shame of your nakedness_ [lacking] may not appear; and _eye salve_ [awakening], so that you may anoint your eyes, _in order that you may see_ [the stark and intense reality of the world]. _As many as I love, I rebuke and discipline_ [so that we can be prudent and steadfast]. Be

zealous [passionate, ideological, eager, fearless] therefore, and repent [change our ways]. Behold, I stand at the door and I am knocking. If anyone hears my voice and opens the door, then I will come in to him and I will dine with him [at the Marriage Supper], and he with me. He that overcomes [the temptation to be passive and mediocre], I will grant to him to sit with me on my throne [in the Millennial Kingdom], as I also overcame and sat down with my Father on His throne. (Revelation 3:15–21 EMTV)

A major change in attitude is needed in believers today if we want to align our thinking with the reality of God's plan for us. We don't need to become obsessed with daily news, political outrages, or the concerns of the day, but rather filled with a longing for this world to be ruled with justice, love, and wisdom, seeing things for how bad they really are.

Consideration: Poverty is all around us

If we would truly heed the warning of Jesus to our church today, we would see that our rich modern society is full of poor people. Not people who are physically starving and naked—our socialist welfare system has taken care of that—but those who are lukewarm and disgusting to Christ. People who are so spiritually ignorant and passive that they are neither hot nor cold. They have no gold "tried by fire", and their eyes are blind to the evil around them. We should care for the poor indeed, but we should start by recognizing that we are all poorer than those hungry Africans we see in advertisements.

REAPING WHAT WAS SOWN

For what is a man profited, if he shall gain the whole world, and lose his own soul? or what shall a man give in exchange for his soul? For the Son of man shall come in the glory of his Father with his angels; and then he shall reward every man according to his works. (Matthew 16:26–27 KJV)

The Millennial Kingdom is the time of rewarding. But it's not just rewarding good people with good things; it's also rewarding "Babylon" with destruction, Satan with imprisonment, the False Prophet and Beast with eternal hellfire, and much more. It's the time of justice on earth. To get a better idea of how this future era is shaped and what we can expect, we need to go back to Isaiah and the old prophets once again, since this is the time they were truly looking forward to and expecting:

> And it shall come to pass in _that day_, that the _remnant of Israel_ [the 144,000 elect], and _they that are escaped of the house of Jacob_ [meaning those who escape "Babylon" and its destruction at the end], shall no more again lean upon him that smote them, but _shall lean upon Jehovah, the Holy One of Israel_ [Jesus Christ and God the Father], _in truth_. A _remnant_ shall return, even the _remnant of Jacob_, unto the mighty God. For though thy people, Israel, be as the sand of the sea, _only a remnant of them_ shall return: a _destruction is determined_ [desolation], overflowing _with righteousness_ [meaning it will be a good desolation]. For a full end, and that determined, will the Lord, Jehovah of hosts, make in the midst of all the earth. (Isaiah 10:20–23 ASV)

Could it be any more clear? This is a condemnation of future Israel, with a warning that only a small, elect portion will be saved. This helps us to accept why the church of today is not the focal point of so much of Revelation, but instead these older and bigger prophecies are. The Gentile church age is meant to provoke Israel to jealousy and give us an opportunity to partake in the covenant, but ultimately the greatest promises belong to the Israelites who love the Lord and trust in Him with all their strength, especially when Satan seems to be the victor over the Messiah himself. This happens during the Abomination of Desolation, and we should be happy that a remnant is saved, not shocked or sad that so many will not believe. Only faith in God and obedience to His command (to flee Jerusalem and not try to save it) will save them, and this is fair.

And it shall come to pass in the last days [during the Millennial Kingdom], that the mountain of the LORD'S house [Zion, in Jerusalem] shall be established in the top of the mountains, and shall be exalted above the hills; and all nations shall flow unto it. And many people shall go and say, Come ye, and let us go up to the mountain of the LORD, to the house of the God of Jacob; and he will teach us of his ways, and we will walk in his paths: for out of Zion shall go forth the law, and the word of the LORD from Jerusalem. And he shall judge among the nations, and shall rebuke many people: and they shall beat their swords into plowshares, and their spears into pruninghooks: nation shall not lift up sword against nation, neither shall they learn war any more. (Isaiah 2:2-4 KJV)

In the Millennial Kingdom nations will not learn war again. Not only will nations flow into Jerusalem, but they will desire to learn God's ways because they will finally see how foolish it is to go against God. He'll judge the nations and rebuke them when they do wrong, through us. With this turn of events, everyone reaps what they have sown in the current world: the god-fearing who have died (or survived by obeying) reap eternal life, resurrection, glorification, power, dignity, and rest. The evil are destroyed and forgotten, and the False Prophet and Beast are already burning for eternity. The neutral nations that did not go along with them aren't resurrected, but they are also not destroyed; they have the opportunity to visit and learn from Christ, and will continue to live on earth without new bodies and blessings. They will effectively be the subjects that we rule over, showing them and their children the way for many generations in the aftermath of the cataclysm God has unleashed. No doubt it will be a unique and important time of God showing His wisdom and setting us as examples, so that we can in turn magnify Him and preach His Word to the world with authority, not with the humble form of preaching we must use today.

For Jesus this is also a joyous time, because he loves each of us personally, and chose us to be his. The Millennial Kingdom is his "marriage" with us and the land that God chose for him:

Let us rejoice and be exceeding glad, and let us give the glory unto him: for the marriage of the Lamb is come, and his wife hath made herself ready. (Revelation 19:7 ASV)

For the husband is the head of the wife, as Christ also is the head of the church, being himself the saviour of the body. But as the church is subject to Christ, so let the wives also be to their husbands in everything. Husbands, love your wives, even as Christ also loved the church, and gave himself up for it; that he might sanctify it, having cleansed it by the washing of water with the word, that he might present the church to himself a glorious church, not having spot or wrinkle or any such thing; but that it should be holy and without blemish. …. For this cause shall a man leave his father and mother, and shall cleave to his wife; and the two shall become one flesh. This mystery is great: but I speak in regard of Christ and of the church. (Ephesians 5:23-32 ASV)

So Jerusalem and the church are together joined in the Marriage Supper, with Christ. We will have feasted and enjoyed the victory, and then be together forever. It is during this period that many promises are fulfilled to the servants of the Lord, such as having cities given to us, and being rewarded according to our works. Salvation is eternal life, but the rewards are meant for this period of justice and compensation.

Jesus gives us the parable of the workers who are given money by their lord, but some are profitable and another only hid the money and gave it back with nothing gained:

"His lord said unto him, Well done, thou good and faithful servant: thou hast been faithful over a few things, I will make thee ruler over many things: enter thou into the joy of thy lord." (Matthew 25:21 KJV)

And to the unprofitable servant he says:

> *His lord answered and said unto him, Thou wicked and slothful servant, thou knewest that I reap where I sowed not, and gather where I have not strawed: Thou oughtest therefore to have put my money to the exchangers, and then at my coming I should have received mine own with usury. Take therefore the talent [money] from him, and give it unto him which hath ten talents. For unto every one that hath shall be given, and he shall have abundance: but from him that hath not shall be taken away even that which he hath. And cast ye the unprofitable servant into outer darkness: there shall be weeping and gnashing of teeth. (Matthew 25:26–30 KJV)*

Jesus will give rulership to those who were faithful and profitable in this life. But without the Millennial Kingdom, this promise doesn't seem to make much sense. In heaven itself, we don't need to rule over anyone or anything, and in "New Creation" there won't be any wayward population to reign over either. This is why the Millennial Kingdom is so important, because we will consciously remember the lives we had, and be able to enjoy the benefits of Christ's rewards.

> *When the Son of man shall come in his glory, and all the holy angels with him [the Day of the Lord], then shall he sit upon the throne of his glory [on earth, in Jerusalem]: And before him shall be gathered all nations: and he shall separate them one from another, as a shepherd divideth his sheep from the goats: And he shall set the sheep on his right hand, but the goats on the left. Then shall the King say unto them on his right hand, Come, ye blessed of my Father, inherit the kingdom prepared for you from the foundation of the world: (Matthew 25:31–34 KJV)*

It is clear that the worldwide kingdom was meant for the faithful sheep, and that this plan was already in place at the foundation of the world, during creation. This world was always meant to belong to God's human family, but the disobedience of Adam and Eve forced the curse to be introduced and the plan to be set back; rebellious spiritual powers led mankind astray. Those spiritual powers have lingered and meddled over and over, culminating in Satan's conspiracy with them. God has been arranging the inevitable fulfillment of that original plan. The Father prepared this world for us to reign on, but in order for justice to be done there needs to be a separation. Just as the two harvests were meant to separate the good from the evil, the Kingdom of Heaven will filter out those who lack the traits he values; specifically, charity and compassion on the innocent and needy.

16

Judgment Day

A final reminder of Satan's futile conspiracy

> *Now <u>after the thousand years</u>, Satan will be released from his prison, and he will come out to deceive the nations which are in the four corners of the earth, <u>Gog and Magog</u>, to gather them together to <u>the war</u>, whose number is like the sand of the sea. (Revelation 20:7-8 EMTV)*

Satan's release coincides with the Second Resurrection, after the thousand years. By that time Jesus Christ and ourselves should have managed to turn the nations toward God and make the world a good place to live again. We know that they will not learn war, so for Satan to be released and gather up a huge army would logically mean he is commanding all of the newly-resurrected unbelievers, not those who survived and multiplied the Armageddon event. Since the Second Resurrection will include everyone else who has died, it ought to easily number in the billions. This overwhelming army will seem unstoppable.

> *And they went up on the breadth of the earth, and compassed <u>the camp of the saints about, and the beloved city</u>: and <u>fire came down from God</u> out of heaven, and devoured them. (Revelation 20:9 KJV)*

This event seems somewhat like an anticlimax, or a footnote, rather than an important fulfillment of prophecy. But it is very important, and will be a final reminder of the supremacy of Jesus Christ, God, and the Millennial Kingdom on earth, for those multitudes of neutral people inhabiting the earth after the thousand years. We are self-centered and tend to only think about our own role in this plan, but God's prophecies also consider future groups within very specific circumstances. Depending on how the Second Resurrection happens, there may be a process of years where Satan deceives the multitudes and builds up the "Gog" and "Magog" army, testing the obedience of those nations who we have been judging and helping during the Millennial Kingdom.

The prophet Ezekiel is the only one besides John in Revelation who mentions Gog and Magog as some kind of evil or threat. This also directly connects John and Ezekiel, increasing the possibility that they are the two witnesses in the last days before the Day of the Lord. In Ezekiel's prophecy about Gog and Magog, he also discuss the birds devouring the flesh of the kings and great warriors, signifying the imagery John uses to describe the Marriage Supper. Ezekiel elaborates on the event by saying how people will cleanse the land for many years afterward by picking up the bones of the evil people who died and burying them in a certain valley, which will be considered a happy thing. However, despite this connection to the Day of the Lord, Revelation only mentions Gog and Magog as something that arrives **after** the Millennial Kingdom, not as part of the Marriage Supper and Armageddon battle. It therefore seems to be a rerun of the last time, and indeed it is: Satan deceives nations and leads an army to try to surround and destroy Christ's empire on earth. He will once again have a leader and a people. But this time, there will be no Abomination of Desolation and apparent success. It is a short and meaningless attempt, and God Himself will devour them with fire.

> And the devil, who deceived them, was <u>thrown into the lake of fire and brimstone where also the Beast and the False Prophet are</u>. And they shall be tormented <u>day and night forever and ever</u>. (Revelation 20:10 EMTV)

Satan is now finally given his eternal destination, burning forever and never dying. Being a celestial figure, or a spirit, Satan will never be consumed despite the hellfire, causing him to be tormented endlessly along with the Beast and False Prophet, who are his servants and tools for persecuting the church and the 144,000 elect. As we will see, this lake of fire will devour and destroy many others, but not everyone who enters will be burned forever.

THE END OF THE WORLD

> *Then I saw <u>a great white throne</u> and He who sat on it, from whose face the earth and the heaven fled. <u>And no place was found for them</u>.*
> *(Revelation 20:11 EMTV)*

The physical universe itself will vanish when God presents Himself on the "great white throne". This is remarkable, but not shocking. God only maintains creation today because He has not yet fulfilled the necessary promises, which is the point of its existence today. But as Jesus said: *"Heaven and earth shall pass away, but my words shall not pass away"* (Matthew 24:35 KJV). This shows that Jesus was correct.

> *And I saw <u>the dead</u> [not the living], the great and the small, standing before the throne, and they opened the books. And another Book was opened, which is <u>the Book of Life</u>. And <u>the dead</u> [not the living] were judged by the things having been written in the books, <u>according to their works</u>. And the sea gave up the dead which were in it; and death and hell [Hades, or the Grave] delivered up the dead which were in them: and they were judged every man <u>according to their works</u>. And death and hell were cast into the lake of fire. <u>This is the second death</u>.*
> *(Revelation 20:12-14 KJV)*

The "lake of fire" is clearly not a physical place, but a spiritual and eternal one, able to affect spiritual beings, souls, and even things like death and the spiritual home of the dead, which we consider to be concepts or metaphysical places.

> *And whosoever was not found written in the book of life*
> *was cast into the lake of fire.*
> *(Revelation 20:15 KJV)*

Remember that the "Second Death" does not affect anyone who was part of the First Resurrection. We are explicitly told that before. Not only that, but it makes sense in the phrasing here, because only the **dead** are judged, which would eliminate living and holy angels, who have never died, and the saints who are incapable of dying with their new bodies. Certainly God will not have us die a second time, after our glorious exaltation; it's not for us, and we won't be judged.

It is during this unique final period of judgment that the souls of the dead will be brought before God. This is where we ought to expect all children and the innocent to be found in the Book of Life; those who never sinned because they did not have the opportunity, and those who lived according to their conscience and the law of nature, just as Paul explained to the Romans:

> *For when the Gentiles, which have not the law, do by nature the things contained in the law, these, having not the law, are a law unto themselves: Which shew the work of the law written in their hearts, their conscience also bearing witness, and their thoughts the mean while accusing or else excusing one another;) In the day when God shall judge the secrets of men by Jesus Christ according to my gospel. (Romans 2:14-16 KJV)*

Many people will not have had the opportunity to "overcome" and be blessed with the Marriage Supper, the Millennial Kingdom, and the beautiful time in the Kingdom of Heaven. This is well enough, because for them it would hold little poetic justice and personal savor. It is unclear if all of these people will be brought back to life for the Second Resurrection, when Satan is released, but presumably this will not resurrect infants into adults, and there will be limitations on who is included in "the rest of the dead" mentioned in that verse. Either way, the martyrs and those who overcome Satan's conspiracy are specially rewarded with the First Resurrection and the Millennial Kingdom blessings because this reward fits their suffering, zeal, belief, and tribulation. But when a child dies, while it is tragic and painful for those who are affected by it, their reward is being found in the Book of Life, which means they will still be rewarded in eternity.

ETERNAL TORMENT, OR DESTRUCTION?

Here are some things to keep in mind about the final punishment. We know that the "Lake of Fire" is an eternal place of punishment, and it will burn forever. Everyone not found in the Book of Life will be cast into it, and this surely will be a horrific torture for them. But there are only a few beings/groups we know for sure are going to spend an **eternity** there:

1. Satan
2. The Beast
3. The False Prophet
4. Those who pledge themselves to the Beast system **after** the Gospel is preached by the three angels who spread the warning to all of mankind in every language (Rev 14)

There is a very strong logic for why these are the **only** people/beings who will suffer **eternally** instead of being consumed by the flames of hell: because each of them has total knowledge of the holiness of the Lord and yet they still reject it and choose to become violent conspiratorial enemies of Jesus Christ himself. The vast majority of people who have ever lived were unaware of who Jesus was, living before he came to this world in the flesh, or only hearing about him afterward, and so they are held to a different standard and receive a different punishment if they are not in the Book of Life. Those who try to be good despite their flaws and ignorance will most likely be in the Book of Life, because God sees their hearts and the law written there.

Others, who sinned without repenting, or defied Christ's salvation offer, or who falsely believed they were saved but were never born again and renewed by the Holy Spirit, will die in this life and be subject to the Second Death—which is truly a "death", in that it is a permanent destruction after being consumed by flame. Who knows how long it takes for a soul to burn in the lake of fire? It may take hours, or it may take years. We are not dealing with typical bodies and flames. One thing I am confident of is that the guilty and condemned, besides the most evil ones who qualify specifically did something to qualify for it, will **not** sit in blistering agony forever and ever and be equally punished as Satan himself and those who rejected the final Gospel offering given by the angels. That doesn't even make sense.

> *And fear not them which kill the body, but are <u>not able to</u>*
> *<u>kill the soul</u>: but rather fear him which is able to <u>destroy</u>*
> *<u>both soul and body in hell</u>.*
> *(Matthew 10:28 KJV)*

God is just and fair. Those who are not found worthy of eternal life will be killed, but not tortured eternally. They will suffer greatly in punishment and lose out on the opportunity for life, but they don't share the same fate as Satan himself, who came down to earth to make war with the saints. Even truly despicable, hateful, and guilty killers and liars will not be burned forever and ever like Satan, but will be consumed eventually and turned into nothing, as a true Second Death. This is what we should expect from fire, which has always been known for consuming and eating up what is put inside. God uses fire to erase things, not to torment. That's why it's so extremely significant when there are people/beings who provoke God to the point of earning themselves eternal torture; billions and trillions of years from that day, they will still be equally suffering and experiencing the reward for their pure evil. This is holy, just and fair, because while we hate the worst offenders in our current day, they are on some level deceived, ignorant, swept up in the misery of their own broken lives. The father of lies, Satan, deserves the punishment on behalf of everyone he recruits.

"And if your eye causes you to stumble, cast it out. It would be better for you to enter into the kingdom of God with one eye, than having two eyes to be <u>cast into the fiery hell, where</u> '<u>Their worm does not die, and the fire is not quenched.</u>'
(Mark 9:47-48 EMTV)

That last phrase in extra quotation marks is a reference back to Isaiah 66.

For <u>as the new heavens and the new earth, which I will</u> <u>make, shall remain before me,</u> saith the LORD, so shall your seed and your name remain. And it shall come to pass, that from one new moon to another, and from one sabbath to another, shall all flesh come to worship before me, saith the LORD. And they shall go forth, and <u>look</u> <u>upon the carcases of the men that have transgressed against</u> <u>me: for their worm shall not die, neither shall their fire be</u> <u>quenched</u>; and they shall be an abhorring unto all flesh.
(Isaiah 66:22-24 KJV)

Here the Lord warns about those who **transgress against Him**: in other words, Satan, the Beast, the False Prophet, and those who ally themselves with these in the final days after hearing the Gospel and the warnings about eternal punishment being the consequence! This is different than the multitudes who are simply not in the Book of Life. Jesus is warning people to not be like those fools, although he does not say that eternal punishment is the only alternative to eternal life. Those who are worthy to live forever will look on those who are punished forever, but there will be billions of people who simply die, suffer, resurrect, and then are burned away and vanish out of existence.

17

LOGIC OF NEW CREATION

And I saw a <u>new heaven</u> [cosmos, sky, universe] and <u>a new earth</u> [physical planet]: for <u>the first heaven and the first earth were passed away</u>; and there was <u>no more sea</u>. (Revelation 21:1 KJV)

Revelation' description of New Creation plays an important role in distinguishing "afterlife" concepts. We must not be short-sighted or hasty to lump the periods and places together. Not only do we **not** go to Heaven forever, but we actually come back down to this very same earth in order to reign in the Millennial Kingdom; then, after the thousand years, there is a final showdown with Satan, where he is finally defeated once and for all and cast into hellfire eternally; only after that is there a Judgment Day, where we are exempt but the rest of the dead stand trial. Once this final sorting process has happened, an entirely new universe is created for us.

A UNIVERSE OF POTENTIAL

Churches have greatly neglected to preach on New Creation, or dared to speculate on what it really means. It's not even part of the narrative of what we should be looking forward to. It's ignored in favor of thinking only of "heaven". But once we realize that a whole new universe will be ours, the prospects of New Creation become much more tangible and exciting than heaven, which is more like a temporary refuge and vantage point. New Creation will be better than heaven, and that shouldn't even be a controversial idea. After all, if God thinks that New Creation is going to be enjoyable for trillions upon trillions of years, for all of eternity, then there must be something extremely amazing about it. We will not miss heaven, or long to go back there.

John's brief description of New Creation shifts our focus to the most important part, which is New Jerusalem and our future with God and Jesus, but this does not rule out all of the other implications about what the new creation is meant for. Those who have studied the logic of the Genesis creation story know that mankind was made "in the image of God" because our function was to "image God", as a verb. What that means is fairly simple: we were not simply made to resemble Him physically, or in spirit, but it is what we are meant to **do**. It's another way of saying we are all made in order to imitate, copy, represent, reflect, function on behalf of God. It turns out that God is not so different from us in the sense that He also loved to have children who reminded Him of Himself. To this day, do we not call Him "Our Father" and try to represent Him on earth? Any father can attest that the joy of children is to see yourself reflected in them, and to watch their growth and maturity into being more like yourself, but also different and special. We will have an eternity to do that, and to grow and learn and be more like God. We will have eternal bodies, immune to fatigue, drowsiness, sickness, lusts, and the constant distractions of life that prevent us from thinking and acting well. But without a new cosmos and planet, our opportunity for growing and learning will be extremely limited. Just as in the Garden of Eden, we will be tasked with tending the creation, exploring it, conquering it, and making it beautiful and perfect. God loves to see us be productive, working, and creating, just as He loves His own creation; not working with sweat and constant struggle and aches, as after the curse was placed on the earth, but the pure and wise work of the engineer, the gardener, and the pioneer.

New Jerusalem will be the eternal centerpiece of the universe, but there is very good reason to believe we will be authorized to go out and explore the whole galaxy from there. Adam was meant to live eternally and eat from the Tree of Life, turning the whole world into his project. Then, when the flood killed mankind and left only Noah's family, God said at the Tower of Babel that if we all had one language and were united, there's nothing we couldn't do. If this is also true for the righteous in New Creation, we should be free to unlock all the mysteries of reality, space travel, chemistry, engineering, mechanics, and everything else that can possibly be learned. Perhaps, millions of years after we get there, we will all have our own planets to call our own and collaborate on, endlessly pioneering and gaining in our appreciation of God's beautiful work.

At minimum, when we consider what we (seem to) know about the science of the planet, with tectonic plates, molten core, oceans, tidal waves, storms, moons, and the relationships between them, it will be fascinating to see what changes there are in the new universe. Those who think that eternity will simply be lounging around, doing nothing, and having no agency or prospects are completely wrong; it's the opposite, and we will be empowered to reflect the glory of God throughout the world, presumably working in harmony under the care and direction of Jesus Christ and God.

AN ETERNAL HOME TO RETURN TO

> Then I saw _the holy city, New Jerusalem,_ coming _down out of heaven_ from God, having been prepared like a bride having been adorned for her husband. And I heard a loud voice from heaven saying, "Behold, the tabernacle of God is with men, and _He shall dwell with them,_ and they shall be His people, and _God Himself shall be with them._ And He shall wipe away every tear from their eyes; and _there shall be no more death, nor sorrow,_ nor crying out; _neither shall there be any more pain, for the former things have passed away._" (Revelation 21:2-4 EMTV)

These are the greatest promises mankind could ever receive, but they become even more exciting in a universe where adventure and exploration are how we will spend untold millennia. Without pain, death, or sorrow, we will be liberated from our worst instincts and encouraged to try things and become the ultimate "imagers" of God, reshaping the universe.

> *Then He who sat on the throne said, "Behold, I am making all things new." And He said to me, "Write, for these words are faithful and true." And He said to me, "I am the Alpha and the Omega, the Beginning and the End. I will give from the spring of the water of life freely to him that is thirsty. He that overcomes I shall give to him these things, and I shall be God to him, and <u>he shall be to me a son</u>. But the cowardly, and unbelieving, and sinners, and abominable, and murderers, and fornicators, and drug users, and idolaters, and all who are false shall <u>have their part</u> in the lake which burns with fire and brimstone, which is <u>the second death</u>." (Revelation 21:5-8 EMTV)*

Everyone who "overcomes" gets the rewards, and everyone who does not is ultimately consumed by the second death; burning away in the lake of fire. It's interesting that cowards are specifically listed here, because that's what it is to value your own life more than the Word of God. He loves those who are willing to suffer and die for His truth and His Son, and those who would spend their lives hiding and ashamed of persecution are not worthy:

> *He that loveth father or mother more than me is <u>not</u> worthy of me: and he that loveth son or daughter more than me is <u>not</u> worthy of me. And he that <u>taketh not his cross and followeth after me</u> [willingness to die a martyr] is not worthy of me. <u>He that findeth his life shall lose it</u>: and he that <u>loseth his life for my sake</u> shall find it. (Matthew 10:37-39 KJV)*

This is what it means to overcome. Remember he also said,

> *"These things I have spoken unto you, that in me ye might have peace. In the world ye shall have tribulation:*

but be of good cheer; I have overcome the world."
(John 16:33 KJV)

Now let's continue with the description of New Jerusalem:

And I saw no temple therein: for the Lord God Almighty
and the Lamb are the temple of it. And the city had no need
of the sun, neither of the moon, to shine in it: for the glory
of God did lighten it, and the Lamb is the light thereof.
(Revelation 21:22-23 KJV)

After a wonderful description of the gates, foundations, dimensions, and material of New Jerusalem, called the "bride, the Lamb's wife", we see this incredible, meaningful description. We've already been told that the city's gates are labeled with the twelve tribes of Israel, and that it has twelve foundations, which have in them the names of the twelve apostles. This shows that even the unremarkable and lesser-known apostles are considered eternally important and wonderful, and that writing books of the Bible is not the only thing God valued in them. Their obedience, their willingness to follow Jesus, and their example to the world must be infinitely more important to God than any of the contributions of those who came later and followed their example. They are each counted as being equivalent to a tribe of Israel! But here, in verses 22 and 23, we see that there is no temple because God and Jesus are the temple; this tells us that in the ideal arrangement, God does not want any sort of legal or ritual system standing in between Him and His children. He wants direct access and communion with us.

The fact that the city does not "need" the sun or the moon does not mean there won't be stars and moons and heavenly lights. It simply means that the city will be sufficiently lit and beautiful by the glory of God and Jesus, so that even if there weren't any sun or moon we could see clearly.

And the nations [Greek: "ethnos", Gentile people] of them
which are saved [saints] shall walk in the light of it: and
the kings of the earth [obviously only those who were

true Christians] do bring their glory and honour into it.
(Revelation 21:24 KJV)

For a first century Jew to see that the Gentiles will be welcomed into New Jerusalem, the ultimate promised homeland of Messianic Jews, would be quite an amazing sight. Gentile kings and those from "nations" (a term for tribes and cultures other than Jews) will be free to walk in the light of God and Christ forever. Not only that, but they will bring glory and honor into it! Make sure to think about what that truly means. These are not idle words or meaningless promises, but powerful revelations by God Himself, about what He loves and wants to spend His eternity in proximity to. The nations have something to offer God's New Jerusalem, and will adorn Christ's bride with extra glory somehow. God's family is bigger than the Jews, as we know from Abraham already. Although it's doubtful that anyone would feel the need to physically alter or personalize New Jerusalem, it is fascinating to think that we humans will have something God wants to show off in His perfect city.

> *And the gates of it shall not be shut at all by day: for there*
> *shall be no night there.*
> *(Revelation 21:25 KJV)*

There will be no night there, in New Jerusalem, but this does not mean night does not exist in the entire planet or universe. We know that the city will be on an extremely high hill, and presumably the brightness of it will be visible from far away, if we feel like exploring and coming back. The city is the final home to return to, where we can worship and socialize, and put our minds together to exalt and cherish the goodness around us. Without cowards or liars there, only the strong in spirit and zealous will be around.

> *And they shall bring the glory and honour of the nations into*
> *it. And there shall in no wise enter into it any thing that*
> *defileth, neither whatsoever worketh abomination, or maketh*

a lie: but they which are written in the Lamb's book of life.
(Revelation 21:26-27 KJV)

John actually repeats the message about the nations bringing glory and honor into New Jerusalem. Think of the imagery of the city descending from the sky and being placed on the mountaintop; we will be somewhere as this happens, perhaps somewhere on the mountain. There will be a question of who can enter, and who the city truly belongs to. For Gentiles to enter seems absurd under ancient Jewish thinking, because God's Kingdom was supposed to be pure and untainted by the Gentile nations. Yet here we see them specifically welcomed, and distinguished from those who create abominations or lies, and those who defile. It's not saying that there will be multitudes of literal nations or countries somewhere out in New Creation, wanting to get in but excluded. We Christian Gentiles are the "nations" discussed here, and the significance must be put into the context of expectations of early church Jews who would be confused about why we would be allowed to enter such a holy city; indeed, to come face to face with God Almighty!

> *And he shewed me a pure river of water of life, clear as crystal, proceeding out of the throne of God and of the Lamb. In the midst of the street of it, and on either side of the river, was there the tree of life, which bare twelve manner of fruits, and yielded her fruit every month [implying the marking of time, days, and months]: and the leaves of the tree were for the healing [Greek: "therapeia", therapeutic attention] of the nations. And there shall be no more curse: but the throne of God and of the Lamb shall be in it; and his servants shall serve him: And they shall see his face; and his name shall be in their foreheads. And there shall be no night there; and they need no candle, neither light of the sun; for the Lord God giveth them light: and they shall reign for ever and ever. (Revelation 22:1-5 KJV)*

Clearly there will be days and cycles, because every month the trees will bare special kinds of fruit. Not just one fruit of life, but twelve, perhaps imbued twelve different virtues, gifts, or blessings for us to try and enjoy. As for the leaves, the Greek word "therapeia" is used only four times in the Bible, and in two of those cases it means "household", as in: *"And the Lord said, Who then is that faithful and wise steward, whom his lord shall make ruler over his **household [therapeia]**, to give them their portion of meat in due season?"* (Luke 12:42 KJV) If this translation were used, the leaves of the trees would be for the households of the nations to eat and gain sustenance, perhaps. If there are many more Gentiles than Jews in New Jerusalem, this could reflect how much we will cluster and eat, enjoying everything on the trees, not just the fruit. For them to have some kind of healing ability is also perfectly logical, but it is unclear what would need healing. We are washed in the blood of Christ and have no need of extra salvation or cleansing; we have white robes without blemish; we have the same new bodies and benefits as anyone else. This causes me to think it is not any particular healing of the nations, but simply good food for the households of the nations.

18

AFTERWORD

I hope that this book has awakened a powerful new appreciation in you of God's masterful strategy for this world. Whether this interpretation is true or not, it stands as a provocation to reconsider and study closely the words of Revelation, Isaiah, Daniel, Jesus and more, and to not be content with the traditional readings and studies that so often seem to lack poetic weight and coherence. At the beginning and end of the book of Revelation we are told that we are blessed if we simply keep the sayings of the book and hold them in our minds. How many can say that they have done this? To meditate on the text should be a daily part of our lives. It's not difficult to keep the sayings, and yet millions of self-professed believers of the Bible have failed to take this blessing for themselves and take advantage of the promise.

Infinitely more could be written and said about Revelation and the deeply interwoven promises of God, and I intend to privately dwell on them with the time God has given me. This book is simply one project, meant to step through the book and stir up a hunger for more. One could research the Italian Renaissance and its morphing into the Enlightenment, along with the modern banking system, democratic republics, modern science, occultism, secret societies, and in short, our modern era. Although not a Christian work, one starting point would be *The Medici* by Paul Strathern, which details the influence of the infamous Italian banking family whose finances shaped Europe, Greco-Roman revivalism, and the Catholic Church during the height of its controversies. Here you see transition into the "image of the Beast" from a ground level, where powerful but ignorant men end up ushering in a new age of wickedness.

Regarding the main discussion of this book, a few important takeaways should be highlighted:

1. That the seals, trumpets, and vials are very different and have their own unique sequence, logic, and symbolic meaning, making it impossible to interchange them or confuse them.

2. That the present day church is not the final group of believers, and that much more must happen after we are killed. The gospel will be preached to the world by angels themselves eventually, surpassing any efforts we could make in our own lives.

3. Israel is very important to prophecy, but for reasons almost nobody seems to appreciate. The 144,000 Israelite elect are central to many prophecies, and we should not assume all promises are given to us only. Rather, we should be happy that God wishes to call His own people again and find a remnant to serve Him.

4. Those who are evil and in the Satanic conspiracy are not aware of the truth, but are deceived, ignorant, and tragically bound to evil spiritual forces that blind them to the truth of Christ. We should pray for them, not seek to destroy them. They often think they are serving God by killing us; and again, Christ himself does not lay the blame at their feet, but rather at the feet of Satan, the Beast, and the spiritual powers of darkness that have been sent to earth to fulfill God's amazing plan.

5. To die for Christ as a martyr is truly a desirable goal. To be sued, slandered, wronged, deprived, and ultimately killed because we love Christ and have taken up our cross to follow him is not simply our duty, but a guaranteed blessing in the next life. There is a great reward waiting for those who are not cowards, who are not lukewarm, and who are not ashamed of the cross. Fight for that with all of your strength, knowing that there will be many who are turned away because they chose the wide path, where many go, rather than the difficult and narrow one.

There is much more we could discuss. What about that strange scene (in Matthew 4:8-9) where Satan tries to tempt Jesus by showing him the kingdoms of the world and their glory, and offers them to Jesus if only he would worship him? If this was a real offer, which we can assume it was, think of the implications! Jesus doesn't mock him for having no authority over the kingdoms, he simply rebukes him and rejects the offer.

I pray that God will bless the reader of this book who turns again toward the Word and rejuvenates his understanding, his passion, and his hunger for truth. This is by no means a perfect interpretation, but I can honestly say that I have tried to be the salt that has savor, not one that is flavorless, lukewarm, or bland.

> Ye are the salt of the earth: but *if the salt have lost his savour*, wherewith shall it be salted? it is thenceforth *good for nothing*, but to be *cast out*, and to be trodden under foot of men. (Matthew 5:13 KJV)

May this book be a blessing, and may you anticipate the return of our Lord. If you wish you to contact me, feel free to email maybewrong@protonmail.com. If you'd like to listen to me reading this book and exploring the topic further, find "The Not Done Yet Podcast", at anchor.fm/maybeeveryoneiswrong or on many other podcast services.

Printed in Great Britain
by Amazon